CAMBRIDGE TEXTS IN THE HISTORY OF
PHILOSOPHY

HUME
An Enquiry Concerning Human Understanding

CAMBRIDGE TEXTS IN THE HISTORY OF PHILOSOPHY

Series editors

KARL AMERIKS
Professor of Philosophy, University of Notre Dame

DESMOND M. CLARKE
Professor of Philosophy, University College Cork

The main objective of Cambridge Texts in the History of Philosophy is to expand the range, variety, and quality of texts in the history of philosophy which are available in English. The series includes texts by familiar names (such as Descartes and Kant) and also by less-well-known authors. Wherever possible, texts are published in complete and unabridged form, and translations are specially commissioned for the series. Each volume contains a critical introduction together with a guide to further reading and any necessary glossaries and textual apparatus. The volumes are designed for student use at undergraduate and postgraduate level and will be of interest not only to students of philosophy but also to a wider audience of readers in the history of science, the history of theology, and the history of ideas.

For a list of titles published in the series, please see end of book.

DAVID HUME

An Enquiry Concerning Human Understanding and Other Writings

EDITED BY

STEPHEN BUCKLE

Australian Catholic University

CAMBRIDGE UNIVERSITY PRESS

CAMBRIDGE
UNIVERSITY PRESS

University Printing House, Cambridge CB2 8BS, United Kingdom

Cambridge University Press is part of the University of Cambridge.

It furthers the University's mission by disseminating knowledge in the pursuit of education, learning and research at the highest international levels of excellence.

www.cambridge.org
Information on this title: www.cambridge.org/9780521604031

© Cambridge University Press 2007

First published 2007
5th printing 2013

A catalogue record for this publication is available from the British Library

ISBN 978-0-521-84340-9 Hardback
ISBN 978-0-521-60403-1 Paperback

Contents

Contents

Acknowledgements

No student of Hume can now escape indebtedness to Tom Beauchamp for his magnificent labours in producing the new critical editions of Hume's two *Enquiries*, and it is a pleasure to acknowledge my own debt. Acknowledgement is also due to the National Library of Scotland, Manuscripts Division, for their assistance and advice concerning the corrected versions of Hume's texts for the essays 'Of Suicide' and 'Of the Immortality of the Soul' (MS 509 in the NLS Manuscripts Collection).

On a more personal level, I would like to thank, first, John Wright and Galen Strawson for their very helpful advice on this project, especially when in its early stages; and, secondly, Sandy Stewart, who may forgive me for disagreeing with his account of the first *Enquiry*'s purposes, but who will not fail to recognize my debt, in the Introduction, to his outstanding articles on the development of Hume's philosophical ideas.

For their invaluable (and prompt) assistance and advice, I would like to thank Desmond Clarke, one of the two general editors of the series, and Hilary Gaskin, of Cambridge University Press. For assisting me with the leave necessary to finish the project, I am indebted to John Ozolins, my Head of Department at the Australian Catholic University, and to Ross Phillips and Robert Young of La Trobe University. Bernadette Tobin, Director of the Plunkett Centre for Ethics at ACU, provided me with the resources and environment in which to complete the work. Finally, my thanks also to Jasmin Chen, David Langsford, Helen McCabe and Leonie Martino for their helpful comments on drafts of the Introduction; and to John Quilter for his expert assistance with Greek fonts.

Introduction

David Hume was born in Edinburgh in 1711, and, after a life lived in England and France as well as Scotland, died there in 1776, a wealthy and famous man. He had become Great Britain's pre-eminent man of letters, notorious for his philosophical works – especially for his critical writings on religion – and (ultimately) applauded for his historical study of England and its institutions. After having established himself as a writer, he enjoyed a successful diplomatic career in Paris and London during the 1760s, before retiring to spend his last years in the town of his birth. There he practised his culinary skills on his friends, in between receiving famous visitors from home and abroad. After his death the great political economist, Adam Smith, published a letter describing his last days, and portraying him as a second Socrates. The greatest architect of the day was commissioned to design a tomb to house his remains. Today, well over two hundred years later, the visitor to Edinburgh is greeted by historical society plaques showing the great man's various places of residence, not to mention a brand-new monumental traffic-hazard in the main street of the Old Town. A better example of a successful life is difficult to imagine.

However, in the middle years of that life, to the man actually living it, such a successful outcome must have been scarcely imaginable. In 1745, Hume's life must have seemed, to his own view, only the most qualified of successes. He was thirty-four years of age, and employed as a tutor to a mentally unstable aristocrat. He had devoted his twenties to writing a philosophical work, *A Treatise of Human Nature* (1739–40), which had received little praise and rather more censure. That work had argued for some decidedly Sceptical[1] views. To focus just on those most relevant for our purposes: it had argued that our beliefs do not arise through distinctively rational processes, but only by our transferring past experience to further, unobserved, cases; in short, that we function not according to reason but by habit. It had further argued that our experience does not give us any idea of the causes by which the world works, and indeed that our very idea of a cause is based on nothing more than observed regularities in our experience; and that even our beliefs in the external world and in our own existence as a coherent self are the result not of reason but of processes in our imagination. In a striking (and subsequently famous) passage, it concluded that Scepticism (of some form) is the only credible philosophical outlook.

These striking and unsettling views were not, however, answered with philosophical replies; instead, they were attacked for their (real or imagined) dangerous consequences for religion. The only notable review had been simply dismissive, devoting more space to the author's errors of literary style than to the content. Admittedly, the young author could take comfort in one undoubtedly positive outcome, the recent success of his *Essays Moral and Political* (1741–2). Even that, however, must have paled in the face of the discovery that the *Treatise* threatened to *prevent* an academic career – when his application for the Chair of Moral Philosophy at Edinburgh University was blocked because of the work's supposed moral and religious implications.

It was in these discouraging circumstances that Hume worked on the *Philosophical Essays on Human Understanding*, now known as *An Enquiry concerning Human Understanding*. The first *Enquiry* (as it is now commonly called) removed some of the more complicated and less persuasive arguments, such as those concerning the origins of the everyday ideas of the external world and the self, and shortened the arguments concerning the origins of our ideas in perceptions and of our knowledge of causes. It also

---

[1] When speaking of Scepticism, I have employed the capital letter throughout, except when referring to modern epistemological or metaphysical views. The reason is that Hume's use of the term retains an awareness of the views of the ancient schools of Sceptics. This awareness has been lost in the ordinary modern philosophical use of the term, which owes most to the hyperbolic doubt entertained by Descartes in the first of the *Meditations*. In brief, ancient Scepticism was a more purely epistemological doubt which denied *knowledge* of a thing's *nature*, but sought to keep ordinary *beliefs* in place; whereas the Cartesian doubt raised questions also about the very *existence* of the thing. Hume's resistance to *excessive* Scepticism is, in part, a resistance to sliding from the first sense to the second.

carried over arguments for the compatibility of human freedom and determinism and for the similarity between animal and human ways of learning from experience. Most strikingly, it included two new sections critical of religion, and a completely rewritten account of the Scepticism implied by the author's philosophy, and concluded with a somewhat ambiguous, but plainly hostile, attack on religion.

This makes it plain that, in contrast to the *Treatise* (at least, as it was published), the *Enquiry* aims to show that Hume's empiricist and Sceptical philosophy is bad news for religion. (The ambiguity is over whether this should mean all religion or only some forms.) Nevertheless, despite this more polemical edge to the *Enquiry*, it is not uncommonly treated as a popular, even a watered-down, rewriting of some of the themes from the *Treatise*. This mistake stems from failing to understand both Hume's conclusions and his purposes. To begin with the latter: if we are to understand those purposes, it is necessary to free ourselves from the tendency to project the views of posterity onto Hume's own circumstances and motivations. To this end, it will be helpful to review Hume's life up to the point of writing the *Enquiry*, and to identify the main intellectual and political currents to which he was responding.

Hume's early career

Hume was the second son of a landed family from Ninewells, near Berwick in the Scottish borders. His father died when he was young, and so, probably because of a lack of family resources, at the unusually early age of ten he accompanied his brother to Edinburgh University. There he studied the standard four-year curriculum of the day: Latin and Greek, Logic and Metaphysics (meaning a systematic approach to the nature of the human being, of God, and of moral and religious duties), and Natural Philosophy (mathematics and natural science). After returning home (without completing the degree, as was common), it came to be expected of him that he would follow in his father's footsteps and enter the law. However, left to find his path through his own reading, he developed a passion for philosophy and literature. He fell under the spell of the ancient moral authors, especially Cicero, Seneca and Plutarch, and also of the modern Stoic philosophy of disciplined self-cultivation advocated by Anthony Ashley Cooper, the third Earl of Shaftesbury, in his *Characteristics of Men, Manners, Opinions, Times*, which had been published in the year of Hume's birth.

At the age of eighteen he suffered a breakdown, apparently from his attempt at rigorous adherence to Shaftesbury's regimen. After his recovery, he developed the idea for a philosophical and literary project, and wrote 'many a quire of paper' over the next few years. In 1734, aged twenty-three, he left Scotland for employment in Bristol, but this lasted only a few months. It may, in any case, have never been intended as more than a stepping-stone in the pursuit of his project, for later that same year he departed for France in order to fulfil his ambitions. After staying for about eight months in Rheims, he settled in the town of La Flèche, in Anjou, at whose Jesuit college René Descartes (1596–1650) had studied a hundred and twenty years earlier. He remained there for just over two years, returning to London in 1737 with the unrevised manuscript of what would become *A Treatise of Human Nature*.

Revisions and the task of finding a publisher finally saw Books I and II of the *Treatise* appear in early 1739. Those volumes, and indeed the whole *Treatise*, can be summarized as an attack on the traditional idea – reinvigorated in the modern rationalist philosophy deriving from Descartes – that the human being is the rational animal. On that view, the human being is a hybrid creature half divine (the immortal, rational part, which resembles the mind of God) and half animal (the material, sensory part).[2] Against that view, Book I denies that humans possess a distinct rational faculty, and that those functions traditionally attributed to reason can be understood to be the result of association and habit. (The late revisions to the work saw the removal of some anti-religious passages, most notably an earlier version of the essay on miracles.[3]) Book II is similarly anti-rationalist: it explains human action in terms of passions, themselves understood in very mechanical terms, and explicitly subordinates reason to the passions. The human being is thus recast as a creature of passion, imagination and habit rather than of reason. This demotion of reason amounts to a denial of the only pathway to certain knowledge, so Scepticism of some form is the unavoidable result.[4]

---

[2] The significance of the idea, in the philosophy of the time, that the human mind resembles the mind of God, and Hume's rejection of it, are brought out in Edward Craig, *The Mind of God and the Works of Man* (Oxford: Clarendon Press, 1987), Chs. 1–2.

[3] Letter to Henry Home, 2 December 1737 (included in this volume).

[4] Hume's essay 'The Sceptic' (included in this volume) illustrates that, for Hume, the demotion of reason is the distinguishing mark of the Sceptical outlook.

On a more positive note, since both passion and imagination are utterly dependent for their functioning on the input provided by the senses, Hume's theory moves the sensory side of human nature to centre-stage. The *Treatise* could therefore be expected to appeal to other philosophies in which the rehabilitation of the senses loomed large. It was, presumably, partly for this reason that Hume's older relative and friend, Henry Home, sent a copy to the most eminent of the Scottish philosophers, the Professor of Moral Philosophy at Glasgow, and advocate of Shaftesburian views, Francis Hutcheson. Hutcheson's response was encouraging, so Hume sent him the manuscript for Book III, 'Of Morals' – but with somewhat unhappy results. Hutcheson did not approve of Hume's occasional swipes at religion; nor, given his Christian Stoic outlook, could he approve of Hume's Epicurean and Sceptical tendencies. To see what was at stake, it is necessary to explain the meaning and contemporary significance of these ancient philosophical viewpoints.

Stoicism, Epicureanism and Scepticism were the major schools of thought of the Hellenistic (later ancient) world. One main source for these philosophies is the philosophical works of Cicero, where the different views are described and assessed in dialogues modelled loosely on Plato's example. The study of Cicero's works was a standard part of the eighteenth-century university curriculum, so these competing views were not only well understood but also employed as standards for categorizing different kinds of contemporary philosophical position. Like all such standards of public debate – consider 'capitalist' and 'communist', or 'liberal' and 'fundamentalist' – the terms were employed crudely, to lump together many different sorts of views. The key differences, however, can be set out as follows. The Stoics believed that the gods exercise a providential concern for the world, and therefore that the surface chaos of life obscures the operation of underlying laws that work for the general good of the creation; that human beings possess reason, a 'divine spark' that distinguishes them from animals and underpins their affinity with the gods; and that through the free exercise of reason human beings can discern the good, constrain their unruly desires, and so attain to happiness through living a virtuous life. Epicureans believed, in contrast, that the gods exercise no concern for the world; that the world is entirely material, all things being made out of atoms; that humans and animals are therefore similar in nature, both driven by their desires for pleasure and the avoidance of pain; and that pleasure and the avoidance of pain, and nothing more, constitute happiness.[5] The Sceptics held that both these schools of thought are 'dogmatic' because they make claims to certain knowledge; that those claims are not justified; and, indeed, that *no* claims to certain knowledge can be justified.

These differences were then translated into the early modern world. The ancient Stoics claimed to know that the world possesses an underlying purpose which justifies it, and which makes religious and moral duty necessary parts of the good life; their early modern Christian descendants can thus be thought of as *philosophical* Christians who held that the central doctrines of Christianity could be established on rational grounds. In contrast, the ancient Epicureans were atomistic materialists, hedonists about motivation, and 'practical atheists'; their early modern descendants revived atomic theory and hedonism about motivation, but (typically) sought to reconcile these themes with Christianity. The ancient Sceptics denied all metaphysical claims, including those in religion and ethics; their early modern descendants did likewise; but both sought to preserve religious faith and an ethics based in custom. To their early modern critics, both Epicureanism and Scepticism were judged to be unreliable foundations for Christian belief, and their defenders were often supposed to be closet atheists. So Christian Stoicism represented, on questions of religion and morals, the 'philosophical high ground'.

To return, then, to Hutcheson. His distaste for Hume's views would have reflected the Stoic's dislike of Scepticism, and, moreover, a Scepticism with evident Epicurean sympathies. So it should come as no surprise that he also complained that Hume's moral philosophy lacked 'a certain warmth in the cause of virtue': this was a recognizably Stoic, and indeed Shaftesburian, complaint, meaning that the writer on morals should *show* the attractiveness of good actions and characters. Hume responded to the charge by letter, and in the course of his defence appealed to the different but complementary roles of anatomist and painter: the anatomist, by pulling the skin off a creature to see what lies within, does not bring about a beautiful result; but, through such studies, the painter is benefited, because enabled to represent the body more accurately, and so the more convincingly to create beauty. 'And in like manner', Hume concluded, 'a metaphysician may be very helpful to a moralist', without engaging in any

---

[5] The differences between Stoic and Epicurean here show the modern dispute between Kantians and utilitarians in ethics to be a modern variation on an old theme.

'warm' moralizing.[6] When Book III of the *Treatise* appeared, at the end of 1740 (almost two years after the first two books), it had been trimmed of passages Hutcheson found offensive; but, in the final paragraph, stubbornly insisted upon, is the contrast between the anatomist and the painter, and the distinct roles of 'abstract speculation' and 'practical morality'. In short, despite concessions, Hume stood his ground against Hutcheson and, by extension, the Shaftesbury-inspired Christian Stoics of whom Hutcheson was the leading figure.[7]

In his short autobiography, *My Own Life*, written in the last year of his life, Hume claimed that the *Treatise* 'fell *dead-born from the press*'. He meant, among other things, that it did not attract readers. (He may also have meant that it contained errors, since the remark is an allusion to a line from Alexander Pope's 'Epilogue to the Satires': 'All, all but truth, drops dead-born from the press'.) If he expected the work to make a major 'splash', then he did indeed have cause to be disappointed, since it attracted reviews only slowly, and sales also were slow. The claim is, nonetheless, exaggerated, since, at least in learned circles, there seems to have been a steady growth in recognition of the author and his talents. But, then as now, the wheels of academe grind slowly, and the book's first serious response, the *Essays on the Principles of Morality and Natural Religion* (1751) by Henry Home (by that stage Lord Kames), still lay well in the future. Hume's response to this slow reception was to write his own review of the book, in order to promote awareness of it. *An Abstract of a Book lately Published, entitled A Treatise of Human Nature* appeared in early 1740, six months before the appearance of Book III. The subsequent success of the *Essays Moral and Political*, however, made Hume feel like a proper man of letters; he responded to this happy turn of events by returning home to brush up on his Greek. This brings us to the fateful year 1745.

Hume's '45

In mid-1744 Hume had been advised that the Chair in Ethics at the University of Edinburgh would soon become vacant. He was encouraged to apply, and duly expressed his interest. But delays ensued, and opposition to Hume's candidature grew. In the meantime, Hume left Edinburgh for

---

[6] Letter to Hutcheson, 17 September 1739 (included in this volume).
[7] *A Treatise of Human Nature*, 3.3.6.6.

Hertfordshire, because he had gained employment there as tutor to the young Marquess of Annandale. With politicking in Edinburgh in full flood, it seems likely that, in his English retreat, Hume turned to what would become the *Enquiry*. It is probable that he began by fleshing out the argument of the *Abstract*, since the argument outlined there closely resembles the *Enquiry*'s epistemological backbone. On that backbone, however, the *Enquiry* constructs a polemic against false philosophy and the religious prejudices to which such philosophy gives shelter. It is not hard to understand why.

In May of 1745, at work on his philosophical reconstructions, news reached him, in a letter, that William Wishart, the Principal of the University, had been circulating a pamphlet against him because of the views expressed in the *Treatise*. The pamphlet was enclosed, so, although he did not have the *Treatise* with him, Hume dashed off a reply to the charges the same day. The letter then came into the hands of Henry Home, who edited and perhaps added some introductions to Hume's various replies, and rushed it into print under the title *A Letter from a Gentleman to his Friend in Edinburgh*. The *Letter* responds to Wishart's charges point by point, and so is a valuable guide to what were taken to be the *Treatise*'s unacceptable implications for religion and morality. It also shares some passages with the *Enquiry*; passages presumably cannibalized from the draft manuscript in the rush to despatch the reply. But the *Letter* did not avail: the position went, eventually – as positions so often do – to the incumbent.

Hume was deemed unsuitable because the *Treatise* was held to contain unacceptable religious and moral positions, expressed or (allegedly) implied. Conspicuous amongst Hume's opponents were Hutcheson and other Shaftesbury-influenced Christian Stoics – despite his attempt to avoid offence by pruning its treatment of religious topics. It is not surprising, then, that he chose to go on the attack. In sharp contrast to the *Treatise* – which had presented itself as contributing to a new spirit in philosophy already abroad amongst English philosophers – the *Enquiry* presents itself as a defence of serious thinking against shallowness, obscurity and superstition. It fleshes out the epistemological skeleton inherited from the *Abstract* with two sections critical of religion, the first a reinstated (probably expanded) critique of miracles, the second a dialogue critical of the argument from design, and so of the philosophical religion characteristic of Stoicism – and set (strikingly) within a defence of philosophy against political interference. Along the way, it also explicitly (and gratuitously) attacks Stoicism, implying it to be no better than the Epicureanism against which it defines itself. Moreover, it begins with a defence of serious philosophy that is plainly a sally against Shaftesburian and Hutchesonian themes. So there is no doubt that Shaftesbury and the Christian Stoics are an important target.[8]

They are not, however, the whole target, nor even the 'official' target. The first section promises that the benefits of serious thinking will be to demolish 'superstition', and the last section concludes that the argument has established that all books of 'divinity and school metaphysics' are fit only to be burnt. These remarks do not fit a Protestant Stoic target. In the first place, 'school metaphysics' – like its synonym, 'scholastic philosophy' – was a common, and commonly abusive, term for the Aristotelian-derived philosophy taught in Catholic universities. Secondly, the term 'superstition' was also, at the time, something of a Protestant code-word for Catholicism, applied because of the latter's emphasis on ceremonies and observances endowed with mysterious powers. Hume himself illustrates the connection in his essay 'Of Superstition and Enthusiasm', where he treats Catholicism as a prime example of the superstitious frame of mind. The (radical) Protestants, in contrast, are classed as 'enthusiasts', meaning those religious believers who believe themselves blessed with divine favours, and so who possess a self-confident frame of mind quite at odds with the anxious or self-doubting mind characteristic of 'superstition'. This is enough to suggest that Shaftesburian Protestant Stoicism is unlikely to be the official target; a conclusion further supported by the fact that Shaftesbury himself referred to his philosophical outlook as a kind of enthusiasm.[9]

So it rather looks as if Hume's official target is Catholicism. If this thought is pursued, there turns out to be a striking piece of supporting evidence. This is the famous section on miracles. The anti-Catholic air of this section tends to be missed because the points of dispute between

[8] These three paragraphs are heavily indebted to M. A. Stewart, 'Two Species of Philosophy: The Historical Significance of the First *Enquiry*', in Peter Millican (ed.), *Reading Hume on Human Understanding* (Oxford: Clarendon Press, 2002), 67–95.
[9] Anthony Ashley Cooper, Third Earl of Shaftesbury, 'A Letter concerning Enthusiasm', in *Characteristics of Men, Manners, Opinions, Times*, ed. Lawrence E. Klein (Cambridge: Cambridge University Press, 1999), 4–28 (esp. 27–8). Cf. also Voltaire's entries for 'enthusiasm' and 'superstition' in the *Philosophical Dictionary* (first published 1764). The latter of these both signals a debt to the works of Cicero, Seneca and Plutarch (Hume's favourite ancient authors), and also mentions, amongst others, the Protestant criticism of Catholicism as superstitious. Voltaire, *Philosophical Dictionary*, ed. Theodore Besterman (London: Penguin, 2004), 187–8, 382–5.

Protestants and Catholics in the shadow of the Reformation have been forgotten by all but specialists, and also because present-day Protestantism
makes much of miracles as a foundation for belief. In Hume's day, however,
the issue was a subject of Protestant attack on Catholicism. It was so because,
although Protestants accept miracles, they allow them to have occurred only
in a past apostolic age, a special period of divine activity in the world. In
contrast, Catholics hold miracles to be a permanent feature of the world:
they are evidence of ongoing divine engagement with the world, primarily
through the activities of particular holy men and women. Thus beatification
requires proof of a miracle, and canonization of saints requires proof of
several. This means that the Catholic, unlike the Protestant, is committed to
the necessity of identifying miracles in the common course of daily life. So a
critique of miracles does fit into a Protestant critique of Catholicism.[10]

Hume plainly exploits this connection. He bookends the section with
Protestant rhetoric: he begins with the former Archbishop of Canterbury's
attack on the Catholic doctrine of transubstantiation, promising a similar
argument that will check 'superstitious delusion'; and he concludes by
insisting that faith, not reason, is the highest court of appeal in religious
matters, thereby invoking not only the characteristic position of the
Christian Sceptic, but also echoing the Protestant dictum of justification
by faith alone.[11] Moreover, his examples of absurdly unbelievable modern
miracle-claims are from France and Spain, both Catholic countries (and
Britain's traditional political enemies). So in this section an anti-Catholic air
is undeniable; and this fact, combined with the anti-Catholic framing of the
whole, plainly shows the *Enquiry* to be packaged as an anti-Catholic tract.

Why might this be? The clue is provided in the political circumstances
obtaining in 1745 and the immediately following years, the period in which

[10] See Hume's letter to George Campbell (included in this volume), which illustrates this source of
dispute between Protestants and Catholics. The focus on miracles in modern Protestantism –
bringing with it a tendency to misread the purpose of Hume's section – owes most to the decline
of natural religion brought about by evolutionary theory, with its non-purposive explanations
for observable natural order. See Stephen Buckle, 'Marvels, Miracles, and Mundane Order',
Australasian Journal of Philosophy 79 (2001), 23–30.

[11] The Catholic Sceptic Michel de Montaigne (1533–92) and the Protestant Sceptic Pierre Bayle
(1647–1706) both accepted that there is no going beyond faith in religious matters. But Hume's
remark also makes sense as an appeal to the Scottish Calvinists against the Christian Stoics. As
such, it can be supposed to be an attempt to persuade conservative elements of the Scottish
Church that a Sceptic in matters of religion, because mindful of the mysterious power of faith,
is, in important respects, more akin to Calvinism than those pretended friends. See James Harris,
'Hume's Use of the Rhetoric of Calvinism', in Marina Frasca-Spada and P. J. E. Kail (eds.), *Impressions of Hume* (Oxford: Clarendon Press, 2005), 141–59.

the *Enquiry* was completed. Just a few months after the Edinburgh affair came to an end, in August, 1745, the Young Pretender, Prince Charles Edward Stuart – now better known as Bonnie Prince Charlie – landed with an army on the west coast of Scotland, and recruited support from the (Catholic) Highlanders for a march on London to reclaim the British throne from the Hanoverians. After early successes, he was soundly defeated at Culloden in April, 1746, finally escaping to France (after five months on the run) in September, 1746.

The episode is now mainly remembered through a romantic lens – for example, in *The Skye Boat Song* – but for supporters of the (Protestant) united crown of England and Scotland, Hume included, it taught an unwelcome but necessary lesson. That lesson was the threat posed by Catholicism and Catholic politics to the peace and prosperity gained through the political settlement of 1688 and the Act of Union of 1707; the threat of a return to the disastrous religious conflicts of the seventeenth century. As things turned out, it was the last gasp of the Jacobite (Stuart) cause in British politics – but that was not to be known at the time. So, for both the English and the Lowland Scots, Catholicism stood not merely for false religion, but also for the possible return to the ruinous civil war of the previous century. Catholicism and its political implications was, thus, a predictable and, indeed, an ideal target for a critic of religious dogma and its harmful effects.

This is to focus on internal British politics. If we turn to international affairs, the Catholic threat also loomed large. Hume tells us, in *My Own Life*, that, after leaving employment with the Marquess of Annandale, he became a secretary to General St Clair, and that this led to his being a party to an ill-starred invasion of France. He then returned to Britain, completing the *Enquiry* in 1747. However, by the time it appeared in 1748, he was again with St Clair, this time on a diplomatic mission in Turin. The two incidents are related. Throughout the whole period, Britain was engaged in the War of the Austrian Succession (1740–8), a series of conflicts arising from opportunistic attempts to take advantage of Maria Theresa's succession to the Austrian throne. Britain allied itself with Austria against Prussian and French attempts to dismember the Austrian empire, and Spain supported France. So, although allied with Catholic Austria (and parts of Italy), Britain was at war with its two powerful Catholic neighbours, France and Spain. The invasion of France, although rather farcical, was nevertheless a hostile action; and the diplomatic mission to Turin was an attempt to get the Italians to accept their fair share of the burden of the war.

So the genesis of the *Enquiry* occurs during a time of war with old Catholic enemies. True, it also involved Catholic friends, but it is not hard to imagine that nearby Catholic enemies loomed larger in the public mind than distant Catholic friends – especially given that one of them, France, had backed Bonnie Prince Charlie's invasion. In short, both at home and abroad, Catholicism and the politics it spawned was an enemy to all Protestant, loyal and progressive-minded Britons, and recognized to be a clear and present danger to political security.

It is not surprising, then, that Hume should have taken advantage of this state of affairs by packaging the *Enquiry* as an attack on Catholicism. This enabled him to wrap up his own personal grievance with the Christian Stoics in a larger and widely popular cause. It also provided him with something of a defensive smokescreen – no small matter in a society where excommunication would result in a partial loss of civil rights. In *A Letter from a Gentleman* he had evaded the issue with replies that are somewhat disingenuous; it seems likely that the anti-Catholic packaging of the *Enquiry* was meant to serve a similar function. Should it have been necessary to do so, it enabled him to argue, with at least some degree of credibility, that the work was aimed only at Catholicism and, in passing, at the fashionable intellectuals' version of Protestantism, not at Christianity (or religion) *per se*; that, if it happened to hit those targets too, doing so had not been his intention. (Would such a defence have *persuaded*? Perhaps not; but it would have provided a coherent answer to official criticism.)

The fact of the matter, though, is that the *Enquiry* is a critique of religion in general – of Christianity in particular – and of its effects on human life. The official attack on Catholicism, and the various sallies against (Christian) Stoicism, are, in the end, merely aspects of this larger critique. Its central epistemological theses – the denial of knowledge of causes, and the restriction of our very idea of causation – are designed to serve a larger ambition. That ambition is to deny the religious picture of the human being, and its consequences: to deny that the human being is the rational animal, that which, by the use of its divine power of reason, can discern fundamental truths about the nature of the universe; to deny (metaphysical) free will; and to deny that reports of miracles, and arguments for the intelligent design of the world, can ever provide good evidence for any system of religious belief. In more constructive vein, the work also defends a 'mitigated' Scepticism capable of being a practical philosophy – 'durable and useful' – because it encourages, within limits, the empirically based research by which common life can be improved. But, lest this more optimistic aspect encourage an excess of toleration, we are reminded, in the closing sentence, that adherence to these useful Sceptical principles spells the end of religious systems. The *Enquiry* is an explicit manifesto for a Sceptical, but aggressively secular, worldview.

Hume's own later account

The account offered here shows Hume's own account of the relationship between the *Treatise* and *Enquiry*, in the posthumously published *My Own Life*, to be seriously misleading. He there says nothing at all about the Edinburgh failure, and he attributes the advent of the *Enquiry* merely to his long-held thought that the failure of the *Treatise* stemmed 'more from the manner than the matter', and from 'a very usual indiscretion' of 'going to the press too early'. Plainly this is a very selective account of its origins, ignoring not only the historical circumstances, personal and political, but also the more hostile approach to religion and its social effects that is so plain a feature of the later work. The best explanation of this difference is to regard *My Own Life* as a somewhat tendentious document, aimed at presenting a portrait of Hume as he wanted to be remembered – a creature of good humour, moral virtue and intellectual constancy who was never soured or discouraged by the prejudicial attacks made on him – rather than as the 'death-bed confession' it is often taken to be.

A second issue raised by *My Own Life* concerns the scope of the *Enquiry*. He says there that he returned to the *Treatise* and 'cast the first part of the work anew', and this has been taken to mean that the *Enquiry* is a rewriting of Book I of the *Treatise*. This is, however, an implausible view, because only about half of the *Enquiry* is, in any straightforward sense, a recasting of Book I. It contains the two new sections on religion, a section on liberty and necessity which derives from Book II, a completely new introduction, and a radically recast treatment of Scepticism in the final section. It also contained, in the early editions, a substantial footnote, in the first section, on moral philosophy,[12] and, in all editions until the final (posthumous) edition, an original discussion, in the third section, of the psychology of aesthetic judgement. In short, especially on its first appearance, the *Enquiry* was much more like a

---

[12] This footnote was removed after the appearance of *An Enquiry concerning the Principles of Morals* in 1751.

concise introduction to Hume's general philosophy – previously suppressed elements included – than a mere recasting of Book I. So the best interpretation of the remark is that the 'first part' to which Hume refers means the first part published – that is, Books I *and* II – together with some short additions that indicated the philosophy's wider implications.

From the *Treatise* to the *Enquiry*: the excision of psychological detail

The *Enquiry* is thus best considered as a shortened and more accessible version of the main elements of Hume's philosophy – with a sting in the tail. This explains the divergences from the *Treatise*. Complex arguments of interest only to the learned are set aside *en masse*. These include, in particular, the detailed account of the mind's psychological mechanisms, and the problems inherent in the modern scientific account of the nature of reality. The latter could have appealed only to those fully engaged in thinking about the new science, so its excision is not surprising. Hume's decision to remove the psychological detail is less obvious – but more instructive. To see why he did it, it will be helpful to understand why it was there in the first place. The *Treatise* presupposes 'faculty psychology', that is, the idea that the mind can be divided into distinct faculties, or kinds of powers. The main such faculties, for epistemological purposes, are the senses, the memory, the imagination and the understanding (or intellect, the faculty of reason). The sensory faculty is the power to receive information through the sense organs; the memory the power to recall those sensory images; and the imagination the power to break up and re-arrange previously sensed images. Since all of these three faculties concern images (their reception, preservation or rearrangement), all three can be thought of as parts of a super-faculty of image-processing. Confusingly, this super-faculty is also called the imagination, but it is usually distinguishable from imagination in the more restricted sense because it is usually the sense in question when, in early modern authors, imagination is contrasted with the understanding. In this broad sense, the imagination is the image-processing power.[13] In both broad and narrow senses, however, the imagination had, ever since Aristotle, been identified with the effect of bodily

---

[13] It is this sense that Hume has in mind when he observes, in the final paragraph of the *Abstract* (§35), that his philosophy affirms 'the empire of the imagination'.

processes on the mind.[14] The understanding or intellect, in contrast, because it deals in reasons, was commonly taken to be a pure activity of the soul, and so possibly independent of any bodily processes.

This distinction, and its dualistic tendencies, were pressed hard by Descartes and his followers. Thus Descartes insists, in the *Meditations*, that ideas in the intellect are not images. The idea of God is a central case; but, in order to establish the point, he appeals to the example of a chiliagon (a thousand-sided figure). It is impossible to form an image of a chiliagon, but that is no bar to understanding what it is; and no bar to discovering its properties through geometrical reasoning.[15] His aim in insisting on the point is to distinguish the intellect sharply from the bodily world of images and image-processing, and thereby to support his dualism of mind and body. The division is taken up in detail by Nicolas Malebranche, one of Descartes's most influential followers, in his massive tome, *The Search after Truth* – a work which Hume recommended a friend to read in order to understand the argument of the *Treatise*.[16] He does so because the whole bent of the *Treatise*'s psychological accounts presupposes the faculty psychology on which Cartesian dualism relies. That is, it presupposes the same distinctions – into sense, imagination and intellect – in order to subvert the Cartesian conclusions: it aims to show that the mental activities the Cartesians attribute to the intellect are in fact processes of the imagination. Thus Hume holds, for example, that ideas, abstract ideas included, are images, and they are connected by association, a process of the imagination rather than of the rational connections drawn by the intellect. In other words, Hume's detailed psychological descriptions in the *Treatise* are there in order to attack Cartesian dualism.

The *Enquiry*'s aim to engage a wider audience is, however, a shift to an audience with only rare attachments to Cartesian kinds of rationalist philosophy, so the detailed psychology of the *Treatise* is actually an obstacle to communicating with that group. In fact, Newton's scientific achievements were popularly regarded as a triumph of British brainpower over the false French physics of Descartes and his followers, an intellectual chauvinism

---

[14] Aristotle says that imagination is a kind of movement in the body, and that it is capable of error for this reason (*On the Soul*, 428b). Hume links the associations of the imagination, bodily processes, and error in a striking passage in the *Treatise* (1.2.5.20).
[15] René Descartes, *Meditations*, Sixth Meditation; in *The Philosophical Writings of Descartes*, trans. John Cottingham, Robert Stoothoff and Dugald Murdoch (Cambridge: Cambridge University Press, 1984), II.50f.
[16] Letter to Michael Ramsay, 26–31 August 1737 (included in this volume).

which did nothing for the popularity of Cartesian metaphysics. So, given the wider British audience he sought to find, the critique of Cartesian psychology threatened both to discourage and to distract, and so was left aside. He may also, of course, have had second thoughts about the details of the *Treatise* accounts, but on his basic commitments he did not change his mind: neither the pre-eminence of the faculty of the imagination nor its particular workings through associative mechanisms disappear from the explanations provided in the *Enquiry*; in fact, they are presumed wherever relevant to the explanatory task. The excisions from the *Treatise* are, then, necessitated by the careful tailoring of the *Enquiry*'s content to the capacities and concerns of its target audience.

From the *Treatise* to the *Enquiry*: the religious critique

The same conclusion can be drawn of the arguments retained: they are preserved because they are central to Hume's basic Sceptical message, but are rewritten with an eye to greater simplicity and clarity. The main thread of argument is this: that the human mind can do no more than receive, preserve and rearrange sensory inputs; that sensory inputs do not give us access to nature's secrets; that we are not, therefore, the rational beings of traditional philosophy, but are incapable of certain knowledge; that, speculative purposes aside, we are not hindered by this lack of knowledge, because practical life depends not on it but on instinctive connections; that we are, therefore, different from animals only in degree, not kind. Onto this framework Hume builds the *Enquiry*'s critique of religion. The basic thrust of the argument is simple enough: if we are merely clever animals, then the religious picture of the human being (derived from ancient philosophy) is wrong; and if we cannot uncover nature's secrets, then neither can we know them to derive from the hand of a divine creator. The religious criticisms of the *Enquiry*'s later sections thus follow naturally from the argument of the preceding sections. (This means, among other things, that they will not be properly understood unless seen in the light of the preceding arguments.)

This should lay to rest the claim that the *Enquiry* is a 'watered-down' version of the *Treatise*. It is no such thing. Such an interpretation reflects the preoccupations of philosophy today rather than in Hume's day. As a result, readers in recent times have restricted Hume's philosophy to his sceptical epistemology and to specific issues in morals and religion. This means that the unity of the philosophy is missed, and is so largely because the Scepticism itself is misunderstood. The problem is that Hume's final Sceptical viewpoint in the *Treatise* is missed because the stages of the enquiry are mistaken for the final viewpoint itself. This means, first, that the very similar viewpoint of the *Enquiry* is taken to be a significant back-down; and, most importantly, that Hume's Scepticism is, in both works, defined by its subordination of reason to other mental faculties.[17] Moreover, once the importance of the religious critique in Hume's thought is recognized, it becomes plain that the *Enquiry* is *more* offensive than the *Treatise* (in its published version). The *Enquiry* is, then, a concise restatement of Hume's central Sceptical principles and their implications: the intellectual credibility only of empirical enquiry into matters affecting human life, and the impossibility of credible systems of religious knowledge.

Experimentalism, Newtonianism, naturalism – and Scepticism

Hume had sub-titled the *Treatise* 'an attempt to introduce the experimental method of reasoning into moral subjects'. He there explicitly connects 'the experimental method of reasoning' with the work of Francis Bacon and the English philosophers he influenced, but Newtonian themes and echoes are also present. In the *Enquiry* the Newtonian connection is very strongly marked. Hume makes reference both to Newton the man and to obviously Newtonian principles of reasoning, in some places even paraphrasing important paragraphs from Newton's main works, the *Principia* and the *Opticks*.

These Newtonian aspects have sometimes been supposed to be at odds with Hume's Scepticism. This is because the early modern idea of 'experimental philosophy' is taken to be the positive (anti-sceptical) commitment to scientific investigation of the world. This is, however, misleading. Early modern experimental philosophy is indeed the ancestor of modern science, and so a commitment to what we mean by scientific investigation. But such a commitment in no way implies that experimental enquiry will ever arrive at ultimate truths about the world; all it requires is

[17] This view is implicit in the *Enquiry*'s limitation of enquiry to the materials provided in common life; it is shown to be the *Treatise*'s settled view in Don Garrett, 'Hume's Conclusions in "Conclusion of this Book"', in Saul Traiger (ed.), *The Blackwell Guide to Hume's Treatise* (Oxford: Blackwell, 2005), 151–75.

that reason should be subordinated to experience. Newton, for his part, makes it plain that he means just that. He insists on the subordination of reason to experiment both explicitly, by insisting that experiments must be accorded authority over mathematical proofs, and implicitly, in, for example, his famous rejection of 'hypotheses' – that is, of speculative first principles. He also restricts both the subjects of enquiry, and the conclusions drawn, to what is observable: natural philosophy should restrict itself to 'manifest' principles. He thus casts the goal of experimental enquiry not as the attainment of ultimate truths about nature, but merely as the progressive harmonizing and simplifying of our best explanatory principles for phenomena: it is what he means by 'laws of nature'.[18]

It seems that, especially in his mature works, it was these features of Newton's outlook that caught Hume's eye. This is made explicit in the *History of England*. He there praises Newton as 'the greatest and rarest genius that ever arose for the ornament and instruction of the species', and also as having 'restored [nature's] ultimate secrets to that obscurity, in which they ever did and ever will remain'.[19] In other words, he commends him not for his experimental method itself, but for his (implicitly) Sceptical outlook. The connection between the two is this: experimental method subordinates reason to experience; but experience limits us to observable properties, not to the underlying powers that cause them. The method is thus built on Scepticism about nature's powers. So, for Hume, Newton's version of experimentalism is distinguished by its Sceptical denial that the fundamental truths about reality are attainable. This immediately explains why Hume thought his Sceptical doubts concerning reason's powers to draw conclusions from experience – what is now known as 'the problem of induction' – to be central to his whole philosophy: experimental philosophy rejects the *a priori* principles ('hypotheses') on which philosophical rationalists rely; but *Newtonian* experimentalism also rejects any claim to establish fundamental truths by experimental means. So, as Hume came to understand it, Newtonian experimentalism also means the Sceptical rejection of the optimistic claims made for inductive empirical enquiry by Francis Bacon and his followers.[20]

---

[18] Isaac Newton, *Principia*, General Scholium (in *Philosophical Writings*, ed. Andrew Janiak (Cambridge: Cambridge University Press, 2004), 92).

[19] Hume, *History of England* (Indianapolis: Liberty Fund, 1983), VI.542.

[20] This means that the famous Section 4 is directed not against rationalism, as often supposed, but against optimistic or dogmatic (including Baconian) empiricism. In fact, the Cartesians not only

Newtonian experimentalism is thus, for Hume, a necessary foundation for his 'durable and useful' Scepticism. Both subordinate reason to the faculty of sense; both restrict empirical enquiry, in subjects of investigation and in conclusions drawn, to what is observable; and both deny the possibility of attaining to ultimate truths. Hume's experimentalism and Newtonianism are, then, aspects of his Sceptical outlook. Furthermore, since Hume's philosophical naturalism is itself summed up in his experimentalism and Newtonianism, it can also be concluded that his naturalism and Scepticism, rather than being at odds with each other, are different sides of the same coin. In short, Hume's philosophy does not betray commitments to a variety of incompatible theses; it is, rather, a single, coherent, philosophical outlook, the unity of which has been obscured by its having been described by a variety of apparently opposed names.

The unity of the *Enquiry*

For the beginning student, the *Enquiry* is encountered as an introduction to philosophy, and especially as an introduction to specific philosophical problems. Discrete sections of the work are read in order to introduce various 'live' philosophical doctrines or problems, such as empiricism, the problem of induction, our knowledge of causation, and, in philosophy of religion classes, the problem of miracles. There is nothing wrong with this, of course, but there is a cost: the idea that the work contains a sustained argument for a coherent philosophy will probably disappear from view. Furthermore, the inertial tendencies of the curriculum entrench not only specific problems but also specific interpretations of them. Thus it is not uncommon to find highly dubitable interpretations of Hume's work continuing to flourish in the classroom. (Every teacher knows the heuristic value of a straw man.) A related problem concerns the survival of anachronistic interpretations of key concepts, for example of scepticism and rationality. The result is confusion, both about Hume's own views and about the threads that bind them. So, as a corrective against that fragmenting tendency, it will be useful to conclude this introduction with a short sketch of the *Enquiry*'s overall argument.

agreed with Hume's denial that powers are perceived – they were his *source*. They themselves had got it from Plato. See Plato, *Theaetetus*, 155e; Nicolas Malebranche, *The Search after Truth*, ed. T. M. Lennon and P. J. Olscamp (Cambridge: Cambridge University Press, 1997), 3.2.3.

After Section 1 makes its case for serious philosophizing, Sections 2–6 put in place the basic account of human psychological functioning, and this account is then put to work in Sections 7–11. Section 2 sets out the raw materials with which the mind works, denying any access to rational first principles by means of which perceptions could be judged for their truthfulness. Instead, perceptions can be classified only according to their order of priority and degree of intensity: the mind's ideas are nothing more than paler copies of vivid perceptions. An exception (the missing shade of blue) is observable, but this exception reflects inertial and associative tendencies in the mind, not innate rational principles, and so actually provides indirect support for the implicitly mechanical story of impressing and copying already provided. Section 3 holds that ideas are connected by association (rather than by logical connections), and so provides another building-block in the development of an account of mental functioning independent of rational processes. (The account offered is strikingly similar to Hobbes's overtly materialistic psychology.)

Section 4 argues that we are able to go beyond immediate experience only through causal reasoning, but that experience does not provide us with the knowledge of causal powers by means of which rational inferences can be made. Neither (veridical) individual perceptions (the Stoic view) nor repeated perceptions over time (the Aristotelian and scholastic view, and also the Epicurean view) can penetrate beyond appearances. Nevertheless, through repeated perceptions we do arrive at causal judgements; so there must be some non-rational means by which these ideas arise in us. Section 5 concludes that this is simply due to custom or habit, an 'instinct or mechanical tendency' of the mind which transfers past experiences to the future, and so forms our expectations. Beliefs in general arise non-rationally, through associations raised by sense experience. Nevertheless, these instinctive features of the mind correspond to the workings of the world, a sort of 'pre-established harmony' between the mind and the world; a harmony that suggests that the mind and the world work according to similar (mechanical) principles. Section 6 holds that the relative frequency of past experience is the basis for our more nuanced expectations, our judgements of probability. All our judgements are therefore determined by our past experience. Mixed past experience leads to qualified confidence, and we express this sense of qualification in the idea of what is probable or improbable, what *may* or *may not* be. Uniform past experience, in contrast, generates in us an unqualified conviction, and so leads to judgements about what *must* or *must not* be. These judgements have, for us, all the force of logical demonstrations, even though they are not such; they are what we commonly regard as *proofs* from experience.

Section 7 argues that our very idea of a cause is generated by just this process. Uniform past experience leads to the feeling that a future event *must* occur, and this feeling of necessity is the impression from which we produce our idea of a causal connection. So our idea of causation is generated independently of whatever causes there may be in nature; and definitions of 'cause', because they pick out only the source of the idea, not the hidden causes themselves, do not ease our ignorance of the real powers in nature. Section 8 argues further that, once this is recognized, the dispute between freedom and determinism can be resolved: that, according to the only definitions of 'cause' we have, our behaviour is determined; and that, according to a plausible (non-metaphysical) definition of freedom, freedom and determination are compatible. But topics of religious importance now arise, since to accept determinism is to reject (metaphysical) free will, and the theodicies that appeal to it; it is to accept that evil is due to prior causes, and (once the Stoic attempt to avoid the problem is set aside) ultimately to the first cause, God. Section 9 then argues that the fundamental divide between human and animal natures – much emphasized in Christian and Stoic views – is in fact a myth.

Sections 10 and 11 directly examine the implications of the preceding account for the foundations of religious belief. These foundations are miraculous events (revealed religion) and arguments for God's existence (natural religion). Section 10 argues that, on the basis of experience alone, the best possible evidence for believing a report of a miracle is insufficient to generate positive belief, since the report implies a collision between two contradictory proofs (in the sense given above). It further argues that, when one adds the other factors that bear on such reports, disbelief is the only proper response. Section 11 has a different air, because it is a dialogue between the author and an imagined Epicurean friend. The friend attacks the (Christian) Stoic argument that there is discernible in nature an underlying design which points to an omnipotent and perfectly good designer; he does so, moreover, by appealing to principles close to Hume's own. The conclusion of this section is, even if only implicitly, that rational argument cannot arrive at theistic conclusions with which to interpret experience. So, with respect to claims to religious knowledge, it returns us to the reliance on uninterpreted experience that was found wanting in the previous section.

The final section then faces an objection that has been waiting in the wings all along. The conclusions reached throughout the *Enquiry* have all been markedly Sceptical – but is Scepticism itself a credible position? If it is not, the attempt to propound a Sceptical philosophy will collapse simply in virtue of that fact. So Section 12 investigates Scepticism. It admits that there is an excessive Scepticism that does defeat itself, but then defends a 'mitigated' Scepticism that is both 'durable and useful', and so is a viable philosophical position. This 'mitigated' Scepticism affirms empirical enquiries into subjects within the bounds of experience, but rejects all metaphysical philosophy. The work concludes in overtly anti-Catholic vein, implying that the Inquisition has burnt the wrong books; but the intent of the argument is to reject all systems of metaphysics and their progeny, systems of religious knowledge.

Other writings

The other writings included in this edition have been chosen for the light they help to throw on Hume's concerns in *An Enquiry concerning Human Understanding*. The place of the first of these, *A Letter from a Gentleman to his Friend in Edinburgh*, has already been indicated above. It answers some of the objections raised against the *Treatise* – its supposed extreme Scepticism, and implied criticisms of religion – and so reveals that, in the *Enquiry*, Hume tried to correct the former impression, but came out fighting on the latter issues.

The essay 'The Sceptic' may mislead, since it does not portray Hume's own view: it is a literary presentation of the viewpoint typical of Scepticism. (It is one in a series of essays that present typical kinds of philosophical outlooks, the others being Stoicism, Epicureanism, and Platonism.) As such, it presents a viewpoint more Pyrrhonian than Hume's own, and so less 'durable and useful' than the Academic Scepticism he champions at the end of the *Enquiry*. The value of the essay lies in its portrayal of Scepticism as then understood – in particular, its denial of the authority of reason – and its contrast with the modern use of 'scepticism' to designate the kind of extreme doubt found in the first of Descartes's *Meditations*.

The two essays unpublished in Hume's lifetime, 'Of Suicide' and 'Of the Immortality of the Soul' can be treated together. 'Of Suicide' can be viewed, in part, as an extension of the argument of *Enquiry* Section 11, in that it restricts reasoning concerning any divinely owed duties of human life to the facts of general providence (laws of nature), thereby excluding appeal to particular providence (special divine provisions concerning human life). This has the effect of reducing specific religious duties to the benefits and burdens of a life, the same perspective allowed for duties to ourselves and others – from which perspective the case for suicide is quickly made. 'Of the Immortality of the Soul' opposes *metaphysical* arguments by identifying analogies – e.g. between human and animal souls – that prove too little or too much; it opposes *moral* arguments by, once again, restricting appeal to divine purposes to the limits imposed by general providence; and it opposes *physical* arguments (arguments drawn from analogies with nature) by running through a series of recognizably Epicurean arguments. Of particular note, given the above account of the *Enquiry*, is its insistence that the organs of the soul are dependent on those of the body. So the argument of this essay renders explicit the implicitly materialist bearing of the *Enquiry*'s psychological theory.

The History of England is primarily concerned with the political history of the Tudors and Stuarts, but to each epoch it appends summaries of important developments in manners and the arts, including thumbnail biographies of the major intellectual figures of the period. These throw light both on Hume's views of these figures, and, indirectly, on his own outlook. Particularly striking is the criticism of Hobbes for his dogmatism, and the praise of Newton for his (implicit) Scepticism.

Hume's letters similarly provide an insight into many of his opinions, both public and private. Those printed here illustrate the circumstances surrounding the publication of the *Treatise*, including the decision to remove the section on miracles; Hume's preference for the *Enquiry* over the *Treatise*, and the instruction to his printer to insert the 'advertisement' in which he effectively disowns the *Treatise* (the latter in a letter with some interesting observations on the American rebellion); his rejection of the charge that he denied causes; and the circumstances – a conversation with a Catholic priest on Protestant criticisms of Catholicism – in which he first formulated the argument against miracles.

Finally, *My Own Life* has often been reprinted, but it is included here more for purposes of critical comparison than simply as a record of the facts of Hume's life. It has not always been read with a critical eye; but its twin concerns, self-justification against living enemies and self-interpretation for the sake of posterity, are no guarantees of the cool detachment of which it seeks to persuade us.

Chronology

1744	Applies for Chair of Moral Philosophy at Edinburgh.
1745	Begins working on *Philosophical Essays*; campaign against his suitability for Edinburgh causes him to compose the letter which becomes *A Letter from a Gentleman to his Friend in Edinburgh*.
1746	Secretary to General St Clair; invades France in September. Death of Hutcheson.
1747	Julien Offray de La Mettrie, *Machine Man*.
1748	Aide-de-camp to St Clair in military embassy to Vienna and Turin. *Philosophical Essays concerning Human Understanding* (later retitled *An Enquiry concerning Human Understanding*).
1749	David Hartley, *Observations on Man*.
1751	*An Enquiry concerning the Principles of Morals*; begins work on *Dialogues concerning Natural Religion*; elected co-secretary of the Edinburgh Philosophical Society (forerunner of the Royal Society of Edinburgh). Henry Home, *Essays on the Principles of Morality and Natural Religion*.
1751– 1752	Denis Diderot and Jean le Rond d'Alembert, *Encyclopedia*. Hume fails in application for Chair in Logic at University of Glasgow; becomes Keeper of the Advocates' Library, Edinburgh; *Political Discourses*; begins work on *History of England*.
1753–4	*Essays and Treatises on Several Subjects* (a collected edition of Hume's works, in which the philosophical works – *Treatise* excluded – are subsequently published).
1754	First volume of *History of England*.
1756	Second volume of *History*.
1757	*Four Dissertations* (containing 'The Natural History of Religion', 'Of the Passions', 'Of Tragedy', and 'Of the Standard of Taste'). Resigns as Keeper of the Advocates' Library.
1759	Third and fourth volumes of *History*.
1761	Last two volumes of *History*.
1763	Goes to Paris as secretary to the British ambassador, Lord Hertford; befriends d'Alembert and other *philosophes*.
1765	For five months, British *chargé d'affaires* in Paris.
1766	Returns to England with Rousseau (who accuses him of treachery).

1767	Under-Secretary of State for Northern Department.
1769	Returns to Edinburgh; settles in New Town, 1771.
1775	Sends the 'Advertisement' to William Strahan, his publisher.
1776	Death of Hume, probably of bowel cancer.
	Adam Smith, *The Wealth of Nations*; American Declaration of Independence.
1777	Final edition of *Essays and Treatises on Several Subjects*.
	Two Essays ('Of Suicide' and 'Of the Immortality of the Soul').
1778	Deaths of Voltaire and Rousseau.
1779	*Dialogues concerning Natural Religion* published by Hume's nephew David.

Further reading

When complete, the new Clarendon Edition of the Works of David Hume (Oxford: Oxford University Press, 1998–) will unite Hume's philosophical works in a complete scholarly edition. It will supersede the now very dated *The Philosophical Works of David Hume*, edited by T.H. Green and T.H. Grose (London: Longman, Green, 1874–5). One of the two Clarendon volumes to have appeared to date is the new edition of the first *Enquiry*, edited by Tom L. Beauchamp; it is an indispensable work for all serious students. The *Enquiry* is also now accessible in electronic form, edited by Peter Millican for the Leeds Hume Project (www.etext.leeds.ac. uk/hume/). The most widely cited edition of the *Enquiry* is the now superseded Oxford edition by L. A. Selby-Bigge, revised by P. H. Nidditch. For Hume's *Essays, Moral, Political, and Literary*, the best available complete edition is that by Eugene F. Miller (Indianapolis: Liberty Fund, revised edn, 1987). The best edition of *Dialogues on Natural Religion* is the companion volume in this series, edited by Dorothy Coleman (Cambridge: Cambridge University Press, 2006).

The classic study of the *Enquiry* is Antony Flew, *Hume's Philosophy of Belief* (London: Routledge and Kegan Paul, 1961; repr. Bristol: Thoemmes Press, 1997). Although quite dated in some ways, Flew is particularly sharp about the religious implications of Hume's arguments. The only other full-length study of the whole work is Stephen Buckle, *Hume's Enlightenment Tract: The Unity and Purpose of* An Enquiry concerning Human Understanding (Oxford: Clarendon Press, 2001). Another recent study focused on some parts of the *Enquiry* is George Stern, *A Faculty Theory of Knowledge: The Aim and Scope of Hume's First* Enquiry (Lewisburg, PA: Bucknell

University Press, 1971). Terence Penelhum, *David Hume: An Introduction to His Philosophical System* (West Lafayette, Indiana: Purdue University Press, 1992) is a valuable introduction to Hume's thought based (primarily) on the *Enquiry*. Finally, Peter Millican (ed.), *Reading Hume on Human Understanding: Essays on the First* Enquiry (Oxford: Clarendon Press, 2002) is a collection of essays on each of the *Enquiry*'s sections, and provides an up-to-date introduction to several key debates about Hume's arguments. Millican interprets the *Enquiry* rather differently from the account offered here.

Of Hume's philosophy more generally, Norman Kemp Smith, *The Philosophy of David Hume*, with a new introduction by Don Garrett (London: Palgrave Macmillan, 2005; originally published 1941), is a classic study. Also of lasting value is John Passmore, *Hume's Intentions*, 3rd edn (London: Duckworth, 1980). Barry Stroud, *Hume* (London: Routledge, 1977) is an accessible work that offers an overall view of Hume's philosophy. A. J. Ayer, *Hume* (Oxford: Oxford University Press, 1980) is brisk and readable, and Georges Dicker, *Hume's Epistemology and Metaphysics* (London: Routledge, 1998) a well-organized introduction to some main themes. More demanding works which offer interpretations of Hume's central philosophical commitments include Don Garrett, *Cognition and Commitment in Hume's Philosophy* (New York: Oxford University Press, 1997); Peter Jones, *Hume's Sentiments: Their Ciceronian and French Context* (Edinburgh: Edinburgh University Press, 1982); Donald W. Livingston, *Hume's Philosophy of Common Life* (Chicago: University of Chicago Press, 1984); David Fate Norton, *David Hume: Common-Sense Moralist, Sceptical Metaphysician* (Princeton: Princeton University Press, 1982); and John P. Wright, *The Sceptical Realism of David Hume* (Manchester: Manchester University Press, 1983).

Of general collections of articles on Hume, the most exhaustive is Stanley Tweyman (ed.), *David Hume: Critical Assessments*, 6 vols. (London: Routledge, 1995). Accessible and very useful collections are David Fate Norton (ed.), *The Cambridge Companion to Hume* (Cambridge: Cambridge University Press, 1993); David Owen (ed.), *Hume: General Philosophy* (Aldershot and Burlington, VT: Ashgate, 2000); and Elizabeth Radcliffe (ed.), *A Companion to Hume* (Malden, MA and Oxford: Blackwell Publishing, 2006). V. C. Chappell (ed.), *Hume* (London: Macmillan, 1966) is an older but still useful collection. M. A. Stewart and John P. Wright (eds.), *Hume and Hume's*

Connexions (Edinburgh: Edinburgh University Press, 1994) and Marina Frasca-Spada and P. J. E. Kail (eds.), *Impressions of Hume* (Oxford: Clarendon Press, 2005) are two other valuable collections of broad scope. Two extremely valuable works which include important chapters on Hume are Edward Craig, *The Mind of God and the Works of Man* (Oxford: Clarendon Press, 1987) and Charles McCracken, *Malebranche and British Philosophy* (Oxford: Clarendon Press, 1983). Steven Nadler (ed.), *A Companion to Early Modern Philosophy* (Malden, MA and Oxford: Blackwell Publishing, 2002) provides a useful context for Hume's thought.

For literature on specific topics, the sheer quantity of literature necessitates being very selective. Harold W. Noonan, *Hume on Knowledge* (London: Routledge, 1999) and David Pears, *Hume's System* (Oxford: Oxford University Press, 1990) are both clear introductions to the purely epistemological topics covered in the *Enquiry*, but, in both cases, are based almost exclusively on the *Treatise*. On reason, induction and causation, the main studies are Tom Beauchamp and Alexander Rosenberg, *Hume and the Problem of Causation* (New York: Oxford University Press, 1981); David Owen, *Hume's Reason* (Oxford: Clarendon Press, 1999); Rupert Read and Kenneth A. Richman (eds.), *The New Hume Debate* (London: Routledge, 2000); and Galen Strawson, *The Secret Connexion: Causation, Realism, and David Hume* (Oxford: Clarendon Press, 1989). On belief and justification, see M. J. Costa, 'Hume and Justified Belief', *Canadian Journal of Philosophy* 11 (1981), 219–28 (Tweyman (ed.), *Hume*, 1.174–82) and Louis E. Loeb, *Stability and Justification in Hume's* Treatise (Oxford: Clarendon Press, 2002). On liberty and necessity, see Paul Russell, *Freedom and Moral Sentiment* (New York: Oxford University Press, 1995) and James A. Harris, *Of Liberty and Necessity* (Oxford: Clarendon Press, 2005), Ch. 3.

On Hume's philosophy of religion, the standard work is J. C. A. Gaskin, *Hume's Philosophy of Religion* (London: Macmillan, 1978). Stephen Buckle, 'Marvels, Miracles, and Mundane Order', *Australasian Journal of Philosophy* 79 (2001), 1–31 offers an account of the roles of Sections 10 and 11 of the *Enquiry* in Hume's overall argument. J. Houston, *Reported Miracles* (Cambridge: Cambridge University Press, 1994) is a major study of miracles, with special reference to Hume. David Fate Norton, *David Hume*, Ch. 6 surveys the variety of meanings of 'scepticism' in the eighteenth century. Hume's Scepticism is held to be Pyrrhonist by Richard H. Popkin, 'David Hume: His Pyrrhonism and His Critique of

Pyrrhonism', *Philosophical Quarterly* 1 (1951), 385–407 (Tweyman (ed.), *Hume*, 2.161–87) and to be genuinely Academic by John P. Wright, 'Hume's Academic Scepticism: A Reappraisal of His Philosophy of Human Understanding', *Canadian Journal of Philosophy* 16 (1986), 407–35 (Tweyman (ed.), *Hume*, 2.222–47, and Owen (ed.), *Hume*, 303–31).

Note on the text

In all, Hume prepared ten editions (and an additional re-issue) of *An Enquiry concerning Human Understanding* for the press. Of these, the last edition, which appeared the year following his death in 1777, was the basis for the Oxford editions of L. A. Selby-Bigge and P. H. Nidditch. Since this edition, however, excises a significant portion of text (from Section 3, illustrating the effect of the association of ideas in aesthetic judgements), and since it was the only edition that he did not himself see through the press, some recent editions have taken the 1772 edition as the definitive text. This is the case with the outstanding new scholarly edition prepared by Tom L. Beauchamp for Oxford University Press. I have followed suit, but with some qualifications, so the text presented here is something of a composite. The material excised in the 1777 edition has been reinstated, but I have included some footnotes later deleted, and the occasional variant reading, where these changes are of genuinely philosophical interest. In keeping with the editorial policy of *Cambridge Texts in the History of Philosophy*, I have modernized the text in several ways: eighteenth-century spellings are replaced with modern spellings; initial capital letters for most nouns or substantives are changed to lower case; '&' is changed to 'and'; contractions are replaced with expanded spellings. Minor inconsistencies in Hume's spelling and punctuation have also been corrected, but for the most part his original punctuation has been preserved. Throughout, my aim has been to produce a text that is both informative and readable, rather than a definitive version of Hume's thoughts. The marginal numbers are the page numbers from the much-cited edition of *Enquiries concerning Human Understanding and concerning the Principles of Morals*, edited by

L. A. Selby-Bigge and revised by P. H. Nidditch, 3rd edn (Oxford: Clarendon Press, 1975). Hume's footnotes are indicated by letter, editorial footnotes by number. Square brackets enclose editorial additions to Hume's footnotes.

For the text of *A Letter from a Gentleman*, I have relied on the Edinburgh facsimile edition of Ernest C. Mossner and John V. Price (Edinburgh: Edinburgh University Press, 1967). The essay 'The Sceptic' is from the 1777 edition of *Essays, Moral, Political, and Literary*, but I have also checked it against the modern editions of Eugene F. Miller (Indianapolis: Liberty Fund, revised edn, 1987) and Stephen Copley and Andrew Edgar (Oxford: Oxford University Press, 1993). For the two posthumously published essays, 'Of Suicide' and 'Of the Immortality of the Soul', I have followed Miller in relying on Hume's own corrected manuscript rather than on the published versions; I am indebted to the National Library of Scotland, Manuscripts Division, for their assistance concerning this version. The extracts from Hume's *History of England* are from the 1778 edition (now reprinted, with a foreword by William B. Todd (Indianapolis: Liberty Fund, 1983)). The text for *My Own Life* is from the 1777 edition of *Essays and Treatises*; I have followed Eugene F. Miller's corrections in his excellent edition of the *Essays*.

The selections from Hume's letters are from J.Y.T. Greig (ed.), *The Letters of David Hume*, 2 vols. (Oxford: Clarendon Press, 1932). The one exception is the letter to Michael Ramsay, 26–31 August 1737, which is taken from Richard H. Popkin, 'So, Hume did Read Berkeley', in Popkin, *The High Road to Pyrrhonism*, ed. Richard A. Watson and James E. Force (Indianapolis: Hackett, 1993), 291. (The letter was originally published in Tadeusz Kozanecki, 'Dawida Hume'a Nieznane Listy w Zbiorach Muzeum Czartoryskich (Polska)', *Archiwum Historii Filozofi i Myśli Społecznej* 9 (1963), 133.)

The sources for the translations of Hume's Greek and Latin quotations are as follows: Aristotle, *Poetics*, trans. Ingram Bywater (Oxford: Oxford University Press, 1920); Cicero, *On Moral Ends*, ed. Julia Annas (Cambridge: Cambridge University Press, 2001); Cicero, *On the Nature of the Gods*, from *De Natura Deorum, Academica*, trans. H. Rackham (Cambridge, MA: Harvard, Loeb Library, 1933); Seneca, *Epistles 1–65*, trans. Richard M. Gummere (Cambridge, MA: Harvard, Loeb Library, 1917); Pliny the Elder, *Natural History*, trans. H. Rackham (Cambridge, MA: Harvard, Loeb Library, 1938). References to works of other authors in the editorial footnotes are to section and paragraph numbers. The exceptions, where references are to page numbers, are Antoine Arnauld and Pierre Nicole, *Logic or the Art of Thinking*, ed. Jill Vance Buroker (Cambridge: Cambridge University Press, 1996); René Descartes, *The Philosophical Writings of Descartes*, trans. John Cottingham, Robert Stoothoff and Dugald Murdoch (Cambridge: Cambridge University Press, 1984); Thomas Hobbes, *Leviathan*, ed. Richard Tuck (Cambridge: Cambridge University Press, 1991); Michel de Montaigne, *The Complete Essays*, ed. M. A. Screech (London: Penguin, 1991); and Isaac Newton, *Philosophical Writings*, ed. Andrew Janiak (Cambridge: Cambridge University Press, 2004).

An enquiry concerning human understanding

Advertisement[1]

Most of the principles, and reasonings, contained in this volume, were published in a work in three volumes, called A *Treatise of Human Nature*: A work which the author had projected before he left college, and which he wrote and published not long after. But not finding it successful, he was sensible of his error in going to the press too early, and he cast the whole anew in the following pieces, where some negligences in his former reasoning and more in the expression, are, he hopes, corrected. Yet several writers, who have honoured the author's philosophy with answers, have taken care to direct all their batteries against that juvenile work, which the author never acknowledged,[2] and have affected to triumph in any advantages, which, they imagined, they had obtained over it: A practice very contrary to all rules of candour and fair-dealing, and a strong instance of those polemical artifices, which a bigoted zeal thinks itself authorized to employ. Henceforth, the author desires, that the following pieces may alone be regarded as containing his philosophical sentiments and principles.

---

[1] Hume enclosed this 'advertisement', or notification, in a letter to his printer, William Strahan, on 26 October 1775 (included in this volume).
[2] The *Treatise* was published anonymously.

I

Of the different species of philosophy

1   Moral philosophy, or the science of human nature,[1] may be treated
after two different manners; each of which has its peculiar merit, and may
contribute to the entertainment, instruction, and reformation of mankind.
The one considers man chiefly as born for action; and as influenced in his
measures by taste and sentiment; pursuing one object, and avoiding
another, according to the value which these objects seem to possess, and
according to the light in which they present themselves. As virtue, of all
objects, is allowed to be the most valuable, this species of philosophers
paint her in the most amiable colours; borrowing all helps from poetry and
eloquence, and treating their subject in an easy and obvious manner, and
such as is best fitted to please the imagination, and engage the affections.
They select the most striking observations and instances from common
life; place opposite characters in a proper contrast; and alluring us into the
paths of virtue by the views of glory and happiness, direct our steps in [6]
these paths by the soundest precepts and most illustrious examples. They
make us *feel* the difference between vice and virtue; they excite and regulate
our sentiments; and so they can but bend our hearts to the love of probity[2]
and true honour, they think, that they have fully attained the end of all their
labours.

2   The other species of philosophers consider man in the light of a
reasonable rather than an active being, and endeavour to form his understanding more than cultivate his manners. They regard human nature as a

---

[1] Moral philosophy, in the broad sense used here, is the study of human nature and action; it is contrasted with natural philosophy, the study of the natural world.
[2] Moral excellence or conscientiousness.

subject of speculation; and with a narrow scrutiny examine it, in order to find those principles, which regulate our understanding, excite our sentiments, and make us approve or blame any particular object, action, or behaviour. They think it a reproach to all literature, that philosophy should not yet have fixed, beyond controversy, the foundation of morals, reasoning, and criticism; and should for ever talk of truth and falsehood, vice and virtue, beauty and deformity, without being able to determine the source of these distinctions. While they attempt this arduous task, they are deterred by no difficulties; but proceeding from particular instances to general principles, they still push on their enquiries to principles more general, and rest not satisfied till they arrive at those original principles, by which, in every science, all human curiosity must be bounded. Though their speculations seem abstract, and even unintelligible to common readers, they aim at the approbation of the learned and the wise; and think themselves sufficiently compensated for the labour of their whole lives, if they can discover some hidden truths, which may contribute to the instruction of posterity.

3   It is certain that the easy and obvious philosophy will always, with the generality of mankind, have the preference above the accurate and abstruse;[3] and by many will be recommended, not only as more agreeable, [7] but more useful than the other. It enters more into common life; moulds the heart and affections; and, by touching those principles which actuate men, reforms their conduct, and brings them nearer to the model of perfection which it describes. On the contrary, the abstruse philosophy, being founded on a turn of mind, which cannot enter into business and action, vanishes when the philosopher leaves the shade, and comes into open day; nor can its principles easily retain any influence over our conduct and behaviour. The feelings of our heart, the agitation of our passions, the vehemence of our affections, dissipate all its conclusions, and reduce the profound philosopher to a mere plebeian.[4]

4   This also must be confessed, that the most durable, as well as justest fame, has been acquired by the easy philosophy, and that abstract reasoners seem hitherto to have enjoyed only a momentary reputation, from the caprice[5] or ignorance of their own age, but have not been able

[3] Difficult to understand.   [4] A member of the common people.
[5] Unpredictable change of mood or outlook.

4

to support their renown with more equitable posterity. It is easy for a profound philosopher to commit a mistake in his subtle reasonings; and one mistake is the necessary parent of another, while he pushes on his consequences, and is not deterred from embracing any conclusion, by its unusual appearance, or its contradiction to popular opinion. But a philosopher, who purposes only to represent the common sense of mankind in more beautiful and more engaging colours, if by accident he falls into error, goes no farther; but renewing his appeal to common sense, and the natural sentiments of the mind, returns into the right path, and secures himself from any dangerous illusions. The fame of Cicero flourishes at present; but that of Aristotle is utterly decayed. La Bruyere passes the seas, and still maintains his reputation: But the glory of Malebranche is confined to his own nation, and to his own age. And Addison, perhaps, will be read with pleasure, when Locke shall be entirely forgotten.[6]

5   The mere philosopher is a character, which is commonly but [8] little acceptable in the world, as being supposed to contribute nothing either to the advantage or pleasure of society; while he lives remote from communication with mankind, and is wrapped up in principles and notions equally remote from their comprehension. On the other hand, the mere ignorant is still more despised; nor is any thing deemed a surer sign of an illiberal genius[7] in an age and nation where the sciences flourish, than to be entirely destitute of all relish for those noble entertainments. The most perfect character is supposed to lie between those extremes; retaining an equal ability and taste for books, company, and business; preserving in conversation that discernment and delicacy[8] which arise from polite letters;[9] and in business, that probity and accuracy which are the natural result of a just philosophy. In order to diffuse and cultivate so accomplished

---

[6] Cicero (106–43 BC), Roman statesman, orator and writer whose works became a model for Latin prose. Aristotle (384–322 BC), Greek philosopher of vast influence but lesser readability, whose principles underpinned the scholastic philosophy of the Middle Ages. Jean de La Bruyère (1645–96), French writer and moralist, satirist of Parisian society. Nicolas Malebranche (1638–1715), French philosopher and priest, influential in the latter half of the seventeenth century for his synthesis of the philosophy of Descartes with (Augustinian) Catholic theology. Joseph Addison (1672–1719), English essayist, poet and dramatist, admired for his unornamented prose style. John Locke (1632–1704), English philosopher whose *Essay Concerning Human Understanding* (1690) shaped the outlook of most empirically minded eighteenth-century scientists and reformers.
[7] Genius: spirit or outlook. Illiberal genius: uncultured or prejudiced resistance to freedom of thought and its consequences.
[8] Accuracy of perception; sensitivity.   [9] Polished writing; literature.

a character, nothing can be more useful than compositions of the easy style and manner, which draw not too much from life, require no deep application or retreat to be comprehended, and send back the student among mankind full of noble sentiments and wise precepts, applicable to every exigency[10] of human life. By means of such compositions, virtue becomes amiable,[11] science agreeable, company instructive, and retirement entertaining.

6   Man is a reasonable being; and as such, receives from science[12] his proper food and nourishment: But so narrow are the bounds of human understanding, that little satisfaction can be hoped for in this particular, either from the extent or security of his acquisitions. Man is a sociable, no less than a reasonable being: But neither can he always enjoy company agreeable and amusing, or preserve the proper relish for them. Man is also an active being; and from that disposition, as well as from the various [9] necessities of human life, must submit to business and occupation: But the mind requires some relaxation, and cannot always support its bent to care and industry. It seems, then, that nature has pointed out a mixed kind of life as most suitable to the human race, and secretly admonished them to allow none of these biases to *draw* too much, so as to incapacitate them for other occupations and entertainments. Indulge your passion for science, says she, but let your science be human, and such as may have a direct reference to action and society. Abstruse thought and profound researches I prohibit, and will severely punish, by the pensive melancholy which they introduce, by the endless uncertainty in which they involve you, and by the cold reception which your pretended discoveries shall meet with, when communicated. Be a philosopher; but, amidst all your philosophy, be still a man.

7   Were the generality of mankind contented to prefer the easy philosophy to the abstract and profound, without throwing any blame or contempt on the latter, it might not be improper, perhaps, to comply with this general opinion, and allow every man to enjoy, without opposition, his own taste and sentiment. But as the matter is often carried farther, even to the absolute rejecting of all profound reasonings, or what is commonly

---

[10] Urgent need or demand.   [11] Pleasing.

[12] Knowledge or learning; philosophy. From Latin *scientia*, meaning 'knowledge'. Hence 'moral sciences' and comparable terms. The modern meaning of the term, denoting empirical enquiry, especially into natural subjects, dates from the nineteenth century.

called *metaphysics*, we shall now proceed to consider what can reasonably be pleaded in their behalf.

8   We may begin with observing, that one considerable advantage, which results from the accurate and abstract philosophy, is, its subserviency to the easy and humane;[13] which, without the former, can never attain a sufficient degree of exactness in its sentiments, precepts, or reasonings. All polite letters are nothing but pictures of human life in various attitudes and situations; and inspire us with different sentiments, of praise or blame, admiration or ridicule, according to the qualities of the object, which they set before us. An artist must be better qualified to succeed in this undertaking, who, besides a delicate taste and a quick apprehen- [10] sion, possesses an accurate knowledge of the internal fabric, the operations of the understanding, the workings of the passions, and the various species of sentiment which discriminate vice and virtue. How painful soever this inward search or enquiry may appear, it becomes, in some measure, requisite to those, who would describe with success the obvious and outward appearances of life and manners. The anatomist presents to the eye the most hideous and disagreeable objects; but his science is useful to the painter in delineating even a Venus or a Helen.[14] While the latter employs all the richest colours of his art, and gives his figures the most graceful and engaging airs; he must still carry his attention to the inward structure of the human body, the position of the muscles, the fabric of the bones, and the use and figure[15] of every part or organ. Accuracy is, in every case, advantageous to beauty, and just reasoning to delicate sentiment. In vain would we exalt the one by depreciating the other.

9   Besides, we may observe, in every art or profession, even those which most concern life or action, that a spirit of accuracy, however acquired, carries all of them nearer their perfection, and renders them more subservient to the interests of society. And though a philosopher may live remote from business, the genius of philosophy, if carefully cultivated

---

[13] Its serving the ends of (not its inferiority to) the easy and humane.

[14] Cf. *Treatise*, 3.3.6.6. The usefulness of anatomy is mentioned by Malebranche, *Search after Truth*, 4.7. In Roman mythology, Venus is the goddess of love (the equivalent of Greek Aphrodite). In Greek mythology, Helen of Troy, wife of Menelaus and the most beautiful woman in the world, is abducted by Paris, thus bringing about the Trojan War – and making her 'the face that launched a thousand ships' (Christopher Marlowe, *Doctor Faustus*, *The Complete Plays*, ed. Frank Romany and Robert Lindsey (London: Penguin, 2003), 13.90).

[15] Shape.

by several, must gradually diffuse itself throughout the whole society, and bestow a similar correctness on every art and calling. The politician will acquire greater foresight and subtlety, in the subdividing and balancing of power; the lawyer more method and finer principles in his reasonings; and the general more regularity in his discipline, and more caution in his plans and operations. The stability of modern governments above the ancient, and the accuracy of modern philosophy, have improved, and probably will still improve, by similar gradations.

[11]   10   Were there no advantage to be reaped from these studies, beyond the gratification of an innocent curiosity, yet ought not even this to be despised; as being one accession to those few safe and harmless pleasures, which are bestowed on the human race. The sweetest and most inoffensive path of life leads through the avenues of science and learning; and whoever can either remove any obstructions in this way, or open up any new prospect, ought so far to be esteemed a benefactor to mankind. And though these researches may appear painful and fatiguing, it is with some minds as with some bodies, which being endowed with vigorous and florid[16] health, require severe exercise, and reap a pleasure from what, to the generality of mankind, may seem burdensome and laborious. Obscurity, indeed, is painful to the mind as well as to the eye; but to bring light from obscurity, by whatever labour, must needs be delightful and rejoicing.

11   But this obscurity in the profound and abstract philosophy, is objected to, not only as painful and fatiguing, but as the inevitable source of uncertainty and error. Here indeed lies the justest and most plausible objection against a considerable part of metaphysics, that they are not properly a science; but arise either from the fruitless efforts of human vanity, which would penetrate into subjects utterly inaccessible to the understanding, or from the craft of popular superstitions, which, being unable to defend themselves on fair ground, raise these entangling brambles to cover and protect their weakness. Chased from the open country, these robbers fly into the forest, and lie in wait to break in upon every unguarded avenue of the mind, and overwhelm it with religious fears and prejudices. The stoutest antagonist, if he remit his watch a moment, is oppressed. And many, through cowardice and folly, open the gates to the

---

[16] Fully flowering; fully developed.

enemies, and willingly receive them with reverence and submission, as their legal sovereigns.

12   But is this a sufficient reason, why philosophers should desist [12] from such researches, and leave superstition still in possession of her retreat? Is it not proper to draw an opposite conclusion, and perceive the necessity of carrying the war into the most secret recesses of the enemy? In vain do we hope, that men, from frequent disappointment, will at last abandon such airy sciences, and discover the proper province of human reason. For, besides that many persons find too sensible an interest in perpetually recalling such topics; besides this, I say, the motive of blind despair can never reasonably have place in the sciences; since, however unsuccessful former attempts may have proved, there is still room to hope, that the industry, good fortune, or improved sagacity of succeeding generations may reach discoveries unknown to former ages. Each adventurous genius will still leap at the arduous prize, and find himself stimulated, rather than discouraged, by the failures of his predecessors; while he hopes that the glory of achieving so hard an adventure is reserved for him alone. The only method of freeing learning, at once, from these abstruse questions, is to enquire seriously into the nature of human understanding, and show, from an exact analysis of its powers and capacity, that it is by no means fitted for such remote and abstruse subjects. We must submit to this fatigue in order to live at ease ever after: And must cultivate true metaphysics with some care, in order to destroy the false and adulterate. Indolence, which, to some persons, affords a safeguard against this deceitful philosophy, is, with others, overbalanced by curiosity; and despair, which, at some moments, prevails, may give place afterwards to sanguine hopes and expectations. Accurate and just reasoning is the only catholic[17] remedy, fitted for all persons and all dispositions; and is alone able to subvert that abstruse philosophy and metaphysical jargon, which, being mixed up with popular superstition, renders it in a manner impenetrable [13] to careless reasoners, and gives it the air of science and wisdom.

13   Besides this advantage of rejecting, after deliberate enquiry, the most uncertain and disagreeable part of learning, there are many positive advantages, which result from an accurate scrutiny into the powers and faculties of human nature. It is remarkable concerning the operations of the mind, that, though most intimately present to us, yet, whenever they

---

[17] Universal or complete.

9

become the object of reflexion, they seem involved in obscurity; nor can the eye readily find those lines and boundaries, which discriminate and distinguish them. The objects are too fine to remain long in the same aspect or situation; and must be apprehended in an instant, by a superior penetration, derived from nature, and improved by habit and reflexion. It becomes, therefore, no inconsiderable part of science barely to know the different operations of the mind, to separate them from each other, to class them under their proper heads, and to correct all that seeming disorder, in which they lie involved, when made the object of reflexion and enquiry. This talk of ordering and distinguishing, which has no merit, when performed with regard to external bodies, the objects of our senses, rises in its value, when directed towards the operations of the mind, in proportion to the difficulty and labour, which we meet with in performing it. And if we can go no farther than this mental geography, or delineation of the distinct parts and powers of the mind, it is at least a satisfaction to go so far; and the more obvious this science may appear (and it is by no means obvious) the more contemptible still must the ignorance of it be esteemed, in all pretenders to learning and philosophy.

14   Nor can there remain any suspicion, that this science is uncertain and chimerical;[18] unless we should entertain such a scepticism as is entirely subversive of all speculation, and even action. It cannot be doubted, that the mind is endowed with several powers and faculties, that these powers are distinct from each other, that what is really distinct to the immediate perception may be distinguished by reflexion; and consequently, that there is a truth and falsehood in all propositions on this subject, and a truth and falsehood, which lie not beyond the compass of human understanding. There are many obvious distinctions of this kind, such as those between the will and understanding, the imagination and passions, which fall within the comprehension of every human creature; and the finer and more philosophical distinctions are no less real and certain, though more difficult to be comprehended. Some instances, especially late ones, of success in these enquiries, may give us a juster notion of the certainty and solidity of this branch of learning. And shall we esteem it worthy the labour of a philosopher to give us a true system of the planets, and adjust the position and order of those remote bodies; while we affect to

[14]

---

[18] Fanciful or illusory. In Greek mythology, the Chimera is a fire-breathing monster with a lion's head, a goat's body and a serpent's tail.

overlook those, who, with so much success, delineate the parts of the mind, in which we are so intimately concerned?[a]

15   But may we not hope, that philosophy, cultivated with care, and encouraged by the attention of the public, may carry its researches still farther, and discover, at least in some degree, the secret springs and principles, by which the human mind is actuated in its operations? Astronomers had long contented themselves with proving, from the phenomena, the true motions, order, and magnitude of the heavenly bodies: Till a philosopher, at last, arose, who seems, from the happiest reasoning, to have also determined the laws and forces, by which the revolutions of the planets are governed and directed.[19] The like has been performed with regard to other parts of nature. And there is no reason to despair of equal success in our enquiries concerning the mental powers and economy, if prosecuted with equal capacity and caution. It is probable, that one operation and [15] principle of the mind depends on another; which, again, may be resolved

---

[a] That faculty, by which we discern truth and falsehood, and that by which we perceive vice and virtue had long been confounded with each other, and all morality was supposed to be built on eternal and immutable relations, which to every intelligent mind were equally invariable as any proposition concerning quantity and number. But a late philosopher [Francis Hutcheson (1694–1746), in his *Inquiry* (1725) and *Essay* (1728)] has taught us, by the most convincing arguments, that morality is nothing in the abstract nature of things, but is entirely relative to the sentiment or mental taste of each particular being; in the same manner as the distinctions of sweet and bitter, hot and cold, arise from the particular feeling of each sense or organ. Moral perceptions therefore, ought not to be classed with the operations of the understanding, but with the tastes or sentiments.

It had been usual with philosophers to divide all the passions of the mind into two classes, the selfish and benevolent, which were supposed to stand in constant opposition and contrariety; nor was it thought that the latter could ever attain their proper object but at the expense of the former. Among the selfish passions were ranked avarice, ambition, revenge: Among the benevolent, natural affection, friendship, public spirit. Philosophers may now perceive the impropriety of this division. It has been proved, beyond all controversy [by Joseph Butler (1692–1752), in his *Sermons* (1729)], that even the passions, commonly esteemed selfish, carry the mind beyond self, directly to the object; that though the satisfaction of these passions gives us enjoyment, yet the prospect of this enjoyment is not the cause of the passion, but on the contrary the passion is antecedent to the enjoyment, and without the former, the latter could never possibly exist; that the case is precisely the same with the passions, denominated benevolent, and consequently that a man is no more interested when he seeks his own glory than when the happiness of his friend is the object of his wishes; nor is he any more disinterested when he sacrifices his ease and quiet to public good than when he labours for the gratification of avarice and ambition. Here therefore is a considerable adjustment in the boundaries of the passions, which had been confounded by the negligence or inaccuracy of former philosophers. These two instances may suffice to show us the nature and importance of this species of philosophy. [Footnote in the 1748 and 1750 editions.]

[19] That is, Sir Isaac Newton (1642–1727). His *Philosophiae Naturalis Principia Mathematica* (Mathematical Principles of Natural Philosophy) (1687) gave a mathematical description of the laws of mechanics and gravitation, and applied them to planetary motion.

into one more general and universal: And how far these researches may possibly be carried, it will be difficult for us, before, or even after, a careful trial, exactly to determine. This is certain, that attempts of this kind are every day made even by those who philosophize the most negligently: And nothing can be more requisite than to enter upon the enterprise with thorough care and attention; that, if it lie within the compass of human understanding, it may at last be happily achieved; if not, it may, however, be rejected with some confidence and security. This last conclusion, surely, is not desirable; nor ought it to be embraced too rashly. For how much must we diminish from the beauty and value of this species of philosophy, upon such a supposition? Moralists have hitherto been accustomed, when they considered the vast multitude and diversity of those actions that excite our approbation or dislike, to search for some common principle, on which this variety of sentiments might depend. And though they have sometimes carried the matter too far, by their passion for some one general principle; it must, however, be confessed, that they are excusable in expecting to find some general principles, into which all the vices and virtues were justly to be resolved. The like has been the endeavour of critics, logicians, and even politicians: Nor have their attempts been wholly unsuccessful; though perhaps longer time, greater accuracy, and more ardent application may bring these sciences still nearer their perfection. To throw up at once all pretensions of this kind may justly be deemed more rash, precipitate, and dogmatical, than even the boldest and most affirmative philosophy, that has ever attempted to impose its crude dictates and principles on mankind.

[16]   16   What though these reasonings concerning human nature seem abstract, and of difficult comprehension? This affords no presumption of their falsehood. On the contrary, it seems impossible, that what has hitherto escaped so many wise and profound philosophers can be very obvious and easy. And whatever pains these researches may cost us, we may think ourselves sufficiently rewarded, not only in point of profit but of pleasure, if by that means, we can make any addition to our stock of knowledge, in subjects of such unspeakable importance.

17   But as, after all, the abstractedness of these speculations is no recommendation, but rather a disadvantage to them, and as this difficulty may perhaps be surmounted by care and art, and the avoiding of all unnecessary detail, we have, in the following enquiry, attempted to throw some light upon subjects, from which uncertainty has hitherto deterred

the wise, and obscurity the ignorant. Happy, if we can unite the boundaries of the different species of philosophy, by reconciling profound enquiry with clearness, and truth with novelty! And still more happy, if, reasoning in this easy manner, we can undermine the foundations of an abstruse philosophy, which seems to have hitherto served only as a shelter to superstition, and a cover to absurdity and error!

2

Of the origin of ideas

1   Every one will readily allow, that there is a considerable difference between the perceptions of the mind, when a man feels the pain of excessive heat, or the pleasure of moderate warmth, and when he afterwards recalls to his memory this sensation, or anticipates it by his imagination. These faculties may mimic or copy the perceptions of the senses; but they never can entirely reach the force and vivacity of the original sentiment.[1] The utmost we say of them, even when they operate with greatest vigour, is, that they represent their object in so lively a manner, that we could *almost* say we feel or see it: But, except the mind be disordered by disease or madness, they never can arrive at such a pitch of vivacity, as to render these perceptions altogether undistinguishable. All the colours of poetry, however splendid, can never paint natural objects in such a manner as to make the description be taken for a real landscape. The most lively thought is still inferior to the dullest sensation.

2   We may observe a like distinction to run through all the other perceptions of the mind. A man, in a fit of anger, is actuated in a very different manner from one who only thinks of that emotion. If you tell me, that any person is in love, I easily understand your meaning, and form a just conception of his situation; but never can mistake that conception for the real disorders and agitations of the passion. When we reflect on our past sentiments [18] and affections, our thought is a faithful mirror, and copies its objects

---

[1] The division of the mind's powers of perception into distinct faculties – sensation, memory, imagination and intellect (or understanding) – derives from Aristotle (*On the Soul*, II–III). The distinction between strong or forceful sensations and weaker imaginings is emphasized in Hobbes (*Leviathan*, 13–16), Malebranche (*The Search after Truth*, 1.12.3–5) and Berkeley (*Principles*, 1.30, 33).

14

truly; but the colours which it employs are faint and dull, in comparison of those in which our original perceptions were clothed. It requires no nice[2] discernment or metaphysical head to mark the distinction between them.

3   Here therefore we may divide all the perceptions of the mind into two classes or species, which are distinguished by their different degrees of force and vivacity.[3] The less forcible and lively are commonly denominated *thoughts* or *ideas*. The other species want a name in our language, and in most others; I suppose, because it was not requisite for any, but philosophical purposes, to rank them under a general term or appellation. Let us, therefore, use a little freedom, and call them *impressions*; employing that word in a sense somewhat different from the usual.[4] By the term *impression*, then, I mean all our more lively perceptions, when we hear, or see, or feel, or love, or hate, or desire, or will. And impressions are distinguished from ideas, which are the less lively perceptions, of which we are conscious, when we reflect on any of those sensations or movements above mentioned.

4   Nothing, at first view, may seem more unbounded than the thought of man, which not only escapes all human power and authority, but is not even restrained within the limits of nature and reality. To form monsters, and join incongruous shapes and appearances, costs the imagination no more trouble than to conceive the most natural and familiar objects. And while the body is confined to one planet, along which it creeps with pain and difficulty; the thought can in an instant transport us into the most distant regions of the universe; or even beyond the universe, into the unbounded chaos, where nature is supposed to lie in total confusion.[5] What never was seen, or heard of, may yet be conceived; nor is any thing beyond the power of thought, except what implies an absolute contradiction.

5   But though our thought seems to possess this unbounded [19] liberty, we shall find, upon a nearer examination, that it is really confined

---

[2] Fine or subtle.

[3] Degree of vivacity or vividness is a measure of perceived intensity, and thus a perceptual standard. Descartes (*Meditations*, Sixth Meditation, 2.52) regards liveliness or vivacity as a marker of sensory, and thus bodily, processes.

[4] The term has a long history in philosophical literature. It derives from Plato's metaphor of the mind as a wax block on which sensations are stamped or impressed (*Theaetetus*, 191c–d), a metaphor which echoes through theories of perception from Aristotle (*On the Soul*, II.12) all the way to Locke (*Essay*, 2.29.3). Both Hobbes and Locke also occasionally use 'impression' as a term for sensation (e.g. *Leviathan*, 16; *Essay*, 2.1.8; 2.21.1). Samuel Clarke attacked Hobbes for reducing (mental) ideas to impressions on the brain (*A Demonstration of the Being and Attributes of God*, X).

[5] In Greek mythology, the universe is created from *chaos*; but this means 'chasm', and so does not imply the disorder or confusion that Hume here supposes.

within very narrow limits, and that all this creative power of the mind amounts to no more than the faculty of compounding, transposing, augmenting, or diminishing the materials afforded us by the senses and experience. When we think of a golden mountain, we only join two consistent ideas, *gold*, and *mountain*, with which we were formerly acquainted. A virtuous horse we can conceive; because, from our own feeling, we can conceive virtue; and this we may unite to the figure and shape of a horse, which is an animal familiar to us. In short, all the materials of thinking are derived either from our outward or inward sentiment: The mixture and composition of these belongs alone to the mind and will. Or, to express myself in philosophical language, all our ideas or more feeble perceptions are copies of our impressions or more lively ones.

6   To prove this, the two following arguments will, I hope, be sufficient. *First*, when we analyse our thoughts or ideas, however compounded or sublime, we always find that they resolve themselves into such simple ideas as were copied from a precedent feeling or sentiment.[6] Even those ideas, which, at first view, seem the most wide of this origin, are found, upon a nearer scrutiny, to be derived from it. The idea of God, as meaning *an infinitely intelligent, wise, and good Being*, arises from reflecting on the operations of our own mind, and augmenting, without limit, those qualities of goodness and wisdom.[7] We may prosecute this enquiry to what length we please; where we shall always find, that every idea which we examine is copied from a similar impression. Those who would assert that this position is not universally true nor without exception, have only one, and that an easy method of refuting it; by producing that idea, which, in [20] their opinion, is not derived from this source. It will then be incumbent on us, if we would maintain our doctrine, to produce the impression, or lively perception, which corresponds to it.

7   *Secondly*, if it happen, from a defect of the organ, that a man is not susceptible of any species of sensation, we always find that he is as little susceptible of the correspondent ideas. A blind man can form no notion of colours; a deaf man of sounds. Restore either of them that sense in which he is deficient; by opening this new inlet for his sensations, you also open an inlet for the ideas; and he finds no difficulty in conceiving these objects.

---

[6] The division of our ideas into simple and compounded (or complex) is a foundation-stone of Locke's philosophy (*Essay*, 2.2ff).

[7] The origin of our idea of God was a litmus test for rationalist and empiricist theories of mental content. Hume follows Locke's account (*Essay*, 1.4.8–11).

The case is the same, if the object, proper for exciting any sensation, has never been applied to the organ. A Laplander or Negro[8] has no notion of the relish of wine. And though there are few or no instances of a like deficiency in the mind, where a person has never felt or is wholly incapable of a sentiment or passion that belongs to his species; yet we find the same observation to take place in a less degree. A man of mild manners can form no idea of inveterate revenge or cruelty; nor can a selfish heart easily conceive the heights of friendship and generosity. It is readily allowed, that other beings may possess many senses of which we can have no conception; because the ideas of them have never been introduced to us in the only manner by which an idea can have access to the mind, to wit, by the actual feeling and sensation.

8   There is, however, one contradictory phenomenon, which may prove that it is not absolutely impossible for ideas to arise, independent of their correspondent impressions. I believe it will readily be allowed, that the several distinct ideas of colour, which enter by the eye, or those of sound, which are conveyed by the ear, are really different from each other; though, at the same time, resembling. Now if this be true of different colours, it must be no less so of the different shades of the same colour; and each shade produces a distinct idea, independent of the rest. For if [21] this should be denied, it is possible, by the continual gradation of shades, to run a colour insensibly into what is most remote from it; and if you will not allow any of the means to be different, you cannot, without absurdity, deny the extremes to be the same. Suppose, therefore, a person to have enjoyed his sight for thirty years, and to have become perfectly acquainted with colours of all kinds except one particular shade of blue, for instance, which it never has been his fortune to meet with. Let all the different shades of that colour, except that single one, be placed before him, descending gradually from the deepest to the lightest; it is plain that he will perceive a blank, where that shade is wanting, and will be sensible that there is a greater distance in that place between the contiguous colour than in any other. Now I ask, whether it be possible for him, from his own imagination, to supply this deficiency, and raise up to himself the idea of that particular shade, though it had never been conveyed to him by his senses? I believe there are few but will be of opinion that he can: And this may serve

---

[8] Laplander: Lapland lies in the extreme north of Scandinavia and north-west Russia, inhabited by the Sami people (previously known by the Swedish term 'Lapp'). Negro (from Spanish and Portuguese for 'black'): the context shows Hume to have in mind the indigenous black African.

as a proof that the simple ideas are not always, in every instance, derived from the correspondent impressions; though this instance is so singular, that it is scarcely worth our observing, and does not merit that for it alone we should alter our general maxim.

9   Here, therefore, is a proposition, which not only seems, in itself, simple and intelligible; but, if a proper use were made of it, might render every dispute equally intelligible, and banish all that jargon, which has so long taken possession of metaphysical reasonings, and drawn disgrace upon them. All ideas, especially abstract ones, are naturally faint and obscure: The mind has but a slender hold of them: They are apt to be confounded
[22]   with other resembling ideas; and when we have often employed any term, though without a distinct meaning, we are apt to imagine it has a determinate idea annexed to it. On the contrary, all impressions, that is, all sensations, either outward or inward, are strong and vivid: The limits between them are more exactly determined: Nor is it easy to fall into any error or mistake with regard to them. When we entertain, therefore, any suspicion that a philosophical term is employed without any meaning or idea (as is but too frequent), we need but enquire, *from what impression is that supposed idea derived?* And if it be impossible to assign any, this will serve to confirm our suspicion.[9] By bringing ideas into so clear a light we may reasonably hope to remove all dispute, which may arise, concerning their nature and reality.[a]

---

[a] It is probable that no more was meant by these, who denied innate ideas, than that all ideas were copies of our impressions; though it must be confessed, that the terms, which they employed, were not chosen with such caution, nor so exactly defined, as to prevent all mistakes about their doctrine. For what is meant by *innate*? If innate be equivalent to natural, then all the perceptions and ideas of the mind must be allowed to be innate or natural, in whatever sense we take the latter word, whether in opposition to what is uncommon, artificial, or miraculous. If by *innate* be meant, *cotemporary to our birth*, the dispute seems to be frivolous; nor is it worth while to enquire at what time thinking begins, whether before, at, or after our birth. Again, the word *idea*, seems to be commonly taken in a very loose sense, by Locke and others; as standing for any of our perceptions, our sensations and passions, as well as thoughts. Now in this sense, I should desire to know, what can be meant by asserting, that self-love, or resentment of injuries, or the passion between the sexes is not innate?

But admitting these terms, *impressions* and *ideas*, in the sense above explained, and understanding by *innate*, what is original or copied from no precedent perception, then may we assert that all our impressions are innate, and our ideas not innate.

To be ingenuous, I must own it to be my opinion, that Locke was betrayed into this question by the schoolmen, who, making use of undefined terms, draw out their disputes to a tedious length, without ever touching the point in question. A like ambiguity and circumlocution seem to run through that philosopher's reasonings on this as well as most other subjects.

[9] The confusions caused by inconsistent or empty uses of words is a recurring theme in seventeenth-century philosophy, particularly amongst critics of scholasticism. See Bacon (*New Organon*, 1.59–60), Hobbes (*Leviathan*, 28, 30–1, 33), Arnauld and Nicole (*Logic or the Art of Thinking*, 58–60) and Locke (*Essay*, 3.2.4–8, 3.10.2–4).

3

Of the association of ideas

1   It is evident, that there is a principle of connexion between the different thoughts or ideas of the mind, and that, in their appearance to the memory or imagination, they introduce each other with a certain degree of method and regularity. In our more serious thinking or discourse, this is so observable, that any particular thought, which breaks in upon the regular tract or chain of ideas, is immediately remarked and rejected. And even in our wildest and most wandering reveries, nay in our very dreams, we shall find, if we reflect, that the imagination ran not altogether at adventures, but that there was still a connexion upheld among the different ideas, which succeeded each other. Were the loosest and freest conversation to be transcribed, there would immediately be observed something which connected it in all its transitions. Or where this is wanting, the person, who broke the thread of discourse, might still inform you, that there had secretly revolved in his mind a succession of thought, which had gradually led him from the subject of conversation. Among different languages, even where we cannot suspect the least connexion or communication, it is found, that the words, expressive of ideas, the most compounded, do yet nearly correspond to each other: A certain proof that the simple ideas, comprehended in the compound ones, were bound together by some universal principle, which had an equal influence on all mankind.

2   Though it be too obvious to escape observation, that [24] different ideas are connected together; I do not find that any philosopher has attempted to enumerate or class all the principles of

association;[1] a subject, however, that seems worthy of curiosity. To me, there appear to be only three principles of connexion among ideas, namely, *resemblance*, *contiguity* in time or place, and *cause* or *effect*.

3   That these principles serve to connect ideas will not, I believe, be much doubted. A picture naturally leads our thoughts to the original:[a] The mention of one apartment in a building naturally introduces an enquiry or discourse concerning the others:[b] And if we think of a wound, we can scarcely forbear reflecting on the pain which follows it.[c] But that this enumeration is complete, and that there are no other principles of association except these, may be difficult to prove to the satisfaction of the reader, or even to a man's own satisfaction. All we can do, in such cases, is to run over several instances, and examine carefully the principle which binds the different thoughts to each other, never stopping till we render the principle as general as possible. The more instances we examine, and the more care we employ, the more assurance shall we acquire, that the enumeration, which we form from the whole, is complete and entire.[2] Instead of entering into a detail of this kind, which would lead into many useless subtleties, we shall consider some of the effects of this connexion upon the passions and imagination; where we may open a field of speculation more entertaining, and perhaps more instructive, than the other.

4   As man is a reasonable being, and is continually in pursuit of happiness, which he hopes to attain by the gratification of some passion or affection, he seldom acts or speaks or thinks without a purpose and intention. He has still some object in view; and however improper the means may sometimes be, which he chooses for the attainment of his end, he never loses view of an end; nor will he so much as throw away his thoughts or reflections, where he hopes not to reap some satisfaction from them.

5   In all compositions of genius, therefore, it is requisite, that the writer have some plan or object; and though he may be hurried from this plan by the vehemence of thought, as in an ode, or drop it carelessly, as in

---

[a] Resemblance.   [b] Contiguity.   [c] Cause and effect.

[1] Associations, or mutual connections, of ideas were a subject of interest to several philosophers. Hobbes (*Leviathan*, 20–1) and Malebranche (*Search after Truth*, 2.1.5.1–2; 2.2.2) explain them by reference to physiological processes. Locke (*Essay*, 2.33) adds a discussion of them as an afterthought, and avoids the speculative physiology.

[2] The remainder of this section appeared in all editions from 1748 to 1772, but was cut from the 1777 edition. Its subject matter, the role of the principles of association in aesthetic perception, follows the lead of Francis Hutcheson (*Inquiry*, 1.6.3, 11–12).

an epistle or essay, there must appear some aim or intention, in his first setting out, if not in the composition of the whole work. A production without a design would resemble more the ravings of a madman,[3] than the sober efforts of genius and learning.

6   As this rule admits of no exception, it follows, that, in narrative compositions, the events or actions, which the writer relates, must be connected together, by some bond or tie: They must be related to each other in the imagination, and form a kind of *unity*, which may bring them under one plan or view, and which may be the object or end of the writer in his first undertaking.

7   This connecting principle among the several events, which form the subject of a poem or history, may be very different, according to the different designs of the poet or historian. Ovid has formed his plan upon the connecting principle of resemblance.[4] Every fabulous transformation, produced by the miraculous power of the gods, falls within the compass of his work. There needs but this one circumstance in any event to bring it under his original plan or intention.

8   An annalist or historian, who should undertake to write the history of Europe during any century, would be influenced by the connexion of contiguity in time and place. All events, which happen in that portion of space and period of time, are comprehended in his design, though in other respects different and unconnected. They have still a species of unity, amidst all their diversity.[5]

9   But the most usual species of connexion among the different events, which enter into any narrative composition, is that of cause and effect; while the historian traces the series of actions according to their natural order, remounts to their secret springs and principles, and delineates their most remote consequences. He chooses for his subject a certain portion of that great chain of events, which compose the history of mankind: Each link in this chain he endeavours to touch in his narration: Sometimes unavoidable ignorance renders all his attempts fruitless: Sometimes, he supplies by conjecture, what is wanting in knowledge: And

---

[3] Locke (*Essay*, 2.11.13; 2.33.3–4) compares associations to madness, because both involve non-rational connections between ideas. Its implication, that rule by the imagination is madness, appears also in Samuel Johnson's *Rasselas* (1759).

[4] Ovid (43 BC–AD c. 17), Roman poet. *Metamorphoses* retells Greek and Roman myths, organized on the theme of changes of shape.

[5] Unity in diversity is much stressed in Hutcheson's aesthetics (e.g. *Inquiry*, 1.3.8–9).

always, he is sensible, that the more unbroken the chain is, which he presents to his reader, the more perfect is his production. He sees, that the knowledge of causes is not only the most satisfactory; this relation or connexion being the strongest of all others; but also the most instructive; since it is by this knowledge alone, we are enabled to control events, and govern futurity.

10   Here therefore we may attain some notion of that *unity* of *action*, about which all critics, after Aristotle, have talked so much:[6] Perhaps, to little purpose, while they directed not their taste or sentiment by the accuracy of philosophy. It appears, that, in all productions, as well as in the epic and tragic, there is a certain unity required, and that, on no occasion, can our thoughts be allowed to run at adventures, if we would produce a work, which will give any lasting entertainment to mankind. It appears also, that even a biographer, who should write the life of Achilles,[7] would connect the events, by showing their mutual dependence and relation, as much as a poet, who should make the anger of that hero, the subject of his narration.[d] Not only in any limited portion of life, a man's actions have a dependence on each other, but also during the whole period of his duration, from the cradle to the grave; nor is it possible to strike off one link, however minute, in this regular chain, without affecting the whole series of events, which follow. The unity of action, therefore, which is to be found in biography or history, differs from that of epic poetry, not in kind, but degree. In epic poetry, the connexion among the events is more close and sensible:[8] The narration is not carried on through such a length of time: And the actors hasten to some remarkable period, which satisfies the curiosity of the reader. This conduct of the epic poet depends on that particular situation of the *imagination* and of the *passions*, which is supposed in that production. The imagination, both of writer and reader,

---

[d] Contrary to Aristotle, Μῦθος δέστὶν εἶζ, οὐχ, ὥσπερ τινὲζ οἴονται, ἐάν περὶ ἕνα ᾖ . Πολλὰ γὰρ καὶ ἄπειρα τῶ γένει συμβαίνει, ἐξ ὧν ἐνίων οὐ δέν ἐστιν ἕν. Οὔτω δὲ καὶ πρὰξειζ ἑνὸζ πολλαὶ εἰσιν, ἐξ ὧν μία οὐδεμὶα γίνεται πρᾶ ξιζ, & c. Κεφ. ή. ['The unity of a plot does not consist, as some suppose, in its having one man as its subject. An infinity of things befall that one man, some of which it is impossible to reduce to unity; and in like manner there are many actions of one man which cannot be made to form one action.' Aristotle, *Poetics*, 1451a15–19.]

[6] Aristotle, *Poetics*, 1451a. A fundamental source for eighteenth-century aesthetics, the *Poetics* distinguishes between two types of poetry, epic and tragic, and sets out their defining features. (Epics are long narrative poems about the actions of ancient heroes, e.g. Homer, *The Iliad*; tragic poetry means ancient Greek tragedy, e.g. Sophocles, *Oedipus the King*.)

[7] The central figure of *The Iliad*, whose anger at being slighted sets in motion a train of tragic events.

[8] Visible.

is more enlivened, and the passions more enflamed than in history, biography, or any species of narration, which confine themselves to strict truth and reality. Let us consider the effect of these two circumstances, an enlivened imagination and enflamed passion; circumstances, which belong to poetry, especially the epic kind, above any other species of composition: And let us examine the reason, why they require a stricter and closer unity in the fable.

11   *First*, all poetry, being a species of painting,[9] brings us nearer to the objects than any other species of narration, throws a stronger light upon them, and delineates more distinctly those minute circumstances, which, though to the historian they seem superfluous, serve mightily to enliven the imagery, and gratify the fancy. If it be not necessary, as in the *Iliad*, to inform us each time the hero buckles his shoes, and ties his garters, it will be requisite, perhaps, to enter into a greater detail than in the *Henriade*;[10] where the events are run over with such rapidity, that we scarcely have leisure to become acquainted with the scene or action. Were a poet, therefore, to comprehend in his subject, any great compass of time or series of events, and trace up the death of Hector to its remote causes, in the rape of Helen, or the judgment of Paris, he must draw out his poem to an immeasurable length, in order to fill this large canvas with just painting and imagery.[11] The reader's imagination, enflamed with such a series of poetical descriptions, and his passions, agitated by a continual sympathy with the actors, must flag long before the period of the narration, and must sink into lassitude and disgust, from the repeated violence of the same movements.

12   *Secondly*, that an epic poet must not trace the causes to any great distance, will farther appear, if we consider another reason, which is drawn from a property of the passions still more remarkable and singular. It is evident, that, in a just composition, all the affections, excited by the different events, described and represented, add mutual force to each

---

[9] Horace (65–8 BC), 'a poem is like a painting', *Art of Poetry*, 360. Horace's passing remark became an aesthetic dogma in the eighteenth century.

[10] Voltaire (1694–1778), French poet and critic. *La Henriade* is an epic poem about the events through which Henri of Navarre became Henri IV of France in 1589.

[11] The point is that this is what Homer, in *The Iliad*, does not do. Instead 'he plunges his hearer into the middle of things' (Horace, *Art of Poetry*, 149), showing how the anger of Achilles leads to the death of Hector, Prince of Troy. The mythological cause of the Trojan War – the judgement of Paris (Hector's brother) that the goddess Aphrodite was fairer than Hera and Athena, for which decision Aphrodite enabled him to abduct Helen and take her to Troy – is simply assumed.

other; and that, while the heroes are all engaged in one common scene, and each action is strongly connected with the whole, the concern is continually awake, and the passions make an easy transition from one object to another. The strong connexion of the events, as it facilitates the passage of the thought or imagination from one to another, facilitates also the transfusion of the passions, and preserves the affections still in the same channel and direction. Our sympathy and concern for Eve prepares the way for a like sympathy with Adam: The affection is preserved almost entire in the transition; and the mind seizes immediately the new object as strongly related to that which formerly engaged its attention. But were the poet to make a total digression from his subject, and introduce a new actor, nowise connected with the personages, the imagination, feeling a breach in the transition, would enter coldly into the new scene; would kindle by slow degrees; and in returning to the main subject of the poem, would pass, as it were, upon foreign ground, and have its concern to excite anew, in order to take part with the principal actors. The same inconvenience follows in a less degree; where the poet traces his events to too great a distance, and binds together actions, which, though not entirely disjoined, have not so strong a connexion as is requisite to forward the transition of the passions. Hence arises the artifice of the oblique narration, employed in the *Odyssey* and *Aeneid*; where the hero is introduced, at first, near the period of his designs, and afterwards shows us, as it were in perspective, the more distant events and causes.[12] By this means, the reader's curiosity is immediately excited: The events follow with rapidity, and in a very close connexion: And the concern is preserved alive, and, by means of the near relation of the objects, continually increases, from the beginning to the end of the narration.

13   The same rule takes place in dramatic poetry; nor is it ever permitted, in a regular composition, to introduce an actor, who has no connexion, or but a small one, with the principal personages of the fable. The spectator's concern must not be diverted by any scenes disjoined and separated by the rest. This breaks the course of the passions, and prevents that communication of the several emotions, by which one scene adds

---

[12] *The Odyssey* is Homer's poem about Odysseus's wanderings after the fall of Troy. *The Aeneid*, by the Roman poet Virgil (70–19 BC), describes the wanderings of Aeneas after the fall of Troy and his foundation of the city of Rome. Oblique narration is the device of telling the story through the main character in retrospect, rather than through the narrator.

force to another, and transfuses the pity and terror,[13] which it excites, upon each succeeding scene, till the whole produces that rapidity of movement, which is peculiar to the theatre. How must it extinguish this warmth of affection, to be entertained, on a sudden, with a new action and new personages, nowise related to the former; to find so sensible a breach or vacuity in the course of the passions, by means of this breach in the connexion of ideas; and instead of carrying the sympathy of one scene into the following, to be obliged, every moment, to excite a new concern, and take part in a new scene of action?

14 To return to the comparison of history and epic poetry, we may conclude, from the foregoing reasonings, that, as a certain unity is requisite in all productions, it cannot be wanting in history more than in any other; that, in history, the connexion among the several events, which unites them into one body, is the relation of cause and effect, the same which takes place in epic poetry; and that, in the latter composition, this connexion is only required to be closer and more sensible, on account of the lively imagination and strong passions, which must be touched by the poet in his narration. The Peloponnesian war is a proper subject for history, the siege of Athens for an epic poem, and the death of Alcibiades for a tragedy.[14]

15 As the difference, therefore, between history and epic poetry consists only in the degrees of connexion, which bind together those several events, of which their subject is composed, it will be difficult, if not impossible, by words, to determine exactly the bounds, which separate them from each other. That is a matter of taste more than of reasoning; and perhaps, this unity may often be discovered in a subject, where, at first view, and from an abstract consideration, we should least expect to find it.

16 It is evident, that Homer, in the course of his narration, exceeds the first proposition of his subject; and that the anger of Achilles, which caused the death of Hector, is not the same with that which produced so many ills to the Greeks. But the strong connexion between these two

---

[13] According to Aristotle, tragedy causes *catharsis*, or purging of the emotions, by arousing pity and fear in the spectator (*Poetics*, 1449b).

[14] Thucydides (c. 455–c. 400 BC) anticipated Hume's advice and wrote the *History of the Peloponnesian War* (about the long war between Sparta and Athens (431–404 BC)). The other two events, falling within the same historical period, have not found an author: the siege of Athens occurred at the end of the Peloponnesian War; Alcibiades (c. 450–404 BC) was an Athenian of exceptional talents who changed sides twice during the War, and later sought refuge with the Persians, only to be murdered by them. (He enjoys a cameo role in Plato's *Symposium*.)

movements, the quick transition from one to another, the contrast[e] between the effects of concord and discord among the princes, and the natural curiosity which we have to see Achilles in action, after so long a repose; all these causes carry on the reader, and produce a sufficient unity in the subject.

17   It may be objected to Milton,[15] that he has traced up his causes to too great a distance, and that the rebellion of the angels produces the fall of man by a train of events, which is both very long and very casual.[16] Not to mention, that the creation of the world, which he has related at length, is no more the cause of that catastrophe, than of the battle of Pharsalia,[17] or any other event, that has ever happened. But if we consider, on the other hand, that all these events, the rebellion of the angels, the creation of the world, and the fall of man, *resemble* each other, in being miraculous and out of the common course of nature; that they are supposed to be *contiguous* in time; and that being detached from all other events, and being the only original facts, which revelation discovers, they strike the eye at once, and naturally recall each other to the thought or imagination: If we consider all these circumstances, I say, we shall find, that these parts of the action have a sufficient unity to make them be comprehended in one fable or narration. To which we may add, that the rebellion of the angels and the fall of man have a peculiar resemblance, as being counterparts to each other, and presenting to the reader the same moral, of obedience to our Creator.

18   These loose hints I have thrown together, in order to excite the curiosity of philosophers, and beget a suspicion at least, if not a full persuasion, that this subject is very copious,[18] and that many operations of the human mind depend on the connexion or association of ideas, which is here explained. Particularly, the sympathy between the passions and imagination will, perhaps, appear remarkable; while we observe that the affections, excited by one object, pass easily to another object connected

---

[e] Contrast or contrariety is a connexion among ideas, which may, perhaps, be considered as a mixture of causation and resemblance. Where two objects are contrary, the one destroys the other, i.e. is the cause of its annihilation, and the idea of the annihilation of an object implies the idea of its former existence. [This footnote, slightly modified, was preserved in the 1777 edition, where it was attached to the end of the penultimate sentence (after 'possible'). See text preceding footnote indicator 2 on p. 20 above.]

[15] John Milton (1608–1704), English poet. His epic poem *Paradise Lost* culminates in the Fall in the Garden of Eden, but precedes it with a long account of the Creation.

[16] Chance or accidental.

[17] Julius Caesar defeated his rival Pompey at the Battle of Pharsalia (or Pharsalus), in 48 BC.

[18] Extensive; providing an abundance of examples.

with it; but transfuse themselves with difficulty, or not at all, along different objects, which have no manner of connexion together. By introducing, into any composition, personages and actions, foreign to each other,[19] an injudicious author loses that communication of emotions, by which alone he can interest the heart, and raise the passions to their proper height and period. The full explication of this principle and all its consequences would lead us into reasonings too profound and too copious for this enquiry. It is sufficient, at present, to have established this conclusion, that the three connecting principles of all ideas are the relations of *resemblance*, *contiguity*, and *causation*.

[19] That is, incapable of unification. See Horace, *Art of Poetry*, 1–23.

4

Sceptical doubts concerning the operations of the understanding

Part 1

1   All the objects of human reason or enquiry may naturally be divided into two kinds, to wit, *relations of ideas* and *matters of fact*.[1] Of the first kind are the sciences of geometry, algebra, and arithmetic; and in short, every affirmation which is either intuitively or demonstratively certain.[2] *That the square of the hypotenuse is equal to the square of the two sides*, is a proposition which expresses a relation between these figures. *That three times five is equal to the half of thirty*, expresses a relation between these numbers. Propositions of this kind are discoverable by the mere operation of thought, without dependence on what is anywhere existent in the universe. Though there never were a circle or triangle in nature, the truths demonstrated by Euclid would for ever retain their certainty and evidence.[3]

2   Matters of fact, which are the second objects of human reason, are not ascertained in the same manner; nor is our evidence of their truth, however great, of a like nature with the foregoing. The contrary of every matter of fact is still possible; because it can never imply a contradiction, and is conceived by the mind with the same facility and distinctness, as if

---

[1] The distinction is clearly stated in Arnauld and Nicole (*Art of Thinking*, 263), and appears in modified form in Malebranche (*Search after Truth*, 6.1.5).

[2] The intuitive and the demonstrative are the two forms of rational certainty. The intuitive is what is known immediately, the demonstrative what is known by means of rational inferences. The distinction is prominent in Descartes, *Rules for the Direction of the Mind*, Rule 3 (1.14–5), and also Locke (*Essay*, 4.2.1–14).

[3] Euclid (c. 300 BC), Greek mathematician, author of *The Elements*, the great textbook of geometry.

ever so conformable to reality. *That the sun will not rise tomorrow* is no [26] less intelligible a proposition, and implies no more contradiction than the affirmation, *that it will rise*. We should in vain, therefore, attempt to demonstrate its falsehood. Were it demonstratively false, it would imply a contradiction, and could never be distinctly conceived by the mind.

3   It may, therefore, be a subject worthy of curiosity, to enquire what is the nature of that evidence which assures us of any real existence and matter of fact, beyond the present testimony of our senses, or the records of our memory.[4] This part of philosophy, it is observable, has been little cultivated, either by the ancients or moderns; and therefore our doubts and errors, in the prosecution of so important an enquiry, may be the more excusable; while we march through such difficult paths without any guide or direction. They may even prove useful, by exciting curiosity, and destroying that implicit faith and security, which is the bane of all reasoning and free enquiry. The discovery of defects in the common philosophy, if any such there be, will not, I presume, be a discouragement, but rather an incitement, as is usual, to attempt something more full and satisfactory than has yet been proposed to the public.

4   All reasonings concerning matter of fact seem to be founded on the relation of *cause* and *effect*. By means of that relation alone we can go beyond the evidence of our memory and senses. If you were to ask a man, why he believes any matter of fact, which is absent; for instance, that his friend is in the country, or in France; he would give you a reason; and this reason would be some other fact; as a letter received from him, or the knowledge of his former resolutions and promises. A man finding a watch or any other machine in a desert island, would conclude that there had once been men in that island. All our reasonings concerning fact are of the same nature. And here it is constantly supposed that there is a con- [27] nexion between the present fact and that which is inferred from it. Were there nothing to bind them together, the inference would be entirely precarious. The hearing of an articulate voice and rational discourse in the dark assures us of the presence of some person: Why? Because these are the effects of the human make and fabric, and closely connected with it. If we anatomize[5] all the other reasonings of this nature, we shall find that they are founded on the relation of cause and effect, and that this relation is

---

[4] Locke (*Essay*, 4.3.5) restricts sensory knowledge of existing things to present impressions.
[5] Analyse in detail.

either near or remote, direct or collateral. Heat and light are collateral effects of fire, and the one effect may justly be inferred from the other.

5   If we would satisfy ourselves, therefore, concerning the nature of that evidence, which assures us of matters of fact, we must enquire how we arrive at the knowledge of cause and effect.

6   I shall venture to affirm, as a general proposition, which admits of no exception, that the knowledge of this relation is not, in any instance, attained by reasonings *a priori*; but arises entirely from experience,[6] when we find that any particular objects are constantly conjoined with each other. Let an object be presented to a man of ever so strong natural reason and abilities; if that object be entirely new to him, he will not be able, by the most accurate examination of its sensible qualities, to discover any of its causes or effects. Adam, though his rational faculties be supposed, at the very first, entirely perfect, could not have inferred from the fluidity and transparency of water that it would suffocate him, or from the light and warmth of fire that it would consume him. No object ever discovers,[7] by the qualities which appear to the senses, either the causes which produced it, or the effects which will arise from it; nor can our reason, unassisted by experience, ever draw any inference concerning real existence and matter of fact.

[28]   7   This proposition, *that causes and effects are discoverable, not by reason but by experience*, will readily be admitted with regard to such objects, as we remember to have once been altogether unknown to us; since we must be conscious of the utter inability, which we then lay under, of fore-telling what would arise from them. Present two smooth pieces of marble to a man who has no tincture of natural philosophy;[8] he will never discover that they will adhere together in such a manner as to require great force to separate them in a direct line, while they make so small a resistance to a lateral pressure. Such events, as bear little analogy to the common course of nature, are also readily confessed to be known only by experience; nor does any man imagine that the explosion of gunpowder, or the attraction of a loadstone,[9] could ever be discovered by arguments *a priori*. In like

---

[6] The *a priori* is what is prior to experience; Hume's use of the term reflects the Aristotelian conception of experience as the fruit of sensations and memories over time. Individual sense-perceptions are thus not experience, which explains why he treats the attempt to draw conclusions from such individual perceptions as *a priori* reasoning. (The modern meaning of *a priori* to mean prior even to sensation derives from Kant.)
[7] Reveals.   [8] In this context, the term means natural science.   [9] A magnetized stone.

manner, when an effect is supposed to depend upon an intricate machinery or secret structure of parts, we make no difficulty in attributing all our knowledge of it to experience. Who will assert that he can give the ultimate reason, why milk or bread is proper nourishment for a man, not for a lion or a tiger?

8   But the same truth may not appear, at first sight, to have the same evidence with regard to events, which have become familiar to us from our first appearance in the world, which bear a close analogy to the whole course of nature, and which are supposed to depend on the simple qualities of objects, without any secret structure of parts. We are apt to imagine that we could discover these effects by the mere operation of our reason, without experience. We fancy, that were we brought on a sudden into this world, we could at first have inferred that one billiard-ball would communicate motion to another upon impulse;[10] and that we needed not to have waited for the event, in order to pronounce with certainty concerning it. Such is the influence of custom, that, where it is strongest, it not only covers our natural ignorance, but even conceals itself, and seems not [29] to take place, merely because it is found in the highest degree.[11]

9   But to convince us that all the laws of nature, and all the operations of bodies without exception, are known only by experience, the following reflections may, perhaps, suffice. Were any object presented to us, and were we required to pronounce concerning the effect, which will result from it, without consulting past observation; after what manner, I beseech you, must the mind proceed in this operation? It must invent or imagine some event, which it ascribes to the object as its effect; and it is plain that this invention must be entirely arbitrary. The mind can never possibly find the effect in the supposed cause, by the most accurate scrutiny and examination. For the effect is totally different from the cause, and consequently can never be discovered in it. Motion in the second billiard-ball is a quite distinct event from motion in the first; nor is there anything in the one to suggest the smallest hint of the other. A stone or piece of metal raised into the air, and left without any support, immediately falls: But to consider the

[10] A collision or impact, resulting in change in motion. The term is employed carefully by Newton, *Principia*, Definition 8 and Scholium, and *Opticks*, Query 31 (64, 86, 132); and also by Locke (*Essay*, 2.8.11–3; 2.21.4).

[11] Malebranche (*Search after Truth*, 3.2.3) uses the example of a moving ball to argue that we are misled by experience into supposing that we perceive causes; Locke (*Essay*, 2.21.4) uses the same example to argue that experience gives only an 'obscure' idea of power. The basic point, that powers are imperceptible, goes back to Plato, *Theaetetus*, 155e.

matter *a priori*, is there anything we discover in this situation which can beget the idea of a downward, rather than an upward, or any other motion, in the stone or metal?

10   And as the first imagination or invention of a particular effect, in all natural operations, is arbitrary, where we consult not experience; so must we also esteem the supposed tie or connexion between the cause and effect, which binds them together, and renders it impossible that any other effect could result from the operation of that cause. When I see, for instance, a billiard-ball moving in a straight line towards another; even suppose motion in the second ball should by accident be suggested to me, as the result of their contact or impulse; may I not conceive, that a hundred different events might as well follow from that cause? May not both these [30] balls remain at absolute rest? May not the first ball return in a straight line, or leap off from the second in any line or direction? All these suppositions are consistent and conceivable. Why then should we give the preference to one, which is no more consistent or conceivable than the rest? All our reasonings *a priori* will never be able to show us any foundation for this preference.

11   In a word, then, every effect is a distinct event from its cause. It could not, therefore, be discovered in the cause, and the first invention or conception of it, *a priori*, must be entirely arbitrary. And even after it is suggested, the conjunction of it with the cause must appear equally arbitrary; since there are always many other effects, which, to reason, must seem fully as consistent and natural. In vain, therefore, should we pretend to determine any single event, or infer any cause or effect, without the assistance of observation and experience.

12   Hence we may discover the reason why no philosopher, who is rational and modest, has ever pretended to assign the ultimate cause of any natural operation, or to show distinctly the action of that power, which produces any single effect in the universe. It is confessed, that the utmost effort of human reason is to reduce the principles, productive of natural phenomena, to a greater simplicity, and to resolve the many particular effects into a few general causes, by means of reasonings from analogy, experience, and observation.[12] But as to the causes of these general causes, we should in vain attempt their discovery; nor shall we ever be able to satisfy ourselves, by any particular explication of them. These ultimate

---

[12] See Newton, *Principia*, 'Rules for the Study of Natural Philosophy', Rules 1–3 (87–9).

springs and principles are totally shut up from human curiosity and enquiry. Elasticity, gravity, cohesion of parts, communication of motion by impulse; these are probably the ultimate causes and principles which we shall ever discover in nature; and we may esteem ourselves sufficiently happy, if, by accurate enquiry and reasoning, we can trace up the particular phenomena to, or near to, these general principles.[13] The most perfect [31] philosophy of the natural kind only staves off our ignorance a little longer: As perhaps the most perfect philosophy of the moral or metaphysical kind serves only to discover larger portions of it. Thus the observation of human blindness and weakness is the result of all philosophy, and meets us at every turn, in spite of our endeavours to elude or avoid it.

13   Nor is geometry, when taken into the assistance of natural philosophy, ever able to remedy this defect, or lead us into the knowledge of ultimate causes, by all that accuracy of reasoning for which it is so justly celebrated. Every part of mixed mathematics[14] proceeds upon the supposition that certain laws are established by nature in her operations; and abstract reasonings are employed, either to assist experience in the discovery of these laws, or to determine their influence in particular instances, where it depends upon any precise degree of distance and quantity. Thus, it is a law of motion, discovered by experience, that the moment or force of any body in motion is in the compound ratio or proportion of its solid contents and its velocity;[15] and consequently, that a small force may remove the greatest obstacle or raise the greatest weight, if, by any contrivance or machinery, we can increase the velocity of that force, so as to make it an overmatch for its antagonist. Geometry assists us in the application of this law, by giving us the just dimensions of all the parts and figures which can enter into any species of machine; but still the discovery of the law itself is owing merely to experience, and all the abstract reasonings in the world could never lead us one step towards the knowledge of it.[16] When we reason *a priori*, and consider merely any object or cause, as it appears to the mind, independent of all observation, it never could suggest to us the notion of any distinct object, such as its effect; much less, show us the inseparable and inviolable connexion between them. A man must be very sagacious who could discover by reasoning that crystal is the effect of heat, and ice of cold, without being [32] previously acquainted with the operation of these qualities.

---

[13] See Newton, *Opticks*, Query 31 (137).   [14] Applied mathematics.
[15] See Newton, *Principia*, Definition 2 (60).   [16] See Newton, *Principia*, Preface to 1st edn (40–1).

Part 2

14   But we have not yet attained any tolerable satisfaction with regard to the question first proposed. Each solution still gives rise to a new question as difficult as the foregoing, and leads us on to farther enquiries. When it is asked, *What is the nature of all our reasonings concerning matter of fact?* the proper answer seems to be, that they are founded on the relation of cause and effect. When again it is asked, *What is the foundation of all our reasonings and conclusions concerning that relation?* it may be replied in one word, Experience. But if we still carry on our sifting humour, and ask, *What is the foundation of all conclusions from experience?* this implies a new question, which may be of more difficult solution and explication. Philosophers, that give themselves airs of superior wisdom and sufficiency, have a hard task when they encounter persons of inquisitive dispositions, who push them from every corner to which they retreat, and who are sure at last to bring them to some dangerous dilemma. The best expedient to prevent this confusion, is to be modest in our pretensions; and even to discover the difficulty ourselves before it is objected to us. By this means, we may make a kind of merit of our very ignorance.

15   I shall content myself, in this section, with an easy task, and shall pretend only to give a negative answer to the question here proposed. I say then, that, even after we have experience of the operations of cause and effect, our conclusions from that experience are *not* founded on reasoning, or any process of the understanding. This answer we must endeavour both to explain and to defend.

16   It must certainly be allowed, that nature has kept us at a great [33] distance from all her secrets, and has afforded us only the knowledge of a few superficial qualities of objects; while she conceals from us those powers and principles on which the influence of those objects entirely depends. Our senses inform us of the colour, weight, and consistence of bread; but neither sense nor reason can ever inform us of those qualities which fit it for the nourishment and support of a human body. Sight or feeling conveys an idea of the actual motion of bodies; but as to that wonderful force or power, which would carry on a moving body for ever in a continued change of place, and which bodies never lose but by communicating it to others;[17] of this we cannot form the most distant

---

[17] Newton, *Principia*, 1st Law of Motion (70–1).

conception. But notwithstanding this ignorance of natural powers[a] and principles, we always presume, when we see like sensible qualities, that they have like secret powers, and expect that effects, similar to those which we have experienced, will follow from them. If a body of like colour and consistence with that bread, which we have formerly eaten, be presented to us, we make no scruple of repeating the experiment, and foresee, with certainty, like nourishment and support. Now this is a process of the mind or thought, of which I would willingly know the foundation. It is allowed on all hands that there is no known connexion between the sensible qualities and the secret powers; and consequently, that the mind is not led to form such a conclusion concerning their constant and regular conjunction, by anything which it knows of their nature. As to past *experience*, it can be allowed to give *direct* and *certain* information of those precise objects only, and that precise period of time, which fell under its cognizance: But why this experience should be extended to future times, and to other objects, which for aught we know, may be only in appearance similar; this is the [34] main question on which I would insist. The bread, which I formerly ate, nourished me; that is, a body of such sensible qualities was, at that time, endowed with such secret powers: But does it follow, that other bread must also nourish me at another time, and that like sensible qualities must always be attended with like secret powers? The consequence seems nowise necessary. At least, it must be acknowledged that there is here a consequence drawn by the mind; that there is a certain step taken; a process of thought, and an inference, which wants to be explained. These two propositions are far from being the same, *I have found that such an object has always been attended with such an effect*, and *I foresee, that other objects, which are, in appearance, similar, will be attended with similar effects*. I shall allow, if you please, that the one proposition may justly be inferred from the other: I know, in fact, that it always is inferred. But if you insist that the inference is made by a chain of reasoning, I desire you to produce that reasoning.[18] The connexion between these propositions is not intuitive. There is required a medium,[19] which may enable the mind to draw such an inference, if indeed it be drawn by reasoning and argument. What that medium is,

---

[a] The word, *power*, is here used in a loose and popular sense. The more accurate explication of it would give additional evidence to this argument. See Section 7. [Footnote added in 1750.]

[18] Inference: any step taken by the mind (any movement from one idea to another), and so not necessarily a *logical* or *just* inference.

[19] An intermediate or linking premise in an argument. See Locke, *Essay*, 4.17.15–16.

I must confess, passes my comprehension; and it is incumbent on those to produce it, who assert, that it really exists, and is the origin of all our conclusions concerning matter of fact.

17   This negative argument must certainly, in process of time, become altogether convincing, if many penetrating and able philosophers shall turn their enquiries this way and no one be ever able to discover any connecting proposition or intermediate step, which supports the understanding in this conclusion. But as the question is yet new, every reader may not trust so far to his own penetration, as to conclude, because an argument escapes his enquiry, that therefore it does not really exist. For [35] this reason it may be requisite to venture upon a more difficult task; and enumerating all the branches of human knowledge, endeavour to show that none of them can afford such an argument.[20]

18   All reasonings may be divided into two kinds, namely, demonstrative reasoning, or that concerning relations of ideas, and moral reasoning, or that concerning matter of fact and existence. That there are no demonstrative arguments in the case seems evident; since it implies no contradiction that the course of nature may change,[21] and that an object, seemingly like those which we have experienced, may be attended with different or contrary effects. May I not clearly and distinctly conceive that a body, falling from the clouds, and which, in all other respects, resembles snow, has yet the taste of salt or feeling of fire? Is there any more intelligible proposition than to affirm, that all the trees will flourish in December and January, and decay in May and June? Now whatever is intelligible, and can be distinctly conceived, implies no contradiction, and can never be proved false by any demonstrative argument or abstract reasoning *a priori*.

19   If we be, therefore, engaged by arguments to put trust in past experience, and make it the standard of our future judgment, these arguments must be probable only, or such as regard matter of fact and real existence according to the division above mentioned. But that there is no argument of this kind, must appear, if our explication of that species of reasoning be admitted as solid and satisfactory. We have said that all arguments concerning existence are founded on the relation of cause and

---

[20] See Descartes, *Rules for the Direction of the Mind*, Rule 7; *Discourse on Method* 2 (1.25, 120).
[21] Newton allows that corpuscles might wear away or break, thereby causing the laws of nature to change (*Opticks*, Query 31 (137)). Lucretius held that the elements – earth, air, fire and water – could undergo change, but that atoms ('indivisibles') could not (*On the Nature of Things*, 5.235–46, 351–79).

effect; that our knowledge of that relation is derived entirely from experience; and that all our experimental conclusions[22] proceed upon the supposition that the future will be conformable to the past. To endeavour, therefore, the proof of this last supposition by probable arguments, or arguments regarding existence, must be evidently going in a circle, and [36] taking that for granted, which is the very point in question.

20   In reality, all arguments from experience are founded on the similarity which we discover among natural objects, and by which we are induced to expect effects similar to those which we have found to follow from such objects. And though none but a fool or madman will ever pretend to dispute the authority of experience, or to reject that great guide of human life,[23] it may surely be allowed a philosopher to have so much curiosity at least as to examine the principle of human nature, which gives this mighty authority to experience, and makes us draw advantage from that similarity which nature has placed among different objects. From causes which appear *similar* we expect similar effects. This is the sum of all our experimental conclusions. Now it seems evident that, if this conclusion were formed by reason, it would be as perfect at first, and upon one instance, as after ever so long a course of experience. But the case is far otherwise. Nothing so like as eggs;[24] yet no one, on account of this appearing similarity, expects the same taste and relish in all of them. It is only after a long course of uniform experiments in any kind, that we attain a firm reliance and security with regard to a particular event. Now where is that process of reasoning which, from one instance, draws a conclusion, so different from that which it infers from a hundred instances that are nowise different from that single one? This question I propose as much for the sake of information, as with an intention of raising difficulties. I cannot find, I cannot imagine any such reasoning. But I keep my mind still open to instruction, if any one will vouchsafe to bestow it on me.

21   Should it be said that, from a number of uniform experiments, we *infer* a connexion between the sensible qualities and the secret powers; this, I must confess, seems the same difficulty, couched in different terms. [37] The question still recurs, on what process of argument this *inference* is founded? Where is the medium, the interposing ideas, which join propositions so very wide of each other? It is confessed that the colour,

---

[22] Conclusions from experience.
[23] Probability is 'the very guide of human life', Joseph Butler, *The Analogy of Religion*, Introduction.
[24] Cf. Cicero, *Academica*, 2.57.

consistence, and other sensible qualities of bread appear not, of themselves, to have any connexion with the secret powers of nourishment and
support. For otherwise we could infer these secret powers from the first
appearance of these sensible qualities, without the aid of experience; contrary to the sentiment of all philosophers, and contrary to plain matter of
fact. Here, then, is our natural state of ignorance with regard to the powers
and influence of all objects. How is this remedied by experience? It only
shows us a number of uniform effects, resulting from certain objects, and
teaches us that those particular objects, at that particular time, were
endowed with such powers and forces. When a new object, endowed with
similar sensible qualities, is produced, we expect similar powers and forces, and look for a like effect. From a body of like colour and consistence
with bread we expect like nourishment and support. But this surely is a
step or progress of the mind, which wants to be explained. When a man
says, *I have found, in all past instances, such sensible qualities conjoined with such
secret powers*: And when he says, *Similar sensible qualities will always be conjoined with similar secret powers*; he is not guilty of a tautology, nor are these
propositions in any respect the same. You say that the one proposition is an
inference from the other. But you must confess that the inference is not
intuitive; neither is it demonstrative: Of what nature is it, then? To say it is
experimental, is begging the question. For all inferences from experience
suppose, as their foundation, that the future will resemble the past, and
that similar powers will be conjoined with similar sensible qualities. If
[38] there be any suspicion that the course of nature may change, and that
the past may be no rule for the future, all experience becomes useless, and
can give rise to no inference or conclusion. It is impossible, therefore, that
any arguments from experience can prove this resemblance of the past to
the future; since all these arguments are founded on the supposition of
that resemblance. Let the course of things be allowed hitherto ever so
regular; that alone, without some new argument or inference, proves not
that, for the future, it will continue so. In vain do you pretend to have
learned the nature[25] of bodies from your past experience. Their secret
nature, and consequently all their effects and influence, may change,
without any change in their sensible qualities. This happens sometimes,
and with regard to some objects: Why may it not happen always, and with
regard to all objects? What logic, what process or argument secures you

---

[25] Essence.

against this supposition? My practice, you say, refutes my doubts. But you mistake the purport of my question. As an agent, I am quite satisfied in the point; but as a philosopher, who has some share of curiosity, I will not say scepticism, I want to learn the foundation of this inference. No reading, no enquiry has yet been able to remove my difficulty, or give me satisfaction in a matter of such importance. Can I do better than propose the difficulty to the public, even though, perhaps, I have small hopes of obtaining a solution? We shall at least, by this means, be sensible[26] of our ignorance, if we do not augment our knowledge.

22   I must confess, that a man is guilty of unpardonable arrogance, who concludes, because an argument has escaped his own investigation, that therefore it does not really exist. I must also confess that, though all the learned, for several ages, should have employed themselves in fruitless search upon any subject, it may still, perhaps, be rash to conclude positively that the subject must, therefore, pass all human comprehension. Even though we examine all the sources of our knowledge, and conclude [39] them unfit for such a subject, there may still remain a suspicion, that the enumeration is not complete, or the examination not accurate. But with regard to the present subject, there are some considerations which seem to remove all this accusation of arrogance or suspicion of mistake.

23   It is certain, that the most ignorant and stupid peasants – nay infants, nay even brute beasts – improve by experience, and learn the qualities of natural objects, by observing the effects which result from them. When a child has felt the sensation of pain from touching the flame of a candle, he will be careful not to put his hand near any candle; but will expect a similar effect from a cause which is similar in its sensible qualities and appearance. If you assert, therefore, that the understanding of the child is led into this conclusion by any process of argument or ratiocination, I may justly require you to produce that argument; nor have you any pretence to refuse so equitable a demand. You cannot say that the argument is abstruse, and may possibly escape your enquiry; since you confess that it is obvious to the capacity of a mere infant. If you hesitate, therefore, a moment, or if, after reflection, you produce any intricate or profound argument, you, in a manner, give up the question, and confess that it is not reasoning which engages us to suppose the past resembling the future, and

---

[26] Aware.

to expect similar effects from causes which are, to appearance, similar. This is the proposition which I intended to enforce in the present section. If I be right, I pretend not to have made any mighty discovery. And if I be wrong, I must acknowledge myself to be indeed a very backward scholar; since I cannot now discover an argument which, it seems, was perfectly familiar to me long before I was out of my cradle.

5

Sceptical solution of these doubts

Part 1

1   The passion for philosophy, like that for religion, seems liable to this inconvenience, that, though it aims at the correction of our manners, and extirpation of our vices, it may only serve, by imprudent management, to foster a predominant inclination, and push the mind, with more determined resolution, towards that side which already *draws* too much, by the bias and propensity of the natural temper. It is certain that, while we aspire to the magnanimous firmness of the philosophic sage, and endeavour to confine our pleasures altogether within our own minds, we may, at last, render our philosophy like that of Epictetus, and other Stoics, only a more refined system of selfishness, and reason ourselves out of all virtue as well as social enjoyment.[1] While we study with attention the vanity of human life, and turn all our thoughts towards the empty and transitory nature of riches and honours, we are, perhaps, all the while flattering our natural indolence, which, hating the bustle of the world, and drudgery of business, seeks a pretence of reason to give itself a full and uncontrolled indulgence. There is, however, one species of philosophy which seems little liable to this inconvenience, and that because it strikes in with no disorderly passion of the human mind, nor can mingle itself with any natural affection or propensity; and that is the Academic or Sceptical [41]

---

[1] The sage is an ideal figure in Stoic philosophy, characterized by a life subordinated to divine Reason and indifferent to pleasure and pain. Epictetus (AD c. 55–c. 135), a leading Stoic, emphasized the importance of the cultivation of the self in the life of virtue. Stoicism is a *more refined* system of selfishness in contrast to the unrefined selfishness of the Epicureans, for whom pleasure is the standard of value.

philosophy.[2] The Academics always talk of doubt and suspense of judgment, of danger in hasty determinations, of confining to very narrow bounds the enquiries of the understanding, and of renouncing all speculations which lie not within the limits of common life and practice. Nothing, therefore, can be more contrary than such a philosophy to the supine indolence of the mind, its rash arrogance, its lofty pretensions, and its superstitious credulity. Every passion is mortified[3] by it, except the love of truth; and that passion never is, nor can be, carried to too high a degree. It is surprising, therefore, that this philosophy, which, in almost every instance, must be harmless and innocent, should be the subject of so much groundless reproach and obloquy.[4] But, perhaps, the very circumstance which renders it so innocent is what chiefly exposes it to the public hatred and resentment. By flattering no irregular passion,[5] it gains few partisans: By opposing so many vices and follies, it raises to itself abundance of enemies, who stigmatize it as libertine, profane, and irreligious.

2   Nor need we fear that this philosophy, while it endeavours to limit our enquiries to common life, should ever undermine the reasonings of common life, and carry its doubts so far as to destroy all action, as well as speculation. Nature will always maintain her rights, and prevail in the end over any abstract reasoning whatsoever. Though we should conclude, for instance, as in the foregoing section, that, in all reasonings from experience, there is a step taken by the mind which is not supported by any argument or process of the understanding; there is no danger that these reasonings, on which almost all knowledge depends, will ever be affected by such a discovery. If the mind be not engaged by argument to make this step, it must be induced by some other principle of equal weight and authority; and that [42] principle will preserve its influence as long as human nature remains the same. What that principle is may well be worth the pains of enquiry.

3   Suppose a person, though endowed with the strongest faculties of reason and reflection, to be brought on a sudden into this world; he would, indeed, immediately observe a continual succession of objects, and

---

[2] Academic philosophy is the moderate form of Scepticism that developed in Plato's Academy from about 270 BC, seventy years after Plato's death. It emphasized a return to Socratic questioning in contrast to the dogmatizing of the Stoics, and came to exercise a considerable influence on Cicero. Academic Scepticism differed from its main rival, Pyrrhonian Scepticism, in emphasizing probability as a standard of judgement intermediate between probability and mere opinion. See Cicero, *Academica*, 2.31; Sextus Empiricus, *Outlines of Scepticism*, 1.226–9.

[3] Subdued by self-discipline.   [4] Strong public criticism or abuse.

[5] A passion which is not, or is not capable of being, a settled principle of action. Cf. *Treatise*, 2.3.4.1.

one event following another; but he would not be able to discover anything farther. He would not, at first, by any reasoning, be able to reach the idea of cause and effect; since the particular powers, by which all natural operations are performed, never appear to the senses; nor is it reasonable to conclude, merely because one event, in one instance, precedes another, that therefore the one is the cause, the other the effect. Their conjunction may be arbitrary and casual. There may be no reason to infer the existence of one from the appearance of the other. And in a word, such a person, without more experience, could never employ his conjecture or reasoning concerning any matter of fact, or be assured of anything beyond what was immediately present to his memory and senses.

4   Suppose, again, that he has acquired more experience, and has lived so long in the world as to have observed familiar objects or events to be constantly conjoined together; what is the consequence of this experience? He immediately infers the existence of one object from the appearance of the other. Yet he has not, by all his experience, acquired any idea or knowledge of the secret power by which the one object produces the other; nor is it by any process of reasoning, he is engaged to draw this inference. But still he finds himself determined to draw it: And though he should be convinced that his understanding has no part in the operation, he would nevertheless continue in the same course of thinking. There is some other principle which determines him to form such a conclusion.

5   This principle is *custom* or *habit*.[6] For wherever the repetition of [43] any particular act or operation produces a propensity to renew the same act or operation, without being impelled by any reasoning or process of the understanding, we always say, that this propensity is the effect of *custom*. By employing that word, we pretend not to have given the ultimate reason of such a propensity. We only point out a principle of human nature, which is universally acknowledged, and which is well known by its effects. Perhaps we can push our enquiries no farther, or pretend to give the cause of this cause; but must rest contented with it as the ultimate principle, which we can assign, of all our conclusions from experience. It is sufficient satisfaction, that we can go so far, without repining[7] at the narrowness of

---

[6] 'Custom settles habits of thinking in the understanding': Locke, *Essay*, 2.33.6. (He adds that this probably reflects the inertial motions of the animal spirits.) See also Hutcheson, *Inquiry*, 1.7. The central role of custom or habit in human behaviour was emphasized by the Pyrrhonians. See Diogenes Laertius, *Lives of Eminent Philosophers*, 'Pyrrho', 9.61–2; Sextus Empiricus, *Outlines of Scepticism*, 1.23–4.

[7] Feeling or expressing discontent.

our faculties because they will carry us no farther. And it is certain we here advance a very intelligible proposition at least, if not a true one, when we assert that, after the constant conjunction of two objects – heat and flame, for instance, weight and solidity – we are determined by custom alone to expect the one from the appearance of the other. This hypothesis seems even the only one which explains the difficulty, why we draw, from a thousand instances, an inference which we are not able to draw from one instance, that is, in no respect, different from them. Reason is incapable of any such variation. The conclusions which it draws from considering one circle are the same which it would form upon surveying all the circles in the universe. But no man, having seen only one body move after being impelled by another, could infer that every other body will move after a like impulse. All inferences from experience, therefore, are effects of custom, not of reasoning.[a]

[a] Nothing is more usual than for writers, even on *moral, political*, or *physical* subjects, to distinguish between *reason* and *experience*, and to suppose, that these species of argumentation are entirely different from each other. The former are taken for the mere result of our intellectual faculties, which, by considering *a priori* the nature of things, and examining the effects, that must follow from their operation, establish particular principles of science and philosophy. The latter are supposed to be derived entirely from sense and observation, by which we learn what has actually resulted from the operation of particular objects, and are thence able to infer, what will, for the future, result from them. Thus, for instance, the limitations and restraints of civil government, and a legal constitution, may be defended, either from *reason*, which reflecting on the great frailty and corruption of human nature, teaches, that no man can safely be trusted with unlimited authority; or from *experience* and history, which inform us of the enormous abuses, that ambition, in every age and country, has been found to make of so imprudent a confidence.

The same distinction between reason and experience is maintained in all our deliberations concerning the conduct of life; while the experienced statesman, general, physician, or merchant is trusted and followed; and the unpractised novice, with whatever natural talents endowed, neglected and despised. Though it be allowed, that reason may form very plausible conjectures with regard to the consequences of such a particular conduct in such particular circumstances; it is still supposed imperfect, without the assistance of experience, which is alone able to give stability and certainty to the maxims, derived from study and reflection.

But notwithstanding that this distinction be thus universally received, both in the active and speculative scenes of life, I shall not scruple to pronounce, that it is, at bottom, erroneous, at least, superficial.

If we examine those arguments, which, in any of the sciences above mentioned, are supposed to be mere effects of reasoning and reflection, they will be found to terminate, at last, in some general principle or conclusion, for which we can assign no reason but observation and experience. The only difference between them and those maxims, which are vulgarly esteemed the result of pure experience, is, that the former cannot be established without some process of thought, and some reflection on what we have observed, in order to distinguish its circumstances, and trace its consequences: Whereas in the latter, the experienced event is exactly and fully familiar to that which we infer as the result of any particular situation. The history of a Tiberius or a Nero makes us dread a like tyranny, were our monarchs freed from the restraints of laws and senates: But the observation of any fraud or cruelty in private life is sufficient, with the aid of a little thought, to give us the same apprehension; while it serves as an instance of the general corruption of human nature, and

6   Custom, then, is the great guide of human life.[8] It is that princi- [44]
ple alone which renders our experience useful to us, and makes us expect,
for the future, a similar train of events with those which have appeared
in the past. Without the influence of custom, we should be entirely [45]
ignorant of every matter of fact beyond what is immediately present to the
memory and senses. We should never know how to adjust means to ends,
or to employ our natural powers in the production of any effect. There
would be an end at once of all action, as well as of the chief part of
speculation.

7   But here it may be proper to remark, that though our conclusions
from experience carry us beyond our memory and senses, and assure us of
matters of fact which happened in the most distant places and most remote
ages, yet some fact must always be present to the senses or memory,[9] from
which we may first proceed in drawing these conclusions.[10] A man, who
should find in a desert country the remains of pompous[11] buildings,
would conclude that the country had, in ancient times, been cultivated by
civilized inhabitants; but did nothing of this nature occur to him, he [46]
could never form such an inference. We learn the events of former ages
from history; but then we must peruse the volumes in which this instruction is contained, and thence carry up our inferences from one testimony
to another, till we arrive at the eyewitnesses and spectators of these distant
events. In a word, if we proceed not upon some fact, present to the memory

shows us the danger which we must incur by reposing an entire confidence in mankind. In both
cases, it is experience which is ultimately the foundation of our inference and conclusion.

   There is no man so young and inexperienced, as not to have formed, from observation, many
general and just maxims concerning human affairs and the conduct of life; but it must be confessed, that, when a man comes to put these in practice, he will be extremely liable to error, till
time and farther experience both enlarge these maxims, and teach him their proper use and application. In every situation or incident, there are many particular and seemingly minute circumstances, which the man of greatest talent is, at first, apt to overlook, though on them the justness
of his conclusions, and consequently the prudence of his conduct, entirely depend. Not to mention, that, to a young beginner, the general observations and maxims occur not always on the
proper occasions, nor can be immediately applied with due calmness and distinction. The truth
is, an unexperienced reasoner could be no reasoner at all, were he absolutely unexperienced; and
when we assign that character to any one, we mean it only in a comparative sense, and suppose him
possessed of experience, in a smaller and more imperfect degree.

[8] An adaptation of Butler's maxim, and a rejection of the ancient (including Stoic) view that philosophy is the guide of life. See Seneca, *Epistles*, 16: 'On Philosophy, the Guide of Life'.
[9] 'The mind, when left to itself, immediately languishes', *Treatise*, 2.3.4.8.
[10] Hobbes argues that expectations about the future are the result of present sensations triggering
   past strings of sensations (in the memory), such that we expect the whole sequence to reoccur, all
   the while relying on the supposition that 'like events will follow like actions' (*Leviathan*, 22).
[11] Grand or impressive.

or senses, our reasonings would be merely hypothetical; and however the particular links might be connected with each other, the whole chain of inferences would have nothing to support it, nor could we ever, by its means, arrive at the knowledge of any real existence. If I ask why you believe any particular matter of fact, which you relate, you must tell me some reason; and this reason will be some other fact, connected with it. But as you cannot proceed after this manner, *in infinitum*, you must at last terminate in some fact, which is present to your memory or senses; or must allow that your belief is entirely without foundation.

8   What, then, is the conclusion of the whole matter? A simple one; though, it must be confessed, pretty remote from the common theories of philosophy. All belief of matter of fact or real existence is derived merely from some object, present to the memory or senses, and a customary conjunction between that and some other object. Or in other words; having found, in many instances, that any two kinds of objects – flame and heat, snow and cold – have always been conjoined together; if flame or snow be presented anew to the senses, the mind is carried by custom to expect heat or cold, and to *believe* that such a quality does exist, and will discover itself upon a nearer approach. This belief is the necessary result of placing the mind in such circumstances. It is an operation of the soul, when we are so situated, as unavoidable as to feel the passion of love, when we receive benefits; or hatred, when we meet with injuries. All these operations are a spe-
[47]   cies of natural instincts, which no reasoning or process of the thought and understanding is able either to produce or to prevent.[12]

9   At this point, it would be very allowable for us to stop our philosophical researches. In most questions we can never make a single step farther; and in all questions we must terminate here at last, after our most restless and curious enquiries. But still our curiosity will be pardonable, perhaps commendable, if it carry us on to still farther researches, and make us examine more accurately the nature of this *belief*, and of the *customary conjunction*, whence it is derived. By this means we may meet with some explications and analogies that will give satisfaction; at least to such as love the abstract sciences, and can be entertained with speculations, which, however accurate, may still retain a degree of doubt and uncertainty. As to readers of a different taste; the remaining part of this section is

---

[12] The mark of instinct is that, in contrast to thought, it operates involuntarily and necessarily when triggered by the relevant stimulus. For the unavoidability of love and hate, see *Treatise*, 2.2.1.

not calculated for them, and the following enquiries may well be understood, though it be neglected.

Part 2

10   Nothing is more free than the imagination of man; and though it
cannot exceed that original stock of ideas furnished by the internal and
external senses,[13] it has unlimited power of mixing, compounding, separ-
ating, and dividing these ideas, in all the varieties of fiction[14] and vision. It
can feign[15] a train of events, with all the appearance of reality, ascribe to
them a particular time and place, conceive them as existent, and paint
them out to itself with every circumstance, that belongs to any historical
fact, which it believes with the greatest certainty. Wherein, therefore, consists the difference between such a fiction and belief? It lies not merely in
any peculiar idea, which is annexed to such a conception as commands our
assent, and which is wanting to every known fiction. For as the mind
has authority over all its ideas, it could voluntarily annex this particular [48]
idea to any fiction, and consequently be able to believe whatever it pleases;
contrary to what we find by daily experience. We can, in our conception,
join the head of a man to the body of a horse;[16] but it is not in our power to
believe that such an animal has ever really existed.

11   It follows, therefore, that the difference between *fiction* and *belief*
lies in some sentiment or feeling, which is annexed to the latter, not to the
former, and which depends not on the will, nor can be commanded at
pleasure.[17] It must be excited by nature, like all other sentiments; and
must arise from the particular situation, in which the mind is placed at any
particular juncture. Whenever any object is presented to the memory or
senses, it immediately, by the force of custom, carries the imagination to
conceive that object, which is usually conjoined to it; and this conception is
attended with a feeling or sentiment, different from the loose reveries of
the fancy.[18] In this consists the whole nature of belief. For as there is no
matter of fact which we believe so firmly that we cannot conceive the

---

[13] Locke (*Essay*, 2.1.4) divides senses into external and internal. The internal sense is our perception
of our own thoughts. Hutcheson (*Inquiry*, 1.1.10–15; 1.6.8–10; 1.8) expands the scope of the term to
include aesthetic and moral perception.
[14] Invention or imagination.   [15] Imagine.   [16] See Horace, *Art of Poetry*, 1.
[17] *Contra* Descartes, for whom the voluntariness of belief is a key doctrine (*Meditations*, Fourth
Meditation, 1.39–42).
[18] The imagination.

47

contrary, there would be no difference between the conception assented to and that which is rejected, were it not for some sentiment which distinguishes the one from the other. If I see a billiard-ball moving toward another, on a smooth table, I can easily conceive it to stop upon contact. This conception implies no contradiction; but still it feels very differently from that conception by which I represent to myself the impulse and the communication of motion from one ball to another.

12   Were we to attempt a *definition* of this sentiment, we should, perhaps, find it a very difficult, if not an impossible task; in the same manner as if we should endeavour to define the feeling of cold or passion of anger, to a creature who never had any experience of these sentiments. [49] *Belief* is the true and proper name of this feeling; and no one is ever at a loss to know the meaning of that term; because every man is every moment conscious of the sentiment represented by it. It may not, however, be improper to attempt a *description* of this sentiment; in hopes we may, by that means, arrive at some analogies, which may afford a more perfect explication of it. I say, then, that belief is nothing but a more vivid, lively, forcible, firm, steady conception of an object, than what the imagination alone is ever able to attain. This variety of terms, which may seem so unphilosophical, is intended only to express that act of the mind, which renders realities, or what is taken for such, more present to us than fictions, causes them to weigh more in the thought, and gives them a superior influence on the passions and imagination. Provided we agree about the thing, it is needless to dispute about the terms. The imagination has the command over all its ideas, and can join and mix and vary them, in all the ways possible. It may conceive fictitious objects with all the circumstances of place and time. It may set them, in a manner, before our eyes, in their true colours, just as they might have existed. But as it is impossible that this faculty of imagination can ever, of itself, reach belief, it is evident that belief consists not in the peculiar nature or order of ideas, but in the *manner* of their conception, and in their *feeling* to the mind. I confess, that it is impossible perfectly to explain this feeling or manner of conception. We may make use of words which express something near it. But its true and proper name, as we observed before, is *belief*; which is a term that every one sufficiently understands in common life. And in philosophy, we can go no farther than assert, that *belief* is something felt by the mind, which distinguishes the ideas of the judgment from the fictions of the imagina- [50] tion. It gives them more weight and influence; makes them appear of

greater importance; enforces them in the mind; and renders them the governing principle of our actions. I hear at present, for instance, a person's voice, with whom I am acquainted; and the sound comes as from the next room. This impression of my senses immediately conveys my thought to the person, together with all the surrounding objects. I paint them out to myself as existing at present, with the same qualities and relations, of which I formerly knew them possessed. These ideas take faster hold of my mind than ideas of an enchanted castle. They are very different to the feeling, and have a much greater influence of every kind, either to give pleasure or pain, joy or sorrow.

13   Let us, then, take in the whole compass of this doctrine, and allow, that the sentiment of belief is nothing but a conception more intense and steady than what attends the mere fictions of the imagination, and that this *manner* of conception arises from a customary conjunction of the object with something present to the memory or senses: I believe that it will not be difficult, upon these suppositions, to find other operations of the mind analogous to it, and to trace up these phenomena to principles still more general.[19]

14   We have already observed that nature has established connexions among particular ideas, and that no sooner one idea occurs to our thoughts than it introduces its correlative, and carries our attention towards it, by a gentle and insensible[20] movement. These principles of connexion or association we have reduced to three, namely, *resemblance*, *contiguity* and *causation*; which are the only bonds that unite our thoughts together, and beget that regular train of reflection or discourse, which, in a greater or less degree, takes place among all mankind. Now here arises a question, on which the solution of the present difficulty will depend. Does it happen, in all these relations, that, when one of the objects is presented to the senses or memory, the mind [51] is not only carried to the conception of the correlative, but reaches a steadier and stronger conception of it than what otherwise it would have been able to attain? This seems to be the case with that belief which arises from the relation of cause and effect. And if the case be the same with the other relations or principles of association, this may be established as a general law, which takes place in all the operations of the mind.

15   We may, therefore, observe, as the first experiment to our present purpose, that, upon the appearance of the picture of an absent friend,

---

[19] Newton, *Principia*, 'Rules for the Study of Natural Philosophy', Rules 1 –3 (87–9).
[20] Imperceptible.

our idea of him is evidently enlivened by the *resemblance*, and that every passion, which that idea occasions, whether of joy or sorrow, acquires new force and vigour. In producing this effect, there concur both a relation and a present impression. Where the picture bears him no resemblance, at least was not intended for him, it never so much as conveys our thought to him: And where it is absent, as well as the person, though the mind may pass from the thought of the one to that of the other, it feels its idea to be rather weakened than enlivened by that transition. We take a pleasure in viewing the picture of a friend, when it is set before us; but when it is removed, rather choose to consider him directly than by reflection in an image, which is equally distant and obscure.

16   The ceremonies of the Roman Catholic religion may be considered as instances of the same nature. The devotees of that superstition usually plead in excuse for the mummeries,[21] with which they are upbraided, that they feel the good effect of those external motions, and postures, and actions, in enlivening their devotion and quickening their fervour, which otherwise would decay, if directed entirely to distant and immaterial [52] objects. We shadow out the objects of our faith, say they, in sensible[22] types and images, and render them more present to us by the immediate presence of these types, than it is possible for us to do merely by an intellectual view and contemplation. Sensible objects have always a greater influence on the fancy than any other; and this influence they readily convey to those ideas to which they are related, and which they resemble. I shall only infer from these practices, and this reasoning, that the effect of resemblance in enlivening the ideas is very common; and as in every case a resemblance and a present impression must concur, we are abundantly supplied with experiments[23] to prove the reality of the foregoing principle.

17   We may add force to these experiments by others of a different kind, in considering the effects of *contiguity* as well as of *resemblance*. It is certain that distance diminishes the force of every idea, and that, upon our approach to any object; though it does not discover itself to our senses; it operates upon the mind with an influence, which imitates an immediate impression. The thinking on any object readily transports the mind to what is contiguous; but it is only the actual presence of an object, that transports it with a superior vivacity. When I am a few miles from home, whatever

---

[21] Ridiculous rituals. The term was a Protestant term of abuse for Catholic rituals. (A mummery is a performance of a masked play.)
[22] Perceptible.   [23] Experiences or examples.

relates to it touches me more nearly than when I am two hundred leagues[24] distant; though even at that distance the reflecting on any thing in the neighbourhood of my friends or family naturally produces an idea of them. But as in this latter case, both the objects of the mind are ideas; notwithstanding there is an easy transition between them; that transition alone is not able to give a superior vivacity to any of the ideas, for want of some immediate impression.[b]

18   No one can doubt but causation has the same influence as [53] the other two relations of resemblance and contiguity. Superstitious people are fond of the relics of saints and holy men, for the same reason, that they seek after types or images, in order to enliven their devotion, and give them a more intimate and strong conception of those exemplary lives, which they desire to imitate. Now it is evident, that one of the best relics, which a devotee could procure, would be the handywork of a saint; and if his clothes and furniture are ever to be considered in this light, it is because they were once at his disposal, and were moved and affected by him; in which respect they are to be considered as imperfect effects, and as connected with him by a shorter chain of consequences than any of those, by which we learn the reality of his existence.

19   Suppose, that the son of a friend, who had been long dead or absent, were presented to us; it is evident, that this object would instantly

---

[b] 'Naturane nobis, inquit, datum dicam, an errore quodam, ut, cum ea loca videamus, in quibus memoria dignos viros acceperimus multim esse versatos, magis moveamur, quam siquando eorum ipsorum aut facta audiamus aut scriptum aliquod legamus? Velut ego nunc moveor. Venit enim mihi Plato in mentem, quem accepimus primum hic disputare solitum; cuius etiam illi hortuli propinqui non memoriam solum mihi afferunt, sed ipsum videntur in conspectu meo hic ponere. Hic Speusippus, hic Xenocrates, hic eius auditor Polemo; cuius ipsa illa sessio fuit, quam videmus. Equidem etiam curiam nostram, Hostiliam dico, non hanc novam, quae mihi minor esse videtur postquam est maior, solebam intuens, Scipionem, Catonem, Laelium, nostrum vero in primis avum cogitare. Tanta vis admonitionis est in locis; ut non sine causa ex iis memoriae ducta sit disciplina.' Cicero, de finibus. lib. v. ['I cannot say whether it is a natural instinct or a kind of illusion, but when we see the places where we are told that the notables of the past spent their time, it is far more moving than when we hear about their achievements or read their writings. This is how I am affected right now. I think of Plato, who they say was the first philosopher to have regularly held discussions here. Those little gardens just nearby not only bring Plato to mind, but actually seem to make him appear before my eyes. Here come Speusippus, Xenocrates and his pupil Polemo, who sat on that very seat we can see over there. Even when I look at our own Senate-house (I mean the original old Hostilia; its enlargement seems to me to have diminished it), I often think of Scipio, Cato, Laelius and above all my grandfather. Such is the evocative power that locations possess. No wonder the training of memory is based on them.' Marcus Piso, in Cicero, *On Moral Ends*, V.2. Speusippus, Xenocrates and Polemo were Plato's immediate successors as leaders of the Academy; Scipio, Cato and Laelius were past Romans of high reputation.]

[24] A league is a measure of distance, approximately equal to three miles.

revive its correlative idea, and recall to our thoughts all past intimacies and familiarities, in more lively colours than they would otherwise have appeared to us. This is another phenomenon, which seems to prove the principle above mentioned.

20   We may observe, that, in these phenomena, the belief of the correlative object is always presupposed; without which the relation could have no effect. The influence of the picture supposes, that we *believe* our
[54] friend to have once existed. Contiguity to home can never excite our ideas of home, unless we believe that it really exists. Now I assert, that this belief, where it reaches beyond the memory or senses, is of a similar nature, and arises from similar causes, with the transition of thought and vivacity of conception here explained. When I throw a piece of dry wood into a fire, my mind is immediately carried to conceive, that it augments, not extinguishes the flame. This transition of thought from the cause to the effect proceeds not from reason. It derives its origin altogether from custom and experience. And as it first begins from an object, present to the senses, it renders the idea or conception of flame more strong and lively than any loose, floating reverie of the imagination. That idea arises immediately. The thought moves instantly towards it, and conveys to it all that force of conception, which is derived from the impression present to the senses. When a sword is levelled at my breast, does not the idea of wound and pain strike me more strongly, than when a glass of wine is presented to me, even though by accident this idea should occur after the appearance of the latter object? But what is there in this whole matter to cause such a strong conception, except only a present object and a customary transition to the idea of another object, which we have been accustomed to conjoin with the former? This is the whole operation of the mind, in all our conclusions concerning matter of fact and existence; and it is a satisfaction to find some analogies, by which it may be explained. The transition from a present object does in all cases give strength and solidity to the related idea.

21   Here, then, is a kind of pre-established harmony between the course of nature and the succession of our ideas;[25] and though the powers

---

[25] A reference to Leibniz's theory that God created the world such that each substance is independent of every other, but that they are so designed that the actions that flow from their independent natures nevertheless remain in harmony. So the human soul's perceptions correspond to the way the world is, even though the perceptions are not caused by the world: 'as the nature of the soul is to represent the universe in a very exact way (though with more or less distinctness), the succession of representations which the soul produces for itself will naturally correspond to the succession of changes in the universe itself'. (G. W. Leibniz, *New System of the Nature of Substances and Their*

and forces, by which the former is governed, be wholly unknown to us; yet our thoughts and conceptions have still, we find, gone on in the same train with the other works of nature. Custom is that principle, by which this [55] correspondence has been effected; so necessary to the subsistence of our species, and the regulation of our conduct, in every circumstance and occurrence of human life. Had not the presence of an object, instantly excited the idea of those objects, commonly conjoined with it, all our knowledge must have been limited to the narrow sphere of our memory and senses; and we should never have been able to adjust means to ends, or employ our natural powers, either to the producing of good, or avoiding of evil. Those, who delight in the discovery and contemplation of *final causes*,[26] have here ample subject to employ their wonder and admiration.[27]

22   I shall add, for a further confirmation of the foregoing theory, that, as this operation of the mind, by which we infer like effects from like causes, and *vice versa*, is so essential to the subsistence of all human creatures, it is not probable, that it could be trusted to the fallacious deductions of our reason, which is slow in its operations; appears not, in any degree, during the first years of infancy; and at best is, in every age and period of human life, extremely liable to error and mistake. It is more conformable to the ordinary wisdom of nature to secure so necessary an act of the mind, by some instinct or mechanical tendency, which may be infallible in its operations, may discover itself at the first appearance of life and thought, and may be independent of all the laboured deductions of the understanding. As nature has taught us the use of our limbs, without giving us the knowledge of the muscles and nerves, by which they are actuated; so has she implanted in us an instinct, which carries forward the thought in a correspondent course to that which she has established among external objects; though we are ignorant of those powers and forces, on which this regular course and succession of objects totally depends.

Communication, 15.) Leibniz's view was discussed by Pierre Bayle, *Historical and Critical Dictionary*, 'Rorarius', Note H.
[26] Aristotle held that there are four 'causes' or explanatory principles, material, formal, efficient and final. A final cause is an end or purpose or goal. See *Metaphysics*, 1013a–b.
[27] See e.g. Alexander Pope, *Essay on Man*, 1.289–94.

6

Of probability[a]

1   Though there be no such thing as *chance* in the world; our ignorance of the real cause of any event has the same influence on the understanding, and begets a like species of belief or opinion.[1]

2   There is certainly a probability, which arises from a superiority of chances on any side; and according as this superiority increases, and surpasses the opposite chances, the probability receives a proportionable increase, and begets still a higher degree of belief or assent to that side, in which we discover the superiority. If a die were marked with one figure or number of spots on four sides, and with another figure or number of spots on the two remaining sides, it would be more probable, that the former would turn up than the latter; though, if it had a thousand sides marked in the same manner, and only one side different, the probability would be much higher, and our belief or expectation of the event more steady and secure. This process of the thought or reasoning may seem trivial and [57] obvious; but to those who consider it more narrowly, it may, perhaps, afford matter for curious speculation.

3   It seems evident, that, when the mind looks forward to discover the event, which may result from the throw of such a die, it considers the turning up of each particular side as alike probable; and this is the very

---

[a] Mr. Locke divides all arguments into demonstrative and probable. In this view, we must say, that it is only probable that all men must die, or that the sun will rise to-morrow. But to conform our language more to common use, we ought to divide arguments into *demonstrations*, *proofs*, and *probabilities*. By *proofs* meaning *such arguments from experience as leave no room for doubt or opposition*. [Cf. Locke, *Essay*, 4.2.1–4; 4.15.1–4; 4.16.6–9.]

[1] The contrast drawn here, between apparent chance and underlying law, echoes Seneca, *Moral Essays*, 'On Providence', 1.2. The role of probability in everyday judgement is also discussed by Butler, *Analogy of Religion*, Introduction.

nature of chance, to render all the particular events, comprehended in it, entirely equal. But finding a greater number of sides concur in the one event than in the other, the mind is carried more frequently to that event, and meets it oftener, in revolving the various possibilities or chances, on which the ultimate result depends. This concurrence of several views in one particular event begets immediately, by an inexplicable contrivance of nature, the sentiment of belief, and gives that event the advantage over its antagonist, which is supported by a smaller number of views, and recurs less frequently to the mind. If we allow, that belief is nothing but a firmer and stronger conception of an object than what attends the mere fictions of the imagination, this operation may, perhaps, in some measure, be accounted for. The concurrence of these several views or glimpses imprints the idea more strongly on the imagination; gives it superior force and vigour; renders its influence on the passions and affections more sensible; and in a word, begets that reliance or security, which constitutes the nature of belief and opinion.

4   The case is the same with the probability of causes, as with that of chance. There are some causes, which are entirely uniform and constant in producing a particular effect; and no instance has ever yet been found of any failure or irregularity in their operation. Fire has always burned, and water suffocated every human creature: The production of motion by impulse and gravity is an universal law, which has hitherto admitted of no exception.[2] But there are other causes, which have been found more irregular and uncertain; nor has rhubarb always proved a purge, or opium [58] a soporific to every one, who has taken these medicines.[3] It is true, when any cause fails of producing its usual effect, philosophers ascribe not this to any irregularity in nature; but suppose, that some secret causes, in the particular structure of parts, have prevented the operation.[4] Our reasonings, however, and conclusions concerning the event are the same as if this principle had no place.[5] Being determined by custom to transfer the past to the future, in all our inferences; where the past has been entirely regular and uniform, we expect the event with the greatest assurance, and leave no room for any contrary supposition. But where different effects have been found to follow from causes, which are to *appearance* exactly similar, all

---

[2] See Newton, *Principia*, Cotes' Preface to 2nd edn, Laws 1–2 and Scholium to Bk 1 Sect. 11 (45, 70–1, 86).
[3] A purge: a laxative. A soporific: a sleep-inducing drug.   [4] See Locke, *Essay*, 4.16.12.
[5] An instance of the 'pre-established harmony' referred to above (5.21).

these various effects must occur to the mind in transferring the past to the future, and enter into our consideration, when we determine the probability of the event. Though we give the preference to that which has been found most usual, and believe that this effect will exist, we must not overlook the other effects, but must assign to each of them a particular weight and authority, in proportion as we have found it to be more or less frequent. It is more probable, in almost every country of Europe, that there will be frost sometime in January, than that the weather will continue open through out that whole month; though this probability varies according to the different climates, and approaches to a certainty[6] in the more northern kingdoms. Here then it seems evident, that, when we transfer the past to the future, in order to determine the effect, which will result from any cause, we transfer all the different events, in the same proportion as they have appeared in the past, and conceive one to have existed a hundred times, for instance, another ten times, and another once. As a great number of views do here concur in one event, they fortify and confirm it to the imagination, beget that sentiment which we call *belief*, and give its object the preference above the contrary event, which is not supported by an
[59] equal number of experiments,[7] and recurs not so frequently to the thought in transferring the past to the future. Let any one try to account for this operation of the mind upon any of the received systems of philosophy, and he will be sensible[8] of the difficulty. For my part, I shall think it sufficient, if the present hints excite the curiosity of philosophers, and make them sensible how defective all common theories are in treating of such curious and such sublime subjects.

[6] That is, to a proof.   [7] Experiences or observations.   [8] Aware.

7

Of the idea of necessary connexion

Part 1

1   The great advantage of the mathematical sciences above the moral consists in this, that the ideas of the former, being sensible, are always clear and determinate, the smallest distinction between them is immediately perceptible, and the same terms are still expressive of the same ideas, without ambiguity or variation.[1] An oval is never mistaken for a circle, nor an hyperbola for an ellipsis.[2] The isosceles and scalenum[3] are distinguished by boundaries more exact than vice and virtue, right and wrong. If any term be defined in geometry, the mind readily, of itself, substitutes, on all occasions, the definition for the term defined: Or even when no definition is employed, the object itself may be presented to the senses, and by that means be steadily and clearly apprehended. But the finer sentiments of the mind, the operations of the understanding, the various agitations of the passions, though really in themselves distinct, easily escape us, when surveyed by reflection; nor is it in our power to recall the original object, as often as we have occasion to contemplate it. Ambiguity, by this means, is gradually introduced into our reasonings: Similar objects are readily taken to be the same: And the conclusion becomes at last very wide of the premises.

---

[1] Hume here assumes the equivalence of geometry and mathematics, established by Descartes in his *Geometry* (1637).
[2] Ellipse.
[3] These are kinds of triangle. The isosceles has two sides of equal length, the scalenum (scalene) has three unequal sides.

[61]   2   One may safely, however, affirm, that, if we consider these sciences in a proper light, their advantages and disadvantages nearly compensate each other, and reduce both of them to a state of equality. If the mind, with greater facility, retains the ideas of geometry clear and determinate, it must carry on a much longer and more intricate chain of reasoning, and compare ideas much wider of each other, in order to reach the abstruser truths of that science. And if moral ideas are apt, without extreme care, to fall into obscurity and confusion, the inferences are always much shorter in these disquisitions, and the intermediate steps, which lead to the conclusion, much fewer than in the sciences which treat of quantity and number. In reality, there is scarcely a proposition in Euclid so simple, as not to consist of more parts, than are to be found in any moral reasoning which runs not into chimera and conceit. Where we trace the principles of the human mind through a few steps, we may be very well satisfied with our progress; considering how soon nature throws a bar to all our enquiries concerning causes, and reduces us to an acknowledgment of our ignorance. The chief obstacle, therefore, to our improvement in the moral or metaphysical sciences is the obscurity of the ideas, and ambiguity of the terms. The principal difficulty in the mathematics is the length of inferences and compass of thought, requisite to the forming of any conclusion. And, perhaps, our progress in natural philosophy is chiefly retarded by the want of proper experiments and phenomena, which are often discovered by chance, and cannot always be found, when requisite, even by the most diligent and prudent enquiry. As moral philosophy seems hitherto to have received less improvement than either geometry or physics, we may conclude, that, if there be any difference in this respect among these sciences, the difficulties, which obstruct the progress of the former, require superior care and capacity to be surmounted.

[62]   3   There are no ideas, which occur in metaphysics, more obscure and uncertain, than those of *power, force, energy* or *necessary connexion*, of which it is every moment necessary for us to treat in all our disquisitions. We shall, therefore, endeavour, in this section, to fix, if possible, the precise meaning of these terms, and thereby remove some part of that obscurity, which is so much complained of in this species of philosophy.

4   It seems a proposition, which will not admit of much dispute, that all our ideas are nothing but copies of our impressions, or, in other words, that it is impossible for us to *think* of anything, which we have not antecedently *felt*, either by our external or internal senses. I have

endeavoured[a] to explain and prove this proposition, and have expressed my hopes, that, by a proper application of it, men may reach a greater clearness and precision in philosophical reasonings, than what they have hitherto been able to attain. Complex ideas, may, perhaps, be well known by definition, which is nothing but an enumeration of those parts or simple ideas, that compose them. But when we have pushed up definitions to the most simple ideas, and find still more ambiguity and obscurity; what resource are we then possessed of? By what invention can we throw light upon these ideas, and render them altogether precise and determinate to our intellectual view? Produce the impressions or original sentiments, from which the ideas are copied. These impressions are all strong and sensible. They admit not of ambiguity. They are not only placed in a full light themselves, but may throw light on their correspondent ideas, which lie in obscurity. And by this means, we may, perhaps, attain a new microscope or species of optics, by which, in the moral sciences, the most minute, and most simple ideas may be so enlarged as to fall readily under our apprehension, and be equally known with the grossest and most sensible[4] ideas, that can be the object of our enquiry.

5   To be fully acquainted, therefore, with the idea of power or [63] necessary connexion, let us examine its impression; and in order to find the impression with greater certainty, let us search for it in all the sources, from which it may possibly be derived.

6   When we look about us towards external objects, and consider the operation of causes, we are never able, in a single instance, to discover any power or necessary connexion; any quality, which binds the effect to the cause, and renders the one an infallible consequence of the other.[5] We only find, that the one does actually, in fact, follow the other. The impulse of one billiard-ball is attended with motion in the second. This is the whole that appears to the *outward* senses. The mind feels no sentiment or *inward* impression from this succession of objects: Consequently, there is not, in any single, particular instance of cause and effect, any thing which can suggest the idea of power or necessary connexion.

7   From the first appearance of an object, we never can conjecture what effect will result from it. But were the power or energy of any cause

---

[a] Section 2.   [4] The largest and most easily perceptible.
[5] That the idea of a cause is an idea of necessary connection is due to Malebranche, *Search after Truth*, 6.2.3.

discoverable by the mind, we could foresee the effect, even without experience; and might, at first, pronounce with certainty concerning it, by mere dint of thought and reasoning.

8   In reality, there is no part of matter, that does ever, by its sensible qualities, discover[6] any power or energy, or give us ground to imagine, that it could produce any thing, or be followed by any other object, which we could denominate its effect. Solidity, extension, motion; these qualities are all complete in themselves, and never point out any other event which may result from them. The scenes of the universe are continually shifting, and one object follows another in an uninterrupted succession; but the power or force, which actuates the whole machine,[7] is entirely concealed from us, [64] and never discovers itself in any of the sensible qualities of body. We know that, in fact, heat is a constant attendant of flame; but what is the connexion between them, we have no room so much as to conjecture or imagine. It is impossible, therefore, that the idea of power can be derived from the contemplation of bodies, in single instances of their operation; because no bodies ever discover any power, which can be the original of this idea.[b]

9   Since, therefore, external objects, as they appear to the senses, give us no idea of power or necessary connexion, by their operation in particular instances, let us see, whether this idea be derived from reflection on the operations of our own minds, and be copied from any internal impression. It may be said, that we are every moment conscious of internal power; while we feel, that, by the simple command of our will, we can move the organs of our body, or direct the faculties of our mind.[8] An act of volition produces motion in our limbs, or raises a new idea in our imagination. This influence of the will we know by consciousness. Hence we acquire the idea of power or energy; and are certain, that we ourselves and all other intelligent beings are possessed of power.[9] This idea, then, is an idea of reflection, since it arises from reflecting on the operations of our own

---

[b] Mr. Locke, in his chapter of power, says that, finding from experience, that there are several new productions in matter, and concluding that there must somewhere be a power capable of producing them, we arrive at last by this reasoning at the idea of power. But no reasoning can ever give us a new, original, simple idea; as this philosopher himself confesses. This, therefore, can never be the origin of that idea. [Locke, *Essay*, 2.21.1, 4.]

[6] Reveal.   [7] The whole universe.

[8] See, e.g., Locke, *Essay*, 2.21.5.

[9] The sentence following replaces these two sentences in the editions of 1748 and 1750:

The operations and mutual influence of bodies are, perhaps, sufficient to prove, that they also are possessed of it. However this may be, the idea of power must certainly be allowed to be an idea of mind, and on the command which is exercised by will, both over the organs of the body and faculties of the soul.

10   We shall proceed to examine this pretension; and first with regard to the influence of volition over the organs of the body. This influence, we may observe, is a fact, which, like all other natural events, can be known only by experience, and can never be foreseen from any apparent energy or power in the cause, which connects it with the effect, and ren- [65] ders the one an infallible consequence of the other. The motion of our body follows upon the command of our will. Of this we are every moment conscious. But the means, by which this is effected; the energy, by which the will performs so extraordinary an operation; of this we are so far from being immediately conscious, that it must for ever escape our most diligent enquiry.

11   For *first*, is there any principle in all nature more mysterious than the union of soul with body; by which a supposed spiritual substance acquires such an influence over a material one, that the most refined thought is able to actuate the grossest matter?[10] Were we empowered, by a secret wish, to remove mountains, or control the planets in their orbit; this extensive authority would not be more extraordinary, nor more beyond our comprehension. But if by consciousness we perceived any power or energy in the will, we must know this power; we must know its connexion with the effect; we must know the secret union of soul and body, and the nature of both these substances;[11] by which the one is able to operate, in so many instances, upon the other.[12]

12   *Secondly*, We are not able to move all the organs of the body with a like authority; though we cannot assign any reason besides experience, for so remarkable a difference between one and the other. Why has the will an influence over the tongue and fingers, not over the heart or liver? This question would never embarrass us, were we conscious of a power in the former case, not in the latter. We should then perceive, independent of

reflection, since it arises from reflecting on the operations of our own mind, and on the command which is exercised by will, both over the organs of the body and faculties of the soul.

[10] Gross (or coarse) matter: the material of solid objects. It was distinguished from subtle matter, the fluids that, e.g., explained nervous impulses. The difference was commonly attributed to the size and shape of their constituent particles.

[11] Hume here accepts Locke's denial that experience acquaints us with substances: *Essay*, 2.23.1; also 4.3.26–8.

[12] This point, repeated below, derives from Malebranche, *Search after Truth*, 6.2.3.

experience, why the authority of will over the organs of the body is circum-scribed within such particular limits. Being in that case fully acquainted with the power or force, by which it operates, we should also know, why its influ-ence reaches precisely to such boundaries, and no farther.

[66]   13   A man, suddenly struck with palsy in the leg or arm, or who had newly lost those members, frequently endeavours, at first to move them, and employ them, in their usual offices. Here he is as much conscious of power to command such limbs, as a man in perfect health is conscious of power to actuate any member which remains in its natural state and con-dition. But consciousness never deceives.[13] Consequently, neither in the one case nor in the other, are we ever conscious of any power. We learn the influence of our will from experience alone. And experience only tea-ches us, how one event constantly follows another; without instructing us in the secret connexion, which binds them together, and renders them inseparable.

14   *Thirdly*, We learn from anatomy, that the immediate object of power in voluntary motion, is not the member itself which is moved, but certain muscles, and nerves, and animal spirits,[14] and, perhaps, some-thing still more minute and more unknown, through which the motion is successively propagated, ere[15] it reach the member itself whose motion is the immediate object of volition. Can there be a more certain proof, that the power, by which this whole operation is performed, so far from being directly and fully known by an inward sentiment or consciousness is, to the last degree, mysterious and unintelligible? Here the mind wills a certain event: Immediately another event, unknown to ourselves, and totally dif-ferent from the one intended, is produced: This event produces another, equally unknown: Till at last, through a long succession, the desired event is produced. But if the original power were felt, it must be known: Were it known, its effect also must be known; since all power is relative to its effect. And *vice versa*, if the effect be not known, the power cannot be known nor felt. How indeed can we be conscious of a power to move our limbs, when we have no such power; but only that to move certain animal
[67] spirits, which, though they produce at last the motion of our limbs, yet operate in such a manner as is wholly beyond our comprehension?[16]

---

[13] That is, about its own contents. See Descartes, *Meditations*, Fourth Meditation (2.39); Locke, *Essay*, 4.9.3.

[14] The subtle fluid in the nerves that communicates sensations and volitions.   [15] Before.

[16] Cf. Malebranche, *Search after Truth*, 6.2.3.

15   We may, therefore, conclude from the whole, I hope, without any temerity, though with assurance; that our idea of power is not copied from any sentiment or consciousness of power within ourselves, when we give rise to animal motion, or apply our limbs to their proper use and office. That their motion follows the command of the will is a matter of common experience, like other natural events: But the power or energy by which this is effected, like that in other natural events, is unknown and inconceivable.[c]

16   Shall we then assert, that we are conscious of a power or energy in our own minds, when, by an act or command of our will, we raise up a new idea, fix the mind to the contemplation of it, turn it on all sides, and at last dismiss it for some other idea, when we think that we have surveyed it with sufficient accuracy? I believe the same arguments will prove, that even this command of the will gives us no real idea of force or energy.

17   *First*, It must be allowed, that, when we know a power, we know that very circumstance in the cause, by which it is enabled to produce the [68] effect: For these are supposed to be synonymous. We must, therefore, know both the cause and effect, and the relation between them. But do we pretend to be acquainted with the nature of the human soul and the nature of an idea, or the aptitude of the one to produce the other? This is a real creation; a production of something out of nothing: Which implies a power so great, that it may seem, at first sight, beyond the reach of any being, less than infinite. At least it must be owned,[17] that such a power is not felt, nor known, nor even conceivable by the mind. We only feel the event, namely, the existence of an idea, consequent to a command of the will: But the manner, in which this operation is performed, the power by which it is produced, is entirely beyond our comprehension.

---

[c] It may be pretended, that the resistance which we meet with in bodies, obliging us frequently to exert our force, and call up all our power, this gives us the idea of force and power. It is this *nisus*, or strong endeavour, of which we are conscious, that is the original impression from which this idea is copied. But, *first*, we attribute power to a vast number of objects, where we never can suppose this resistance or exertion of force to take place; to the Supreme Being, who never meets with any resistance; to the mind in its command over its ideas and limbs, in common thinking and motion, where the effect follows immediately upon the will, without any exertion or summoning up of force; to inanimate matter, which is not capable of this sentiment. *Secondly*, This sentiment of an endeavour to overcome resistance has no known connexion with any event: What follows it, we know by experience; but could not know it *a priori*. It must, however, be confessed, that the animal *nisus*, which we experience, though it can afford no accurate precise idea of power, enters very much into that vulgar, inaccurate idea, which is formed by it. [Final sentence added in 1756.]

[17] Admitted.

18   *Secondly,* The command of the mind over itself is limited, as well as its command over the body; and these limits are not known by reason, or any acquaintance with the nature of cause and effect, but only by experience and observation, as in all other natural events and in the operation of external objects. Our authority over our sentiments and passions is much weaker than that over our ideas; and even the latter authority is circumscribed within very narrow boundaries. Will any one pretend to assign the ultimate reason of these boundaries, or show why the power is deficient in one case, not in another.

19   *Thirdly,* This self-command is very different at different times. A man in health possesses more of it than one languishing with sickness.[18] We are more master of our thoughts in the morning than in the evening: Fasting, than after a full meal. Can we give any reason for these variations, except experience? Where then is the power, of which we pretend to be conscious? Is there not here, either in a spiritual or material substance, or both, some secret mechanism or structure of parts, upon which the effect [69] depends, and which, being entirely unknown to us, renders the power or energy of the will equally unknown and incomprehensible?

20   Volition is surely an act of the mind, with which we are sufficiently acquainted. Reflect upon it. Consider it on all sides. Do you find anything in it like this creative power, by which it raises from nothing a new idea, and with a kind of *fiat*,[19] imitates the omnipotence of its Maker, if I may be allowed so to speak, who called forth into existence all the various scenes of nature? So far from being conscious of this energy in the will, it requires as certain experience as that of which we are possessed, to convince us that such extraordinary effects do ever result from a simple act of volition.

21   The generality of mankind never find any difficulty in accounting for the more common and familiar operations of nature – such as the descent of heavy bodies, the growth of plants, the generation of animals, or the nourishment of bodies by food: But suppose that, in all these cases, they perceive the very force or energy of the cause, by which it is connected with its effect, and is for ever infallible in its operation. They acquire, by long habit, such a turn of mind, that, upon the appearance of the cause, they immediately expect with assurance its usual attendant, and hardly

---

[18] Lucretius, *Nature of Things*, 3.463f.
[19] Creative act (from the Latin, 'let it be done'); an allusion to the creation story in Genesis 1.

conceive it possible that any other event could result from it. It is only on
the discovery of extraordinary phenomena, such as earthquakes, pestilence, and prodigies of any kind, that they find themselves at a loss to
assign a proper cause, and to explain the manner in which the effect is
produced by it. It is usual for men, in such difficulties, to have recourse to
some invisible intelligent principle[d] as the immediate cause of that event
which surprises them, and which, they think, cannot be accounted for
from the common powers of nature. But philosophers, who carry their
scrutiny a little farther, immediately perceive that, even in the most [70]
familiar events, the energy of the cause is as unintelligible as in the most
unusual, and that we only learn by experience the frequent *conjunction* of
objects, without being ever able to comprehend anything like *connexion*
between them. Here, then, many philosophers[20] think themselves obliged
by reason to have recourse, on all occasions, to the same principle, which
the vulgar never appeal to but in cases that appear miraculous and supernatural. They acknowledge mind and intelligence to be, not only the ultimate and original cause of all things, but the immediate and sole cause of
every event which appears in nature. They pretend[21] that those objects
which are commonly denominated *causes*, are in reality nothing but *occasions*; and that the true and direct principle of every effect is not any power
or force in nature, but a volition of the Supreme Being, who wills that such
particular objects should for ever be conjoined with each other. Instead of
saying that one billiard-ball moves another by a force which it has derived
from the author of nature, it is the Deity himself, they say, who, by a particular volition, moves the second ball, being determined to this operation
by the impulse of the first ball, in consequence of those general laws which
he has laid down to himself in the government of the universe. But

---

[d] Θεὸς ἀπὸ μηχανῆς. [Literally, 'a god out of a machine'; in Latin (as it appears in the 1748 and
1750 editions), *deus ex machina*. The phrase derives from ancient Greek tragedy, especially that of
Euripides, in which a god is lowered to the stage to sort out the problems of the human characters. The term thus means to resolve a difficulty by a miraculous or otherwise non-natural
device. Hume refers (1750 edition) to Cicero's *On the Nature of the Gods*. The relevant passage
there is as follows: 'For in so far as you cannot see how nature can cause this without some intelligent mind, you have recourse to a god, like the tragic poets when unable to arrange the conclusion of a plot' (1. 20. 53). Hume's objection itself derives from Leibniz; he probably became aware
of it through Bayle's criticism of Leibniz's view in the *Dictionary*, 'Rorarius', Note H. Interest-
ingly, both Leibniz and Bayle use the better-known Latin term, as does Hume in the 1748 edition. He has, presumably, shifted to the original Greek term to show off his learning.]
[20] Malebranche (*Search after Truth*, 6.2.3) and other Cartesians. The extent to which Descartes shared
the view is controversial.
[21] Claim.

65

philosophers advancing still in their enquiries, discover that, as we are totally ignorant of the power on which depends the mutual operation of bodies, we are no less ignorant of that power on which depends the operation of mind on body, or of body on mind, nor are we able, either from our senses or consciousness, to assign the ultimate principle in one case more than in the other. The same ignorance, therefore, reduces them to the same conclusion. They assert that the Deity is the immediate cause of the union between soul and body; and that they are not the organs of sense, which, being agitated by external objects, produce sensations in the [71] mind; but that it is a particular volition of our omnipotent Maker, which excites such a sensation, in consequence of such a motion in the organ. In like manner, it is not any energy in the will that produces local motion in our members: It is God himself, who is pleased to second our will, in itself impotent, and to command that motion which we erroneously attribute to our own power and efficacy. Nor do philosophers stop at this conclusion. They sometimes extend the same inference to the mind itself, in its internal operations. Our mental vision or conception of ideas is nothing but a revelation made to us by our Maker. When we voluntarily turn our thoughts to any object, and raise up its image in the fancy, it is not the will which creates that idea: It is the universal Creator, who discovers it to the mind, and renders it present to us.

22   Thus, according to these philosophers, every thing is full of God. Not content with the principle, that nothing exists but by his will, that nothing possesses any power but by his concession: They rob nature, and all created beings, of every power, in order to render their dependence on the Deity still more sensible and immediate. They consider not that, by this theory, they diminish, instead of magnifying, the grandeur of those attributes, which they affect so much to celebrate. It argues surely more power in the Deity to delegate a certain degree of power to inferior creatures than to produce every thing by his own immediate volition. It argues more wisdom to contrive at first the fabric of the world with such perfect foresight that, of itself, and by its proper operation, it may serve all the purposes of providence, than if the great Creator were obliged every moment to adjust its parts, and animate by his breath all the wheels of that stupendous machine.

23   But if we would have a more philosophical confutation of this theory, perhaps the two following reflections may suffice.

24　　*First*, It seems to me that this theory of the universal energy and [72] operation of the Supreme Being is too bold ever to carry conviction with it to a man, sufficiently apprized of the weakness of human reason, and the narrow limits to which it is confined in all its operations. Though the chain of arguments which conduct to it were ever so logical, there must arise a strong suspicion, if not an absolute assurance, that it has carried us quite beyond the reach of our faculties, when it leads to conclusions so extraordinary, and so remote from common life and experience. We are got into fairy land, long ere we have reached the last steps of our theory; and *there* we have no reason to trust our common methods of argument, or to think that our usual analogies and probabilities have any authority. Our line is too short to fathom such immense abysses. And however we may flatter ourselves that we are guided, in every step which we take, by a kind of verisimilitude and experience, we may be assured that this fancied experience has no authority when we thus apply it to subjects that lie entirely out of the sphere of experience. But on this we shall have occasion to touch afterwards.[e]

25　　*Secondly*, I cannot perceive any force in the arguments on which this theory is founded. We are ignorant, it is true, of the manner in which bodies operate on each other: Their force or energy is entirely incomprehensible: But are we not equally ignorant of the manner or force by which a mind, even the supreme mind, operates either on itself or on body? Whence, I beseech you, do we acquire any idea of it? We have no sentiment or consciousness of this power in ourselves. We have no idea of the supreme being but what we learn from reflection on our own faculties. Were our ignorance, therefore, a good reason for rejecting any thing, we [73] should be led into that principle of denying all energy in the Supreme Being as much as in the grossest matter. We surely comprehend as little the operations of one as of the other. Is it more difficult to conceive that motion may arise from impulse than that it may arise from volition? All we know is our profound ignorance in both cases.[f]

---

[e] Section 12.

[f] I need not examine at length the *vis inertiae* which is so much talked of in the new philosophy, and which is ascribed to matter. We find by experience, that a body at rest or in motion continues for ever in its present state, till put from it by some new cause; and that a body impelled takes as much motion from the impelling body as it acquires itself. These are facts. When we call this a *vis inertiae*, we only mark these facts, without pretending to have any idea of the inert power; in the same manner as, when we talk of gravity, we mean certain effects, without comprehending that active power. It was never the meaning of Sir Isaac Newton to rob second causes of all force or energy; though

Part 2

26   But to hasten to a conclusion of this argument, which is already drawn out to too great a length: We have sought in vain for an idea of power or necessary connexion in all the sources from which we could suppose it to be derived. It appears that, in single instances of the operation of bodies, we never can, by our utmost scrutiny, discover any thing but one event following another, without being able to comprehend any force or power [74] by which the cause operates, or any connexion between it and its supposed effect. The same difficulty occurs in contemplating the operations of mind on body; where we observe the motion of the latter to follow upon the volition of the former, but are not able to observe or conceive the tie which binds together the motion and volition, or the energy by which the mind produces this effect. The authority of the will over its own faculties and ideas is not a whit more comprehensible: So that, upon the whole, there appears not, throughout all nature, any one instance of connexion which is conceivable by us. All events seem entirely loose and separate. One event follows another; but we never can observe any tie between them. They seem *conjoined*, but never *connected*. And as we can have no idea of any thing which never appeared to our outward sense or inward sentiment, the necessary conclusion *seems* to be that we have no idea of connexion or power at all, and that these words are absolutely without any meaning, when employed either in philosophical reasonings or common life.

27   But there still remains one method of avoiding this conclusion, and one source which we have not yet examined. When any natural object or event is presented, it is impossible for us, by any sagacity or penetration,

---

some of his followers have endeavoured to establish that theory upon his authority. On the contrary, that great philosopher had recourse to an etherial active fluid to explain his universal attraction; though he was so cautious and modest as to allow, that it was a mere hypothesis, not to be insisted on, without more experiments. I must confess, that there is something in the fate of opinions a little extraordinary. Descartes insinuated that doctrine of the universal and sole efficacy of the Deity, without insisting on it. Malebranche and other Cartesians made it the foundation of all their philosophy. It had, however, no authority in England. Locke, Clarke, and Cudworth, never so much as take notice of it, but suppose all along, that matter has a real, though subordinate and derived power. By what means has it become so prevalent among our modern metaphysicians? [The *vis inertiae* is inertial force: Newton, *Principia*, Definition 3, 1st Law of Motion; *Opticks*, Query 31 (60, 70–1, 135). 'Second causes' are causes that derive their power from a first cause (e.g. God). So all ordinary natural causes are 'second causes'. Hume introduced the term in the editions after 1750, to replace 'matter'. This latter term was also removed – replaced by 'fluid' – from the succeeding sentence. That is, in the 1748 and 1750 editions, the text read 'to rob matter of all force' in the first instance, and 'etherial active matter' in the second. See also *A Letter from a Gentleman*.]

to discover, or even conjecture, without experience, what event will result from it, or to carry our foresight beyond that object which is immediately present to the memory and senses. Even after one instance or experiment where we have observed a particular event to follow upon another, we are not entitled to form a general rule, or foretell what will happen in like cases; it being justly esteemed an unpardonable temerity to judge of the whole course of nature from one single experiment, however accurate or certain. But when one particular species of event has always, in all instances, been conjoined with another, we make no longer any scruple of fore- [75] telling one upon the appearance of the other, and of employing that reasoning, which can alone assure us of any matter of fact or existence. We then call the one object, *cause*; the other, *effect*. We suppose that there is some connexion between them; some power in the one, by which it infallibly produces the other, and operates with the greatest certainty and strongest necessity.

28   It appears, then, that this idea of a necessary connexion among events arises from a number of similar instances which occur of the constant conjunction of these events; nor can that idea ever be suggested by any one of these instances, surveyed in all possible lights and positions. But there is nothing in a number of instances, different from every single instance, which is supposed to be exactly similar; except only, that after a repetition of similar instances, the mind is carried by habit, upon the appearance of one event, to expect its usual attendant, and to believe that it will exist. This connexion, therefore, which we *feel* in the mind, this customary transition of the imagination from one object to its usual attendant, is the sentiment or impression from which we form the idea of power or necessary connexion. Nothing farther is in the case. Contemplate the subject on all sides; you will never find any other origin of that idea. This is the sole difference between one instance, from which we can never receive the idea of connexion, and a number of similar instances, by which it is suggested. The first time a man saw the communication of motion by impulse, as by the shock of two billiard balls, he could not pronounce that the one event was *connected*; but only that it was *conjoined* with the other. After he has observed several instances of this nature, he then pronounces them to be *connected*. What alteration has happened to give rise to this new idea of *connexion*? Nothing but that he now *feels* these events to be *connected* [76] in his imagination, and can readily foretell the existence of one from the appearance of the other. When we say, therefore, that one object is

connected with another, we mean only that they have acquired a connexion in our thought, and give rise to this inference, by which they become proofs of each other's existence: A conclusion which is somewhat extraordinary, but which seems founded on sufficient evidence. Nor will its evidence be weakened by any general diffidence of the understanding, or sceptical suspicion concerning every conclusion which is new and extraordinary. No conclusions can be more agreeable to scepticism than such as make discoveries concerning the weakness and narrow limits of human reason and capacity.

29   And what stronger instance can be produced of the surprising ignorance and weakness of the understanding than the present? For surely, if there be any relation among objects which it imports to us to know perfectly, it is that of cause and effect. On this are founded all our reasonings concerning matter of fact or existence. By means of it alone we attain any assurance concerning objects which are removed from the present testimony of our memory and senses. The only immediate utility of all sciences, is to teach us, how to control and regulate future events by their causes. Our thoughts and enquiries are, therefore, every moment, employed about this relation. Yet so imperfect are the ideas which we form concerning it, that it is impossible to give any just definition of cause, except what is drawn from something extraneous and foreign to it. Similar objects are always conjoined with similar. Of this we have experience. Suitably to this experience, therefore, we may define a cause to be *an object, followed by another, and where all the objects similar to the first are followed by objects similar to the second.* Or in other words *where, if the first object had not* [77] *been, the second never had existed.* The appearance of a cause always conveys the mind, by a customary transition, to the idea of the effect. Of this also we have experience. We may, therefore, suitably to this experience, form another definition of cause, and call it, *an object followed by another, and whose appearance always conveys the thought to that other.* But though both these definitions be drawn from circumstances foreign to the cause, we cannot remedy this inconvenience, or attain any more perfect definition, which may point out that circumstance in the cause, which gives it a connexion with its effect. We have no idea of this connexion, nor even any distant notion what it is we desire to know, when we endeavour at a conception of it. We say, for instance, that the vibration of this string is the cause of this particular sound. But what do we mean by that affirmation? We either mean *that this vibration is followed by this sound, and that all similar*

vibrations have been followed by similar sounds: Or, *that this vibration is followed by this sound, and that upon the appearance of one the mind anticipates the senses, and forms immediately an idea of the other.* We may consider the relation of cause and effect in either of these two lights; but beyond these, we have no idea of it.[g]

30   To recapitulate, therefore, the reasonings of this section: Every [78] idea is copied from some preceding impression or sentiment; and where we cannot find any impression, we may be certain that there is no idea. In all single instances of the operation of bodies or minds, there is nothing that produces any impression, nor consequently can suggest any idea of power or necessary connexion. But when many uniform instances appear, and the same object is always followed by the same event; we then begin to entertain the notion of cause and connexion. We then *feel* a new sentiment or impression, to wit, a customary connexion in the thought or imagination between one object and its usual attendant; and this sentiment is the original of that idea which we seek for. For as this idea arises from a number of similar instances, and not from any single instance, it must arise from that circumstance, in which the number of instances differ from every individual instance. But this customary connexion or transition of the imagination is the only circumstance in which they differ. In every

---

[g] According to these explications and definitions, the idea of *power* is relative as much as that of *cause*; and both have a reference to an effect, or some other event constantly conjoined with the former. When we consider the *unknown* circumstance of an object, by which the degree or quantity of its effect is fixed and determined, we call that its power: and accordingly, it is allowed by all philosophers, that the effect is the measure of the power. But if they had any idea of power, as it is in itself, why could not they measure it in itself? The dispute whether the force of a body in motion be as its velocity, or the square of its velocity; this dispute, I say, need not be decided by comparing its effects in equal or unequal times; but by a direct mensuration and comparison. As to the frequent use of the words, *force, power, energy, etc*, which every where occur in common conversation, as well as in philosophy; that is no proof, that we are acquainted, in any instance, with the connecting principle between cause and effect, or can account ultimately for the production of one thing to another. These words, as commonly used, have very loose meanings annexed to them; and their ideas are very uncertain and confused. No animal can put external bodies in motion without the sentiment of a *nisus* or endeavour; and every animal has a sentiment or feeling from the stroke or blow of an external object, that is in motion. These sensations, which are merely animal, and from which we can *a priori* draw no inference, we are apt to transfer to inanimate objects, and to suppose, that they have some such feelings, whenever they transfer or receive motion. With regard to energies, which are exerted, without our annexing to them any idea of communicated motion, we consider only the constant experienced conjunction of the events; and as we *feel* a customary connexion between the ideas, we transfer that feeling to the objects; as nothing is more usual than to apply to external bodies every internal sensation, which they occasion. [Footnote added in 1750, enlarged in 1756. The dispute concerning the force of a body was between Leibniz and the Cartesians and Newtonians. The concluding clause derives from Malebranche, *Search after Truth*, 1.12.5.]

other particular they are alike. The first instance which we saw of motion communicated by the shock of two billiard balls (to return to this obvious illustration) is exactly similar to any instance that may, at present, occur to us; except only, that we could not, at first, *infer* one event from the other; which we are enabled to do at present, after so long a course of uniform experience. I know not whether the reader will readily apprehend this reasoning. I am afraid that, should I multiply words about it, or throw it into a greater variety of lights, it would only become more obscure and intricate. In all abstract reasonings there is one point of view which, if we can happily hit, we shall go farther towards illustrating the subject than by all the eloquence and copious expression in the world. This point of view we should endeavour to reach, and reserve the flowers of rhetoric for subjects which are more adapted to them.

[79]

8

Of liberty and necessity

Part I

1   It might reasonably be expected, in questions which have been canvassed and disputed with great eagerness, since the first origin of science, and philosophy, that the meaning of all the terms, at least, should have been agreed upon among the disputants; and our enquiries, in the course of two thousand years, been able to pass from words to the true and real subject of the controversy. For how easy may it seem to give exact definitions of the terms employed in reasoning, and make these definitions, not the mere sound of words, the object of future scrutiny and examination? But if we consider the matter more narrowly, we shall be apt to draw a quite opposite conclusion. From this circumstance alone, that a controversy has been long kept on foot, and remains still undecided, we may presume that there is some ambiguity in the expression, and that the disputants affix different ideas to the terms employed in the controversy. For as the faculties of the mind are supposed to be naturally alike in every individual; otherwise nothing could be more fruitless than to reason or dispute together; it were impossible, if men affix the same ideas to their terms, that they could so long form different opinions of the same subject; especially when they communicate their views, and each party turn themselves on all sides, in search of arguments which may give them the victory over their [81] antagonists. It is true, if men attempt the discussion of questions which lie entirely beyond the reach of human capacity, such as those concerning the origin of worlds, or the economy of the intellectual system or region of

73

spirits,[1] they may long beat the air in their fruitless contests, and never arrive at any determinate conclusion. But if the question regard any subject of common life and experience, nothing, one would think, could preserve the dispute so long undecided but some ambiguous expressions, which keep the antagonists still at a distance, and hinder them from grappling with each other.

2   This has been the case in the long disputed question concerning liberty and necessity; and to so remarkable a degree that, if I be not much mistaken, we shall find, that all mankind, both learned and ignorant, have always been of the same opinion with regard to this subject, and that a few intelligible definitions would immediately have put an end to the whole controversy. I own that this dispute has been so much canvassed on all hands, and has led philosophers into such a labyrinth of obscure sophistry, that it is no wonder, if a sensible reader indulge his ease so far as to turn a deaf ear to the proposal of such a question, from which he can expect neither instruction or entertainment. But the state of the argument here proposed may, perhaps, serve to renew his attention; as it has more novelty, promises at least some decision of the controversy, and will not much disturb his ease by any intricate or obscure reasoning.

3   I hope, therefore, to make it appear that all men have ever agreed in the doctrine both of necessity and of liberty, according to any reasonable sense, which can be put on these terms; and that the whole controversy has hitherto turned merely upon words. We shall begin with examining the doctrine of necessity.

[82]   4   It is universally allowed that matter, in all its operations, is actuated by a necessary force, and that every natural effect is so precisely determined by the energy of its cause that no other effect, in such particular circumstances, could possibly have resulted from it.[2] The degree and direction of every motion is, by the laws of nature, prescribed with such exactness that a living creature may as soon arise from the shock of two bodies as motion in any other degree or direction than what is actually produced by it.[3] Would we, therefore, form a just and precise idea of *necessity*, we must consider whence that idea arises when we apply it to the operation of bodies.

---

[1] The nature and workings of minds or spirits. Cf. Locke, *Essay*, 4.3.27.
[2] 'Nature does nothing in vain', Newton, *Principia*, Rules for the Study of Natural Philosophy, Rule 1 (87).
[3] Newton, *Principia*, Laws of Motion (70–1).

5   It seems evident that, if all the scenes of nature were continually shifted in such a manner that no two events bore any resemblance to each other, but every object was entirely new, without any similitude to whatever had been seen before, we should never, in that case, have attained the least idea of necessity, or of a connexion among these objects. We might say, upon such a supposition, that one object or event has followed another; not that one was produced by the other. The relation of cause and effect must be utterly unknown to mankind. Inference and reasoning concerning the operations of nature would, from that moment, be at an end; and the memory and senses remain the only canals,[4] by which the knowledge of any real existence could possibly have access to the mind. Our idea, therefore, of necessity and causation arises entirely from the uniformity observable in the operations of nature, where similar objects are constantly conjoined together, and the mind is determined by custom to infer the one from the appearance of the other. These two circumstances form the whole of that necessity, which we ascribe to matter. Beyond the constant *conjunction* of similar objects, and the consequent *inference* from one to the other, we have no notion of any necessity or connexion.

6   If it appear, therefore, that all mankind have ever allowed, with- [83] out any doubt or hesitation, that these two circumstances take place in the voluntary actions of men, and in the operations of mind; it must follow, that all mankind have ever agreed in the doctrine of necessity, and that they have hitherto disputed, merely for not understanding each other.

7   As to the first circumstance, the constant and regular conjunction of similar events, we may possibly satisfy ourselves by the following considerations. It is universally acknowledged that there is a great uniformity among the actions of men, in all nations and ages, and that human nature remains still the same, in its principles and operations. The same motives always produce the same actions: The same events follow from the same causes. Ambition, avarice, self-love, vanity, friendship, generosity, public spirit; these passions, mixed in various degrees, and distributed through society, have been, from the beginning of the world, and still are, the source of all the actions and enterprises, which have ever been observed among mankind. Would you know the sentiments, inclinations, and course of life of the Greeks and Romans? Study well the temper and actions of the

---

[4] An allusion to the theory of animal spirits, according to which the nerves are channels (canals) along which the animal spirits that convey sensations and memories flow.

French and English: You cannot be much mistaken in transferring to the former *most* of the observations which you have made with regard to the latter. Mankind are so much the same, in all times and places, that history informs us of nothing new or strange in this particular. Its chief use is only to discover the constant and universal principles of human nature, by showing men in all varieties of circumstances and situations, and furnishing us with materials from which we may form our observations and become acquainted with the regular springs of human action and behaviour. These records of wars, intrigues, factions, and revolutions, are so [84] many collections of experiments, by which the politician or moral philosopher fixes the principles of his science, in the same manner as the physician or natural philosopher becomes acquainted with the nature of plants, minerals, and other external objects, by the experiments which he forms concerning them. Nor are the earth, water, and other elements, examined by Aristotle, and Hippocrates, more like to those which at present lie under our observation than the men described by Polybius and Tacitus are to those who now govern the world.[5]

8   Should a traveller, returning from a far country, bring us an account of men, wholly different from any with whom we were ever acquainted; men, who were entirely divested of avarice, ambition, or revenge; who knew no pleasure but friendship, generosity, and public spirit; we should immediately, from these circumstances, detect the falsehood, and prove him a liar, with the same certainty as if he had stuffed his narration with stories of centaurs and dragons, miracles and prodigies. And if we would explode any forgery in history, we cannot make use of a more convincing argument, than to prove, that the actions ascribed to any person are directly contrary to the course of nature, and that no human motives, in such circumstances, could ever induce him to such a conduct. The veracity of Quintus Curtius[6] is as much to be suspected, when he describes the supernatural courage of Alexander, by which he was hurried

---

[5] Aristotle recognized the four elements of earth, water, air and fire as the primary material causes; however, he rejected reliance, in scientific explanation, on material causes alone (*Metaphysics* 983a–985b). Hippocrates (c. 460–377 BC), Greek physician, traditionally regarded as the father of medicine. In 'The Nature of Man', a popular lecture on physiology attributed to him, the author rejects speculative theories based on these elements, and replaces them with appeal to the four humours, blood, phlegm, yellow bile and black bile. Polybius (c. 200–c. 118 BC) and Tacitus (AD c. 56–c. 120) were Roman historians, both of whom sought to go beyond mere narration of events to underlying principles about human nature and history.

[6] Quintus Curtius Rufus (1st century AD), author of *The History of Alexander*, a colourful but unreliable history of Alexander the Great.

on singly to attack multitudes, as when he describes his supernatural force and activity, by which he was able to resist them. So readily and universally do we acknowledge a uniformity in human motives and actions as well as in the operations of body.

9   Hence likewise the benefit of that experience, acquired by long life and a variety of business and company, in order to instruct us in the principles of human nature, and regulate our future conduct, as well as speculation. By means of this guide, we mount up to the knowledge of men's inclinations and motives, from their actions, expressions, and [85] even gestures; and again descend to the interpretation of their actions from our knowledge of their motives and inclinations. The general observations treasured up by a course of experience, give us the clue of human nature, and teach us to unravel all its intricacies. Pretexts and appearances no longer deceive us. Public declarations pass for the specious colouring of a cause.[7] And though virtue and honour be allowed their proper weight and authority, that perfect disinterestedness, so often pretended to, is never expected in multitudes and parties; seldom in their leaders; and scarcely even in individuals of any rank or station. But were there no uniformity in human actions, and were every experiment which we could form of this kind irregular and anomalous, it were impossible to collect any general observations concerning mankind; and no experience, however accurately digested by reflection, would ever serve to any purpose. Why is the aged husbandman more skilful in his calling than the young beginner, but because there is a certain uniformity in the operation of the sun, rain, and earth towards the production of vegetables; and experience teaches the old practitioner the rules by which this operation is governed and directed?

10   We must not, however, expect that this uniformity of human actions should be carried to such a length as that all men, in the same circumstances, will always act precisely in the same manner, without making any allowance for the diversity of characters, prejudices, and opinions. Such a uniformity in every particular, is found in no part of nature. On the contrary, from observing the variety of conduct in different men, we are enabled to form a greater variety of maxims, which still suppose a degree of uniformity and regularity.

11   Are the manners of men different in different ages and coun- [86] tries? We learn thence the great force of custom and education, which

---

[7] That is, are recognized to be distorted by the political interests they serve.

mould the human mind from its infancy and form it into a fixed and established character.[8] Is the behaviour and conduct of the one sex very unlike that of the other? It is thence we become acquainted with the different characters which nature has impressed upon the sexes, and which she preserves with constancy and regularity. Are the actions of the same person much diversified in the different periods of his life, from infancy to old age? This affords room for many general observations concerning the gradual change of our sentiments and inclinations, and the different maxims which prevail in the different ages of human creatures. Even the characters, which are peculiar to each individual, have a uniformity in their influence; otherwise our acquaintance with the persons and our observation of their conduct could never teach us their dispositions, or serve to direct our behaviour with regard to them.

12   I grant it possible to find some actions, which seem to have no regular connexion with any known motives, and are exceptions to all the measures of conduct which have ever been established for the government of men. But if we would willingly know what judgment should be formed of such irregular and extraordinary actions, we may consider the sentiments commonly entertained with regard to those irregular events which appear in the course of nature, and the operations of external objects. All causes are not conjoined to their usual effects with like uniformity. An artificer, who handles only dead matter, may be disappointed of his aim, as well as the politician, who directs the conduct of sensible and intelligent agents.

13   The vulgar,[9] who take things according to their first appearance, attribute the uncertainty of events to such an uncertainty in the causes as makes the latter often fail of their usual influence; though they meet with [87] no impediment in their operation. But philosophers, observing that, almost in every part of nature, there is contained a vast variety of springs and principles, which are hid, by reason of their minuteness or remoteness,[10] find, that it is at least possible the contrariety of events may not proceed from any contingency in the cause, but from the secret operation of contrary causes. This possibility is converted into certainty by farther observation, when they remark that, upon an exact scrutiny, a contrariety of effects always betrays a contrariety of causes, and proceeds from their mutual opposition. A peasant can give no better reason for the stopping of

---

[8] Hume pursues this topic in the essay 'Of National Characters'.   [9] The masses.
[10] Locke, *Essay*, 4.3.24–5.

any clock or watch than to say that it does not commonly go right: But an artist easily perceives that the same force in the spring or pendulum has always the same influence on the wheels; but fails of its usual effects, perhaps by reason of a grain of dust, which puts a stop to the whole movement. From the observation of several parallel instances, philosophers form a maxim that the connexion between all causes and effects is equally necessary, and that its seeming uncertainty in some instances proceeds from the secret opposition of contrary causes.

14   Thus, for instance, in the human body, when the usual symptoms of health or sickness disappoint our expectation; when medicines operate not with their wonted[11] powers; when irregular events follow from any particular cause; the philosopher and physician are not surprised at the matter, nor are ever tempted to deny, in general, the necessity and uniformity of those principles by which the animal economy[12] is conducted. They know that a human body is a mighty complicated machine: That many secret powers lurk in it, which are altogether beyond our comprehension: That to us it must often appear very uncertain in its operations: And that therefore the irregular events, which outwardly discover themselves, can be no proof that the laws of nature are not observed with the greatest regularity in its internal operations and government.

15   The philosopher, if he be consistent, must apply the same rea- [88] soning to the actions and volitions of intelligent agents. The most irregular and unexpected resolutions of men may frequently be accounted for by those who know every particular circumstance of their character and situation. A person of an obliging disposition gives a peevish answer: But he has the toothache, or has not dined. A stupid fellow discovers an uncommon alacrity in his carriage:[13] But he has met with a sudden piece of good fortune. Or even when an action, as sometimes happens, cannot be particularly accounted for, either by the person himself or by others; we know, in general, that the characters of men are, to a certain degree, inconstant and irregular. This is, in a manner, the constant character of human nature; though it be applicable, in a more particular manner, to some persons who have no fixed rule for their conduct, but proceed in a continued course of caprice and inconstancy. The internal principles and motives may operate in a uniform manner, notwithstanding these seeming

---

[11] Usual.   [12] The physical organization of animals; their structure and function.
[13] A normally vague or slow fellow has an uncharacteristic spring in his step.

irregularities; in the same manner as the winds, rain, cloud, and other variations of the weather are supposed to be governed by steady principles; though not easily discoverable by human sagacity and enquiry.

16   Thus it appears, not only that the conjunction between motives and voluntary actions is as regular and uniform as that between the cause and effect in any part of nature; but also that this regular conjunction has been universally acknowledged among mankind, and has never been the subject of dispute, either in philosophy or common life. Now, as it is from past experience that we draw all inferences concerning the future, and as we conclude that objects will always be conjoined together which we find to have always been conjoined; it may seem superfluous to prove that this experienced uniformity in human actions is a source whence we draw [89] *inferences* concerning them. But in order to throw the argument into a greater variety of lights we shall also insist, though briefly, on this latter topic.

17   The mutual dependence of men is so great in all societies that scarce any human action is entirely complete in itself, or is performed without some reference to the actions of others, which are requisite to make it answer fully the intention of the agent. The poorest artificer, who labours alone, expects at least the protection of the magistrate, to ensure him the enjoyment of the fruits of his labour. He also expects that, when he carries his goods to market, and offers them at a reasonable price, he shall find purchasers, and shall be able, by the money he acquires, to engage others to supply him with those commodities which are requisite for his subsistence. In proportion as men extend their dealings, and render their intercourse with others more complicated, they always comprehend, in their schemes of life, a greater variety of voluntary actions, which they expect, from the proper motives, to co-operate with their own. In all these conclusions they take their measures from past experience, in the same manner as in their reasonings concerning external objects; and firmly believe that men, as well as all the elements, are to continue, in their operations, the same that they have ever found them. A manufacturer reckons upon the labour of his servants for the execution of any work as much as upon the tools which he employs, and would be equally surprised were his expectations disappointed. In short, this experimental inference and reasoning concerning the actions of others enters so much into human life that no man, while awake, is ever a moment without employing it. Have we not reason, therefore, to affirm that all mankind have always agreed in

the doctrine of necessity according to the foregoing definition and explication of it?

18   Nor have philosophers ever entertained a different opinion from the people in this particular. For, not to mention that almost every action of their life supposes that opinion, there are even few of the speculative [90] parts of learning to which it is not essential. What would become of *history*, had we not a dependence on the veracity of the historian according to the experience which we have had of mankind? How could *politics* be a science, if laws and forms of government had not a uniform influence upon society?[14] Where would be the foundation of *morals*, if particular characters had no certain or determinate power to produce particular sentiments, and if these sentiments had no constant operation on actions? And with what pretence could we employ our *criticism* upon any poet or polite author, if we could not pronounce the conduct and sentiments of his actors either natural or unnatural to such characters, and in such circumstances? It seems almost impossible, therefore, to engage either in science[15] or action of any kind without acknowledging the doctrine of necessity, and this *inference* from motives to voluntary actions, from characters to conduct.

19   And indeed, when we consider how aptly *natural* and *moral* evidence link together, and form only one chain of argument, we shall make no scruple to allow that they are of the same nature, and derived from the same principles. A prisoner, who has neither money nor interest, discovers the impossibility of his escape, as well when he considers the obstinacy of the gaoler, as the walls and bars with which he is surrounded; and, in all attempts for his freedom, chooses rather to work upon the stone and iron of the one, than upon the inflexible nature of the other. The same prisoner, when conducted to the scaffold, foresees his death as certainly from the constancy and fidelity of his guards, as from the operation of the axe or wheel.[16] His mind runs along a certain train of ideas: The refusal of the soldiers to consent to his escape; the action of the executioner; the separation of the head and body; bleeding, convulsive motions, and death. Here is a connected chain of natural causes and voluntary actions; but the mind feels no difference between them in passing from one link to [91] another: Nor is less certain of the future event than if it were connected with the objects present to the memory or senses, by a train of causes,

---

[14] A topic pursued in Hume's essay 'That Politics may be Reduced to a Science'.
[15] Theoretical enquiry.   [16] An instrument of torture.

cemented together by what we are pleased to call a *physical* necessity. The same experienced union has the same effect on the mind, whether the united objects be motives, volition, and actions; or figure and motion.[17] We may change the name of things; but their nature and their operation on the understanding never change.

20   Were a man, whom I know to be honest and opulent, and with whom I live in intimate friendship, to come into my house, where I am surrounded with my servants, I rest assured that he is not to stab me before he leaves it in order to rob me of my silver standish;[18] and I no more suspect this event than the falling of the house itself, which is new, and solidly built and founded – *But he may have been seized with a sudden and unknown frenzy.* – So may a sudden earthquake arise, and shake and tumble my house about my ears. I shall therefore change the suppositions. I shall say that I know with certainty that he is not to put his hand into the fire and hold it there till it be consumed: And this event, I think I can foretell with the same assurance, as that, if he throw himself out at the window, and meet with no obstruction, he will not remain a moment suspended in the air. No suspicion of an unknown frenzy can give the least possibility to the former event, which is so contrary to all the known principles of human nature. A man who at noon leaves his purse full of gold on the pavement at Charing Cross, may as well expect that it will fly away like a feather, as that he will find it untouched an hour after. Above one half of human reasonings contain inferences of a similar nature, attended with more or less degrees of certainty proportioned to our experience of the usual conduct of mankind in such particular situations.[19]

[92]   21   I have frequently considered, what could possibly be the reason why all mankind, though they have ever, without hesitation, acknowledged the doctrine of necessity in their whole practice and reasoning, have yet discovered such a reluctance to acknowledge it in words, and have rather shown a propensity, in all ages, to profess the contrary opinion. The matter, I think, may be accounted for after the following manner. If we examine the operations of body, and the production of effects from their causes, we shall find that all our faculties can never carry us farther in our knowledge of this relation than barely to observe that particular objects are *constantly conjoined* together, and that the mind is

---

[17] The shapes and motions of particles, i.e. explanations in physics.
[18] A desk-stand for pens and ink.   [19] This paragraph was added in the 1772 edition.

carried, by a *customary transition*, from the appearance of one to the belief of the other. But though this conclusion concerning human ignorance be the result of the strictest scrutiny of this subject, men still entertain a strong propensity to believe that they penetrate farther into the powers of nature, and perceive something like a necessary connexion between the cause and the effect. When again they turn their reflections towards the operations of their own minds, and *feel* no such connexion of the motive and the action; they are thence apt to suppose, that there is a difference between the effects which result from material force, and those which arise from thought and intelligence. But being once convinced that we know nothing farther of causation of any kind than merely the *constant conjunction* of objects, and the consequent *inference* of the mind from one to another, and finding that these two circumstances are universally allowed to have place in voluntary actions; we may be more easily led to own the same necessity common to all causes. And though this reasoning may contradict the systems of many philosophers, in ascribing necessity to the determinations of the will, we shall find, upon reflection, that they dissent from it in words only, not in their real sentiment. Necessity, according to the sense in which it is here [93] taken, has never yet been rejected, nor can ever, I think, be rejected by any philosopher. It may only, perhaps, be pretended[20] that the mind can perceive, in the operations of matter, some farther connexion between the cause and effect; and a connexion that has not place in voluntary actions of intelligent beings. Now whether it be so or not, can only appear upon examination; and it is incumbent on these philosophers to make good their assertion, by defining or describing that necessity, and pointing it out to us in the operations of material causes.

22   It would seem, indeed, that men begin at the wrong end of this question concerning liberty and necessity, when they enter upon it by examining the faculties of the soul, the influence of the understanding, and the operations of the will. Let them first discuss a more simple question, namely, the operations of body and of brute unintelligent matter; and try whether they can there form any idea of causation and necessity, except that of a constant conjunction of objects, and subsequent inference of the mind from one to another. If these circumstances form, in reality, the whole of that necessity, which we conceive in matter, and if these circumstances be also universally acknowledged to take place in the operations of

---

[20] Claimed.

the mind, the dispute is at an end; at least, must be owned to be thenceforth merely verbal. But as long as we will rashly suppose, that we have some farther idea of necessity and causation in the operations of external objects; at the same time, that we can find nothing farther in the voluntary actions of the mind; there is no possibility of bringing the question to any determinate issue, while we proceed upon so erroneous a supposition. The only method of undeceiving us is to mount up higher; to examine the narrow extent of science[21] when applied to material causes; and to convince ourselves that all we know of them is the constant con-

[94] junction and inference above mentioned. We may, perhaps, find that it is with difficulty we are induced to fix such narrow limits to human understanding: But we can afterwards find no difficulty when we come to apply this doctrine to the actions of the will. For as it is evident that these have a regular conjunction with motives and circumstances and characters, and as we always draw inferences from one to the other, we must be obliged to acknowledge in words that necessity, which we have already avowed, in every deliberation of our lives, and in every step of our conduct and behaviour.[a]

---

[a] The prevalence of the doctrine of liberty may be accounted for, from another cause, *viz.* a false sensation of seeming experience which we have, or may have, of liberty or indifference, in many of our actions. The necessity of any action, whether of matter or of mind, is not, properly speaking, a quality in the agent, but in any thinking or intelligent being, who may consider the action; and it consists chiefly in the determination of his thoughts to infer the existence of that action from some preceding objects; as liberty, when opposed to necessity, is nothing but the want of that determination, and a certain looseness or indifference, which we feel, in passing, or not passing, from the idea of one object to that of any succeeding one.⟩ Now we may observe, that, though, in *reflecting* on human actions, we seldom feel such a looseness, or indifference, but are commonly able to infer them with considerable certainty from their motives, and from the dispositions of the agent; yet it frequently happens, that, in *performing* the actions themselves, we are sensible of something like it: And as all resembling objects are readily taken for each other, this has been employed as a demonstrative and even intuitive proof of human liberty. We feel, that our actions are subject to our will, on most occasions; and imagine we feel, that the will itself is subject to nothing, because, when by a denial of it we are provoked to try, we feel, that it moves easily every way, and produces an image of itself (or a *velleity*, as it is called in the schools) even on that side, on which it did not settle. This image, or faint motion, we persuade ourselves, could, at that time, have been completed into the thing itself; because, should that be denied, we find, upon a second trial, that, at present, it can. We consider not, that the fantastical desire of showing liberty, is here the motive of our actions. And it seems certain, that, however we may imagine we feel a liberty within ourselves, a spectator can commonly infer our actions from our motives and character; and even where he cannot, he concludes in general, that he might, were he perfectly acquainted with every circumstance of our situation and temper, and the most secret springs of our complexion and disposition. Now this is the very essence of necessity, according to the foregoing doctrine. [A velleity is a mere wish, an inclination that does not lead to action, and so contrasted with a volition. To be 'called in the schools' is to be academic jargon.]

[21] Knowledge.

23   But to proceed in this reconciling project with regard to the [95] question of liberty and necessity; the most contentious question of metaphysics, the most contentious science; it will not require many words to prove, that all mankind have ever agreed in the doctrine of liberty as well as in that of necessity, and that the whole dispute, in this respect also, has been hitherto merely verbal. For what is meant by *liberty*, when applied to voluntary actions? We cannot surely mean that actions have so little connexion with motives, inclinations, and circumstances, that one does not follow with a certain degree of uniformity from the other, and that one affords no inference by which we can conclude the existence of the other. For these are plain and acknowledged matters of fact. By liberty, then, we can only mean *a power of acting or not acting, according to the determinations of the will*; that is, if we choose to remain at rest, we may; if we choose to move, we also may.[22] Now this hypothetical liberty is universally allowed to belong to every one who is not a prisoner and in chains. Here then is no subject of dispute.

24   Whatever definition we may give of *liberty*, we should be careful to observe two requisite circumstances; *first*, that it be consistent with plain matter of fact; *secondly*, that it be consistent with itself. If we observe these circumstances, and render our definition intelligible, I am persuaded that all mankind will be found of one opinion with regard to it.

25   It is universally allowed that nothing exists without a cause of its existence, and that *chance*, when strictly examined, is a mere negative word, and means not any real power which has anywhere a being in nature.[23] But it is pretended that some causes are necessary, some not necessary. Here then is the advantage of definitions. Let any one *define* a cause, without comprehending, as a part of the definition, a *necessary connexion* with its effect; and let him show distinctly the origin of the idea, expressed by the [96] definition; and I shall readily give up the whole controversy. But if the foregoing explication of the matter be received, this must be absolutely impracticable. Had not objects a regular conjunction with each other, we should never have entertained any notion of cause and effect; and this regular conjunction produces that inference of the understanding, which is the only connexion, that we can have any comprehension of. Whoever attempts a definition of *cause*, exclusive of these circumstances, will be

---

[22] Comparable definitions are to be found in Hobbes (*Leviathan*, 145–7) and Locke (*Essay*, 2.21.7–14).
[23] See Seneca, *Moral Essays*, 'On Providence', 1.2.

obliged either to employ unintelligible terms or such as are synonymous to the term which he endeavours to define.[b] And if the definition above mentioned be admitted; liberty, when opposed to necessity, not to constraint, is the same thing with chance; which is universally allowed to have no existence.

Part 2

26   There is no method of reasoning more common, and yet none more blameable, than, in philosophical disputes, to endeavour the refutation of any hypothesis, by a pretence of its dangerous consequences to religion and morality. When any opinion leads to absurdities, it is certainly false; but it is not certain that an opinion is false, because it is of dangerous consequence. Such topics, therefore, ought entirely to be forborne; as serving nothing to the discovery of truth, but only to make the person of an

[97]   antagonist odious. This I observe in general, without pretending to draw any advantage from it. I frankly submit to an examination of this kind, and shall venture to affirm that the doctrines, both of necessity and of liberty, as above explained, are not only consistent with morality, but are absolutely essential to its support.

27   *Necessity* may be defined two ways, conformably to the two definitions of *cause*, of which it makes an essential part. It consists either in *the constant conjunction of like objects*, or in *the inference of the understanding from one object to another*. Now necessity, in both these senses, (which, indeed, are at bottom the same) has universally, though tacitly, in the schools, in the pulpit, and in common life, been allowed to belong to the will of man; and no one has ever pretended to deny that we can draw inferences concerning human actions, and that those inferences are founded on the experienced union of like actions, with like motives, inclinations, and circumstances. The only particular in which any one can differ, is, that either, perhaps, he will refuse to give the name of *necessity* to this property of human actions: But as long as the meaning is understood, I hope the word can do

---

[b] Thus, if a cause be defined, *that which produces any thing*; it is easy to observe, that *producing* is synonymous to *causing*. In like manner, if a cause be defined, *that by which any thing exists*; this is liable to the same objection. For what is meant by these words, *by which*? Had it been said, that a cause is *that* after which *any thing constantly exists*; we should have understood the terms. For this is, indeed, all we know of the matter. And this constancy forms the very essence of necessity, nor have we any other idea of it.

no harm: Or that he will maintain it possible to discover something farther in the operations of matter. But this, it must be acknowledged, can be of no consequence to morality or religion, whatever it may be to natural philosophy or metaphysics. We may here be mistaken in asserting that there is no idea of any other necessity or connexion in the actions of body: But surely we ascribe nothing to the actions of the mind, but what everyone does, and must readily allow of. We change no circumstance in the received orthodox system with regard to the will, but only in that with regard to material objects and causes. Nothing, therefore, can be more innocent, at least, than this doctrine.

28   All laws being founded on rewards and punishments, it is supposed as a fundamental principle, that these motives have a regular and [98] uniform influence on the mind, and both produce the good and prevent the evil actions.[24] We may give to this influence what name we please; but, as it is usually conjoined with the action, it must be esteemed a *cause*, and be looked upon as an instance of that necessity, which we would here establish.

29   The only proper object of hatred or vengeance is a person or creature, endowed with thought and consciousness; and when any criminal or injurious actions excite that passion, it is only by their relation to the person, or connexion with him. Actions are, by their very nature, temporary and perishing; and where they proceed not from some *cause* in the character and disposition of the person who performed them, they can neither redound[25] to his honour, if good; nor infamy, if evil. The actions themselves may be blameable; they may be contrary to all the rules of morality and religion: But the person is not answerable for them; and as they proceeded from nothing in him that is durable and constant, and leave nothing of that nature behind them, it is impossible he can, upon their account, become the object of punishment or vengeance. According to the principle, therefore, which denies necessity, and consequently causes, a man is as pure and untainted, after having committed the most horrid crime, as at the first moment of his birth, nor is his character anywise concerned in his actions; since they are not derived from it, and the wickedness of the one can never be used as a proof of the depravity of the other.

30   Men are not blamed for such actions as they perform ignorantly and casually, whatever may be the consequences. Why? but because the

---

[24] Locke, *Essay*, 2.28.6.   [25] Contribute greatly.

principles of these actions are only momentary, and terminate in them alone. Men are less blamed for such actions as they perform hastily and unpremeditatedly than for such as proceed from deliberation. For what
[99] reason? but because a hasty temper, though a constant cause or principle in the mind, operates only by intervals, and infects not the whole character. Again, repentance wipes off every crime, if attended with a reformation of life and manners. How is this to be accounted for? but by asserting that actions render a person criminal merely as they are proofs of criminal principles in the mind; and when, by an alteration of these principles, they cease to be just proofs, they likewise cease to be criminal. But, except upon the doctrine of necessity, they never were just proofs, and consequently never were criminal.

31   It will be equally easy to prove, and from the same arguments, that *liberty*, according to that definition above mentioned, in which all men agree, is also essential to morality, and that no human actions, where it is wanting, are susceptible of any moral qualities, or can be the objects either of approbation or dislike. For as actions are objects of our moral sentiment, so far only as they are indications of the internal character, passions, and affections; it is impossible that they can give rise either to praise or blame, where they proceed not from these principles, but are derived altogether from external violence.

32   I pretend not to have obviated or removed all objections to this theory, with regard to necessity and liberty. I can foresee other objections, derived from topics which have not here been treated of. It may be said, for instance, that, if voluntary actions be subjected to the same laws of necessity with the operations of matter, there is a continued chain of necessary causes, pre-ordained and pre-determined, reaching from the original cause of all to every single volition of every human creature. No contingency anywhere in the universe; no indifference; no liberty. While we act, we are, at the same time, acted upon. The ultimate author of all our volitions is the Creator of the world, who first bestowed motion on this immense machine, and placed all beings in that particular position,
[100] whence every subsequent event, by an inevitable necessity, must result. Human actions, therefore, either can have no moral turpitude at all, as proceeding from so good a cause; or if they have any turpitude, they must involve our Creator in the same guilt, while he is acknowledged to be their ultimate cause and author. For as a man, who fired a mine, is answerable for all the consequences whether the train he employed be long

or short;[26] so wherever a continued chain of necessary causes is fixed, that being, either finite or infinite, who produces the first, is likewise the author of all the rest, and must both bear the blame and acquire the praise which belong to them. Our clear and unalterable ideas of morality establish this rule, upon unquestionable reasons, when we examine the consequences of any human action; and these reasons must still have greater force when applied to the volitions and intentions of a Being infinitely wise and powerful. Ignorance or impotence may be pleaded for so limited a creature as man; but those imperfections have no place in our Creator. He foresaw, he ordained, he intended all those actions of men, which we so rashly pronounce criminal. And we must therefore conclude, either that they are not criminal, or that the Deity, not man, is accountable for them. But as either of these positions is absurd and impious, it follows, that the doctrine from which they are deduced cannot possibly be true, as being liable to all the same objections. An absurd consequence, if necessary, proves the original doctrine to be absurd; in the same manner as criminal actions render criminal the original cause, if the connexion between them be necessary and inevitable.

33   This objection consists of two parts, which we shall examine separately; *first*, that, if human actions can be traced up, by a necessary chain, to the Deity, they can never be criminal; on account of the infinite perfection of that Being from whom they are derived, and who can intend nothing but what is altogether good and laudable. Or, *secondly*, if they be [101] criminal, we must retract the attribute of perfection, which we ascribe to the Deity, and must acknowledge him to be the ultimate author of guilt and moral turpitude in all his creatures.

34   The answer to the first objection seems obvious and convincing. There are many philosophers who, after an exact scrutiny of all the phenomena of nature, conclude, that the *whole*, considered as one system, is, in every period of its existence, ordered with perfect benevolence; and that the utmost possible happiness will, in the end, result to all created beings, without any mixture of positive or absolute ill or misery. Every physical ill, say they, makes an essential part of this benevolent system, and could not possibly be removed, even by the Deity himself, considered as a wise agent, without giving entrance to greater ill, or excluding greater good, which will

---

[26] Presumably a reference to mining by detonating explosives; in which case the 'train' is a trail of gunpowder, and its length implies the time available for retreating to a safe distance.

result from it. From this theory, some philosophers, and the ancient Stoics among the rest, derived a topic of consolation under all afflictions, while they taught their pupils that those ills under which they laboured were, in reality, goods to the universe; and that to an enlarged view, which could comprehend the whole system of nature, every event became an object of joy and exultation.[27] But though this topic be specious[28] and sublime, it was soon found in practice weak and ineffectual. You would surely more irritate than appease a man lying under the racking pains of the gout by preaching up to him the rectitude of those general laws, which produced the malignant humours in his body, and led them through the proper canals, to the sinews and nerves, where they now excite such acute torments. These enlarged views may, for a moment, please the imagination of a speculative man, who is placed in ease and security; but neither can they dwell with constancy on his mind, even though undisturbed by the [102] emotions of pain or passion; much less can they maintain their ground when attacked by such powerful antagonists. The affections take a narrower and more natural survey of their object; and by an economy,[29] more suitable to the infirmity of human minds, regard alone the beings around us, and are actuated by such events as appear good or ill to the private system.

35   The case is the same with *moral* as with *physical* ill. It cannot reasonably be supposed, that those remote considerations, which are found of so little efficacy with regard to one, will have a more powerful influence with regard to the other. The mind of man is so formed by nature that, upon the appearance of certain characters, dispositions, and actions, it immediately feels the sentiment of approbation or blame; nor are there any emotions more essential to its frame and constitution. The characters which engage our approbation are chiefly such as contribute to the peace and security of human society; as the characters which excite blame are chiefly such as tend to public detriment and disturbance: Whence it may reasonably be presumed, that the moral sentiments arise, either mediately or immediately, from a reflection of these opposite interests. What though philosophical meditations establish a different opinion or conjecture; that everything is right with regard to the *whole*, and that the qualities, which disturb society, are, in the main, as beneficial, and are as suitable to the

---

[27] See Seneca, 'On Providence'; Pope, *Essay on Man*, 1; also William Leechman, 'Preface', in Francis Hutcheson, *A System of Moral Philosophy* (1755).
[28] Attractive or plausible.   [29] System of organization.

primary intention of nature, as those which more directly promote its happiness and welfare? Are such remote and uncertain speculations able to counterbalance the sentiments which arise from the natural and immediate view of the objects? A man who is robbed of a considerable sum; does he find his vexation for the loss anywise diminished by these sublime reflections? Why then should his moral resentment against the crime be supposed incompatible with them? Or why should not the acknowledgment of a real distinction between vice and virtue be reconcil- [103] able to all speculative systems of philosophy, as well as that of a real distinction between personal beauty and deformity? Both these distinctions are founded in the natural sentiments of the human mind: And these sentiments are not to be controlled or altered by any philosophical theory or speculation whatsoever.

36   The *second* objection admits not of so easy and satisfactory an answer; nor is it possible to explain distinctly, how the Deity can be the mediate[30] cause of all the actions of men, without being the author of sin and moral turpitude. These are mysteries, which mere natural and unassisted reason is very unfit to handle; and whatever system she embraces, she must find herself involved in inextricable difficulties, and even contradictions, at every step which she takes with regard to such subjects. To reconcile the indifference and contingency of human actions with prescience; or to defend absolute decrees, and yet free the Deity from being the author of sin, has been found hitherto to exceed all the power of philosophy. Happy, if she be thence sensible of her temerity, when she pries into these sublime mysteries; and leaving a scene so full of obscurities and perplexities, return, with suitable modesty, to her true and proper province, the examination of common life; where she will find difficulties enough to employ her enquiries, without launching into so boundless an ocean of doubt, uncertainty, and contradiction!

[30] Indirect.

9

Of the reason of animals

1   All our reasonings concerning matter of fact are founded on a species of *analogy*, which leads us to expect from any cause the same events,
which we have observed to result from similar causes.[1] Where the causes
are entirely similar, the analogy is perfect, and the inference, drawn from
it, is regarded as certain and conclusive: Nor does any man ever entertain a
doubt, where he sees a piece of iron, that it will have weight and cohesion
of parts; as in all other instances, which have ever fallen under his observation. But where the objects have not so exact a similarity, the analogy is
less perfect, and the inference is less conclusive; though still it has some
force, in proportion to the degree of similarity and resemblance. The ana-
tomical observations, formed upon one animal, are, by this species of
reasoning, extended to all animals; and it is certain, that when the circulation of the blood, for instance, is clearly proved to have place in one
creature, as a frog, or fish, it forms a strong presumption, that the same
principle has place in all.[2] These analogical observations may be carried
farther, even to this science, of which we are now treating; and any theory,
by which we explain the operations of the understanding, or the origin and
connexion of the passions in man, will acquire additional authority, if we
find, that the same theory is requisite to explain the same phenomena in all
[105] other animals.[3] We shall make trial of this, with regard to the hypothesis,
by which we have, in the foregoing discourse, endeavoured to account for

---

[1] For the role of analogy, see Locke (*Essay*, 4.16.12) and Butler (*Analogy of Religion*, Introduction). For
the rule that like causes produce like effects, see Hobbes, *Leviathan*, 22.
[2] William Harvey (1578–1657) established the circulation of the blood in animals by means of experiments on frogs and fish.
[3] Hume pursues a further implication of such analogies in 'Of the Immortality of the Soul'.

92

all experimental reasonings; and it is hoped, that this new point of view will serve to confirm all our former observations.[4]

2   *First*, It seems evident, that animals as well as men learn many things from experience, and infer, that the same events will always follow from the same causes. By this principle they become acquainted with the more obvious properties of external objects, and gradually, from their birth, treasure up a knowledge of the nature of fire, water, earth, stones, heights, depths, *etc.*, and of the effects which result from their operation. The ignorance and inexperience of the young are here plainly distinguishable from the cunning and sagacity of the old, who have learned, by long observation, to avoid what hurt them, and to pursue what gave ease or pleasure. A horse, that has been accustomed to the field, becomes acquainted with the proper height which he can leap, and will never attempt what exceeds his force and ability. An old greyhound will trust the more fatiguing part of the chase to the younger, and will place himself so as to meet the hare in her doubles;[5] nor are the conjectures, which he forms on this occasion, founded in any thing but his observation and experience.

3   This is still more evident from the effects of discipline and education on animals, who, by the proper application of rewards and punishments, may be taught any course of action, and most contrary to their natural instincts and propensities. Is it not experience, which renders a dog apprehensive of pain, when you menace him, or lift up the whip to beat him? Is it not even experience, which makes him answer to his name, and infer, from such an arbitrary sound, that you mean him rather than any of his fellows, and intend to call him, when you pronounce it in a certain manner, and with a certain tone and accent?[6]

4   In all these cases, we may observe, that the animal infers some [106] fact beyond what immediately strikes his senses; and that this inference is altogether founded on past experience, while the creature expects from the

---

[4] The rationality of animals, and therefore their close kinship with human beings, is a favourite topic of Sceptics; see Sextus Empiricus, *Outlines of Scepticism* (1.65ff); Michel de Montaigne, 'An Apology for Raymond Sebond' (505–42). In contrast, the Stoics emphasized the distance between humans and animals (e.g. Seneca, *Moral Essays*, 'On Anger', 1.3.3–8). Locke (*Essay*, 2.11.10–11) allows some measure of reason in animals, but denies them the power of abstraction, and so of what is necessary for speech.

[5] That is, to intercept the hare when it doubles back. The example is from Sir Kenelm Digby (1603–65), *Two Treatises* (1644), First Treatise (*Of the Nature of Bodies*), 36–8.

[6] On animal capacity for learning, see Montaigne, 'An Apology for Raymond Sebond' (518–20). The specific examples are to be found in Sextus Empiricus (*Outlines of Scepticism*, 1.66) and Hobbes (*Leviathan*, 19).

present object the same consequences, which it has always found in its observation to result from similar objects.

5   *Secondly,* It is impossible, that this inference of the animal can be founded on any process of argument or reasoning, by which he concludes, that like events must follow like objects, and that the course of nature will always be regular in its operations. For if there be in reality any arguments of this nature, they surely lie too abstruse for the observation of such imperfect understandings; since it may well employ the utmost care and attention of a philosophic genius to discover and observe them. Animals, therefore, are not guided in these inferences by reasoning: Neither are children: Neither are the generality of mankind, in their ordinary actions and conclusions: Neither are philosophers themselves, who, in all the active parts of life, are, in the main, the same with the vulgar, and are governed by the same maxims. Nature must have provided some other principle, of more ready, and more general use and application; nor can an operation of such immense consequence in life, as that of inferring effects from causes, be trusted to the uncertain process of reasoning and argumentation. Were this doubtful with regard to men, it seems to admit of no question with regard to the brute creation; and the conclusion being once firmly established in the one, we have a strong presumption, from all the rules of analogy, that it ought to be universally admitted, without any exception or reserve. It is custom alone, which engages animals, from every object, that strikes their senses, to infer its usual attendant, and carries their imagination, from the appearance of the one, to conceive the other, in that particular manner, which we denominate *belief*.[7] No [107] other explication can be given of this operation, in all the higher, as well as lower classes of sensitive beings, which fall under our notice and observation.[a]

---

[7] A similar account of animal functioning is offered by Leibniz, *Monadology*, 25–8; *Principles of Nature and Grace*, 5. He then goes on sharply to distinguish animal from human function.

[a] Since all reasoning concerning facts or causes is derived merely from custom, it may be asked how it happens, that men so much surpass animals in reasoning, and one man so much surpasses another? Has not the same custom the same influence on all?
We shall here endeavour briefly to explain the great difference in human understandings: After which the reason of the difference between men and animals will easily be comprehended.
  1. When we have lived any time, and have been accustomed to the uniformity of nature, we acquire a general habit, by which we always transfer the known to the unknown, and conceive the latter to resemble the former. By means of this general habitual principle, we regard even one experiment as the foundation of reasoning, and expect a similar event with some degree of certainty, where the experiment has been made accurately, and free from all foreign circumstances. It is

6   But though animals learn many parts of their knowledge from [108] observation, there are also many parts of it, which they derive from the original hand of nature; which much exceed the share of capacity they possess on ordinary occasions; and in which they improve, little or nothing, by the longest practice and experience. These we denominate *instincts*, and are so apt to admire, as something very extraordinary, and inexplicable by all the disquisitions of human understanding. But our wonder will, perhaps, cease or diminish, when we consider, that the experimental reasoning itself, which we possess in common with beasts, and on which the whole conduct of life depends, is nothing but a species of instinct or mechanical power,[8] that acts in us unknown to ourselves; and in its chief operations, is not directed by any such relations or comparisons of ideas, as are the proper objects of our intellectual faculties. Though the instinct be different, yet still it is an instinct, which teaches a man to avoid the fire; as much as that, which teaches a bird, with such exactness, the art of incubation, and the whole economy and order of its nursery.

therefore considered as a matter of great importance to observe the consequences of things; and as one man may very much surpass another in attention and memory and observation, this will make a very great difference in their reasoning.

2. Where there is a complication of causes to produce any effect, one mind may be much larger than another, and better able to comprehend the whole system of objects, and to infer justly their consequences.

3. One man is able to carry on a chain of consequences to a greater length than another.

4. Few men can think long without running into a confusion of ideas, and mistaking one for another; and there are various degrees of this infirmity.

5. The circumstance, on which the effect depends, is frequently involved in other circumstances, which are foreign and extrinsic. The separation of it often requires great attention, accuracy, and subtlety.

6. The forming of general maxims from particular observation is a very nice operation; and nothing is more usual, from haste or a narrowness of mind, which sees not on all sides, than to commit mistakes in this particular.

7. When we reason from analogies, the man, who has the greater experience or the greater promptitude of suggesting analogies, will be the better reasoner.

8. Biases from prejudice, education, passion, party, *etc.* hang more upon one mind than another.

9. After we have acquired a confidence in human testimony, books and conversation enlarge much more the sphere of one man's experience and thought than those of another.

It would be easy to discover many other circumstances that make a difference in the understandings of men. [Footnote added in 1750.]

[8] Mechanisms are organizations of matter, so the implication is that experimental reasoning depends on some physical process. Cf. Locke, *Essay*, 2.33.6; and La Mettrie, *Machine Man* (1747), 13, 35.

10

Of miracles

Part 1

1   There is, in Dr. Tillotson's writings, an argument against the *real presence*, which is as concise, and elegant, and strong as any argument can possibly be supposed against a doctrine, so little worthy of a serious refutation.[1] It is acknowledged on all hands, says that learned prelate, that the authority, either of the scripture or of tradition, is founded merely in the testimony of the Apostles, who were eye-witnesses to those miracles of our Saviour, by which he proved his divine mission. Our evidence, then, for, the truth of the Christian religion is less than the evidence for the truth of our senses; because, even in the first authors of our religion, it was no greater; and it is evident it must diminish in passing from them to their disciples; nor can any one rest such confidence in their testimony, as in the immediate object of his senses. But a weaker evidence can never destroy a stronger; and therefore, were the doctrine of the real presence ever so clearly revealed in scripture, it were directly contrary to the rules of just reasoning to give our assent to it. It contradicts sense, though both the scripture and tradition, on which it is supposed to be built, carry not such evidence with them as sense; when they are considered merely as external evidences, and are not brought home to every one's breast, by the immediate operation of the Holy Spirit.

[1] John Tillotson (1630–94), English theologian, ultimately Archbishop of Canterbury, an outspoken critic of Catholic doctrines. The doctrine of the real presence, or transubstantiation, is the Catholic doctrine that, in the sacrament of the Eucharist, the substance (but not the appearance) of the bread and wine becomes, at its consecration, the body and blood of Christ – that Christ becomes a real presence.

2   Nothing is so convenient as a decisive argument of this kind, [110] which must at least *silence* the most arrogant bigotry and superstition,[2] and free us from their impertinent solicitations. I flatter myself, that I have discovered an argument of a like nature, which, if just, will, with the wise and learned, be an everlasting check to all kinds of superstitious delusion, and consequently, will be useful as long as the world endures. For so long, I presume, will the accounts of miracles and prodigies be found in all history, sacred and profane.

3   Though experience be our only guide in reasoning concerning matters of fact; it must be acknowledged, that this guide is not altogether infallible, but in some cases is apt to lead us into errors. One, who in our climate, should expect better weather in any week of June than in one of December, would reason justly, and conformably to experience; but it is certain, that he may happen, in the event, to find himself mistaken. However, we may observe, that, in such a case, he would have no cause to complain of experience; because it commonly informs us beforehand of the uncertainty, by that contrariety of events, which we may learn from a diligent observation. All effects follow not with like certainty from their supposed causes. Some events are found, in all countries and all ages, to have been constantly conjoined together: Others are found to have been more variable, and sometimes to disappoint our expectations; so that, in our reasonings concerning matter of fact, there are all imaginable degrees of assurance, from the highest certainty to the lowest species of moral evidence.[3]

4   A wise man, therefore, proportions his belief to the evidence. In such conclusions as are founded on an infallible experience, he expects the event with the last degree of assurance, and regards his past experience as a full *proof* of the future existence of that event.[4] In other cases, he [111] proceeds with more caution: He weighs the opposite experiments: He considers which side is supported by the greater number of experiments: To that side he inclines, with doubt and hesitation; and when at last he fixes his judgment, the evidence exceeds not what we properly call *probability*. All probability, then, supposes an opposition of experiments and

---

[2] Credulous belief in supernatural causes or mysteries; a term of abuse, including by Protestants of Catholicism. See Hume's essay 'Of Superstition and Enthusiasm'.

[3] Moral evidence is evidence concerning (unobservable) human motivations.

[4] A proof in the sense explained in Section 6. Note that the argument here concerns arguments from experience (proofs and probabilities) and not *a priori* arguments (demonstrations).

observations, where the one side is found to overbalance the other, and to produce a degree of evidence, proportioned to the superiority. A hundred instances or experiments on one side, and fifty on another, afford a doubtful expectation of any event; though a hundred uniform experiments, with only one that is contradictory, reasonably beget a pretty strong degree of assurance. In all cases, we must balance the opposite experiments, where they are opposite, and deduct the smaller number from the greater, in order to know the exact force of the superior evidence.

5   To apply these principles to a particular instance; we may observe, that there is no species of reasoning more common, more useful, and even necessary to human life, than that which is derived from the testimony of men, and the reports of eye-witnesses and spectators. This species of reasoning, perhaps, one may deny to be founded on the relation of cause and effect. I shall not dispute about a word. It will be sufficient to observe that our assurance in any argument of this kind is derived from no other principle than our observation of the veracity of human testimony, and of the usual conformity of facts to the reports of witnesses. It being a general maxim, that no objects have any discoverable connexion together, and that all the inferences, which we can draw from one to another, are founded merely on our experience of their constant and regular conjunction; it is evident, that we ought not to make an exception to this maxim in favour of human testimony, whose connexion with any event seems, in itself, as little necessary as any other. Were not the memory tenacious to a certain degree; had not [112] men commonly an inclination to truth and a principle of probity; were they not sensible to shame, when detected in a falsehood: Were not these, I say, discovered by *experience* to be qualities, inherent in human nature, we should never repose the least confidence in human testimony. A man delirious, or noted for falsehood and villainy, has no manner of authority with us.

6   And as the evidence, derived from witnesses and human testimony, is founded on past experience, so it varies with the experience, and is regarded either as a *proof* or a *probability*, according as the conjunction between any particular kind of report and any kind of object has been found to be constant or variable. There are a number of circumstances to be taken into consideration in all judgments of this kind; and the ultimate standard, by which we determine all disputes, that may arise concerning them, is always derived from experience and observation. Where this experience is not entirely uniform on any side, it is attended with an unavoidable contrariety in our judgments, and with the same opposition

and mutual destruction of argument as in every other kind of evidence. We frequently hesitate concerning the reports of others. We balance the opposite circumstances, which cause any doubt or uncertainty; and when we discover a superiority on any side, we incline to it; but still with a diminution of assurance, in proportion to the force of its antagonist.

7   This contrariety of evidence, in the present case, may be derived from several different causes; from the opposition of contrary testimony; from the character or number of the witnesses; from the manner of their delivering their testimony; or from the union of all these circumstances. We entertain a suspicion concerning any matter of fact, when the witnesses contradict each other; when they are but few, or of a doubtful character; when they have an interest in what they affirm; when they deliver [113] their testimony with hesitation, or on the contrary, with too violent asseverations.[5] There are many other particulars of the same kind, which may diminish or destroy the force of any argument, derived from human testimony.

8   Suppose, for instance, that the fact, which the testimony endeavours to establish, partakes of the extraordinary and the marvellous;[6] in that case, the evidence, resulting from the testimony, admits of a diminution, greater or less, in proportion as the fact is more or less unusual. The reason why we place any credit in witnesses and historians, is not derived from any *connexion*, which we perceive *a priori*, between testimony and reality, but because we are accustomed to find a conformity between them. But when the fact attested is such a one as has seldom fallen under our observation, here is a contest of two opposite experiences; of which the one destroys the other, as far as its force goes, and the superior can only operate on the mind by the force, which remains. The very same principle of experience, which gives us a certain degree of assurance in the testimony of witnesses, gives us also, in this case, another degree of assurance against the fact, which they endeavour to establish; from which contradiction there necessarily arises a counterpoise, and mutual destruction of belief and authority.

---

[5] Emphatic declarations.
[6] The extraordinary and the marvellous are degrees of nonconformity with the ordinary course of things. (The miraculous is the limit case of maximum nonconformity.) See also Hume, *The History of England*, 2.398ff.

99

9   *I should not believe such a story were it told me by Cato*, was a proverbial saying in Rome, even during the lifetime of that philosophical patriot.[a] The incredibility of a fact, it was allowed, might invalidate so great an authority.[7]

10   The Indian prince, who refused to believe the first relations concerning the effects of frost, reasoned justly; and it naturally required very strong testimony to engage his assent to facts, that arose from a state [114] of nature, with which he was unacquainted, and which bore so little analogy to those events, of which he had had constant and uniform experience. Though they were not contrary to his experience, they were not conformable to it.[b]

11   But in order to increase the probability against the testimony of witnesses, let us suppose, that the fact, which they affirm, instead of being only marvellous, is really miraculous; and suppose also, that the testimony considered apart and in itself, amounts to an entire proof; in that case, there is proof against proof, of which the strongest must prevail, but still with a diminution of its force, in proportion to that of its antagonist.

12   A miracle is a violation of the laws of nature;[8] and as a firm and unalterable experience has established these laws, the proof against a miracle, from the very nature of the fact, is as entire as any argument from experience can possibly be imagined.[9] Why is it more than probable, that all men must die; that lead cannot, of itself, remain suspended in the air; that fire consumes wood, and is extinguished by water; unless it be, that [115] these events are found agreeable to the laws of nature, and there is

[a] Plutarch, in vita Catonis. [Plutarch, *Lives*, 'Cato the Younger', 19.4.768b–c.]
[b] No Indian, it is evident, could have experience that water did not freeze in cold climates. This is placing nature in a situation quite unknown to him; and it is impossible for him to tell *a priori* what will result from it. It is making a new experiment, the consequence of which is always uncertain. One may sometimes conjecture from analogy what will follow; but still this is but conjecture. And it must be confessed, that, in the present case of freezing, the event follows contrary to the rules of analogy, and is such as a rational Indian would not look for. The operations of cold upon water are not gradual, according to the degrees of cold; but whenever it comes to the freezing point, the water passes in a moment, from the utmost liquidity to perfect hardness. Such an event, therefore, may be denominated *extraordinary*, and requires a pretty strong testimony, to render it credible to people in a warm climate: But still it is not *miraculous*, nor contrary to uniform experience of the course of nature in cases where all the circumstances are the same. The inhabitants of Sumatra have always seen water fluid in their own climate, and the freezing of their rivers ought to be deemed a prodigy: But they never saw water in Muscovy during the winter; and therefore they cannot reasonably be positive what would there be the consequence. [Paragraph in text added in 1750, footnote added in 1756. Hume's Indian example seems to conflate two different examples from Locke (*Essay*, 2.13.19, 2.23.2; 4.15.5). Muscovy: the region around Moscow.]
[7] Paragraph added in 1756.
[8] See Bayle, *Dictionary*, 'Rorarius', Note L; 'Spinoza', Note R.
[9] Cf. Locke, *Essay*, 4.1.6.13.

required a violation of these laws, or in other words, a miracle to prevent them? Nothing is esteemed a miracle, if it ever happen in the common course of nature. It is no miracle that a man, seemingly in good health, should die on a sudden; because such a kind of death, though more unusual than any other, has yet been frequently observed to happen. But it is a miracle, that a dead man should come to life; because that has never been observed in any age or country. There must, therefore, be a uniform experience against every miraculous event, otherwise the event would not merit that appellation. And as a uniform experience amounts to a proof, there is here a direct and full *proof*, from the nature of the fact, against the existence of any miracle; nor can such a proof be destroyed, or the miracle rendered credible, but by an opposite proof, which is superior.^c

13   The plain consequence is (and it is a general maxim worthy of our attention),'That no testimony is sufficient to establish a miracle, unless the [116] testimony be of such a kind, that its falsehood would be more miraculous, than the fact, which it endeavours to establish: And even in that case there is a mutual destruction of arguments, and the superior only gives us an assurance suitable to that degree of force, which remains, after deducting the inferior.' When anyone tells me, that he saw a dead man restored to life, I immediately consider with myself, whether it be more probable, that this person should either deceive or be deceived, or that the fact, which he relates, should really have happened. I weigh the one miracle against the other; and according to the superiority, which I discover, I pronounce my decision, and always reject the greater miracle. If the falsehood of his testimony would be more miraculous, than the event which he relates; then, and not till then, can he pretend to command my belief or opinion.

---

^c Sometimes an event may not, *in itself*, *seem* to be contrary to the laws of nature, and yet, if it were real, it might, by reason of some circumstances, be denominated a miracle; because, *in fact*, it is contrary to these laws. Thus if a person, claiming a divine authority, should command a sick person to be well, a healthful man to fall down dead, the clouds to pour rain, the winds to blow, in short, should order many natural events, which immediately follow upon his command; these might justly be esteemed miracles, because they are really, in this case, contrary to the laws of nature. For if any suspicion remain, that the event and command concurred by accident, there is no miracle and no transgression of the laws of nature. If this suspicion be removed, there is evidently a miracle, and a transgression of these laws; because nothing can be more contrary to nature than that the voice or command of a man should have such an influence. A miracle may be accurately defined, *a transgression of a law of nature by a particular volition of the Deity, or by the interposition of some invisible agent*. A miracle may either be discoverable by men or not. This alters not its nature and essence. The raising of a house or ship into the air is a visible miracle. The raising of a feather, when the wind wants ever so little of a force requisite for that purpose, is as real a miracle, though not so sensible with regard to us. [Footnote added in 1750.]

Part 2

14   In the foregoing reasoning we have supposed, that the testimony, upon which a miracle is founded, may possibly amount to an entire proof, and that the falsehood of that testimony would be a real prodigy:[10] But it is easy to show, that we have been a great deal too liberal in our concession, and that there never was a miraculous event established on so full an evidence.

15   For *first*, there is not to be found, in all history, any miracle attested by a sufficient number of men, of such unquestioned good-sense, education, and learning, as to secure us against all delusion in themselves; of such undoubted integrity, as to place them beyond all suspicion of any design to deceive others; of such credit and reputation in the eyes of mankind, as to have a great deal to lose in case of their being detected in any falsehood; and at the same time, attesting facts performed in such a public manner and in so celebrated a part of the world, as to render the [117] detection unavoidable: All which circumstances are requisite to give us a full assurance in the testimony of men.

16   *Secondly*, We may observe in human nature a principle which, if strictly examined, will be found to diminish extremely the assurance, which we might, from human testimony, have in any kind of prodigy. The maxim, by which we commonly conduct ourselves in our reasonings, is, that the objects, of which we have no experience, resemble those, of which we have; that what we have found to be most usual is always most probable; and that where there is an opposition of arguments, we ought to give the preference to such as are founded on the greatest number of past observations. But though, in proceeding by this rule, we readily reject any fact which is unusual and incredible in an ordinary degree; yet in advancing farther, the mind observes not always the same rule; but when anything is affirmed utterly absurd and miraculous, it rather the more readily admits of such a fact, upon account of that very circumstance, which ought to destroy all its authority. The passion of *surprise* and *wonder*, arising from miracles, being an agreeable emotion, gives a sensible[11] tendency towards the belief of those events, from which it is derived. And this goes so far, that even those who cannot enjoy this pleasure immediately, nor can

---

[10] An amazing or unnatural event. Hume's choice of the term in this context is to emphasize his point that testimonies as well as natural events can be measured for degrees of extraordinariness.
[11] Perceptible.

believe those miraculous events, of which they are informed, yet love to partake of the satisfaction at second-hand or by rebound, and place a pride and delight in exciting the admiration of others.

17   With what greediness are the miraculous accounts of travellers received, their descriptions of sea and land monsters, their relations of wonderful adventures, strange men, and uncouth manners? But if the spirit of religion join itself to the love of wonder, there is an end of common sense; and human testimony, in these circumstances, loses all pretensions to authority. A religionist may be an enthusiast,[12] and imagine he sees what has no reality: He may know his narrative to be false, and yet persevere in it, [118] with the best intentions in the world, for the sake of promoting so holy a cause: Or even where this delusion has not place, vanity, excited by so strong a temptation, operates on him more powerfully than on the rest of mankind in any other circumstances; and self-interest with equal force. His auditors may not have, and commonly have not, sufficient judgment to canvass his evidence: What judgment they have, they renounce by principle, in these sublime and mysterious subjects: Or if they were ever so willing to employ it, passion and a heated imagination disturb the regularity of its operations. Their credulity increases his impudence: And his impudence overpowers their credulity.

18   Eloquence, when at its highest pitch, leaves little room for reason or reflection; but addressing itself entirely to the fancy or the affections, captivates the willing hearers, and subdues their understanding. Happily, this pitch it seldom attains. But what a Tully or a Demosthenes could scarcely effect over a Roman or Athenian audience, every Capuchin, every itinerant or stationary teacher can perform over the generality of mankind, and in a higher degree, by touching such gross and vulgar passions.[13]

19   The many instances of forged miracles, and prophecies, and supernatural events, which, in all ages, have either been detected by contrary evidence, or which detect themselves by their absurdity, prove sufficiently the strong propensity of mankind to the extraordinary and the marvellous, and ought reasonably to beget a suspicion against all relations

---

[12] Someone who believes themselves to be divinely inspired or possessed; a religious visionary; a radical Protestant. See Hume's essay 'Of Superstition and Enthusiasm'.

[13] Tully (i.e. Cicero) and Demosthenes (384–322 BC) were, respectively, the Latin and Greek speakers most famed for their eloquence or oratory. Capuchins are Franciscan friars dedicated to missionary work.

of this kind. This is our natural way of thinking, even with regard to the most common and most credible events. For instance: There is no kind of report which rises so easily, and spreads so quickly, especially in country places and provincial towns, as those concerning marriages; insomuch [119] that two young persons of equal condition never see each other twice, but the whole neighbourhood immediately join them together. The pleasure of telling a piece of news so interesting, of propagating it, and of being the first reporters of it, spreads the intelligence. And this is so well known, that no man of sense gives attention to these reports, till he find them confirmed by some greater evidence. Do not the same passions, and others still stronger, incline the generality of mankind to believe and report, with the greatest vehemence and assurance, all religious miracles?

20   *Thirdly*, It forms a strong presumption against all supernatural and miraculous relations, that they are observed chiefly to abound among ignorant and barbarous nations; or if a civilized people has ever given admission to any of them, that people will be found to have received them from ignorant and barbarous ancestors, who transmitted them with that inviolable sanction and authority, which always attend received opinions. When we peruse the first histories of all nations, we are apt to imagine ourselves transported into some new world; where the whole frame of nature is disjointed, and every element performs its operations in a different manner, from what it does at present. Battles, revolutions, pestilence, famine and death, are never the effect of those natural causes, which we experience. Prodigies, omens, oracles, judgments, quite obscure the few natural events, that are intermingled with them. But as the former grow thinner every page, in proportion as we advance nearer the enlightened ages, we soon learn, that there is nothing mysterious or supernatural in the case, but that all proceeds from the usual propensity of mankind towards the marvellous, and that, though this inclination may at intervals receive a check from sense and learning, it can never be thoroughly extirpated from human nature.

21   *It is strange*, a judicious reader is apt to say, upon the perusal of [120] these wonderful historians, *that such prodigious events never happen in our days*. But it is nothing strange, I hope, that men should lie in all ages. You must surely have seen instances enough of that frailty. You have yourself heard many such marvellous relations started, which, being treated with scorn by all the wise and judicious, have at last been abandoned even by the vulgar. Be assured, that those renowned lies, which have spread and

flourished to such a monstrous height, arose from like beginnings; but being sown in a more proper soil, shot up at last into prodigies almost equal to those which they relate.

22   It was a wise policy in that false prophet, Alexander, who though now forgotten, was once so famous, to lay the first scene of his impostures in Paphlagonia, where, as Lucian tells us, the people were extremely ignorant and stupid, and ready to swallow even the grossest delusion.[14] People at a distance, who are weak enough to think the matter at all worth enquiry, have no opportunity of receiving better information. The stories come magnified to them by a hundred circumstances. Fools are industrious in propagating the imposture; while the wise and learned are contented, in general, to deride its absurdity, without informing themselves of the particular facts, by which it may be distinctly refuted. And thus the impostor above mentioned was enabled to proceed, from his ignorant Paphlagonians, to the enlisting of votaries, even among the Grecian philosophers, and men of the most eminent rank and distinction in Rome; nay, could engage the attention of that sage emperor Marcus Aurelius;[15] so far as to make him trust the success of a military expedition to his delusive prophecies.

23   The advantages are so great, of starting an imposture among an ignorant people, that, even though the delusion should be too gross to impose on the generality of them (*which, though seldom, is sometimes the case*) it has a much better chance for succeeding in remote countries, than if the first scene had been laid in a city renowned for arts and knowledge. [121] The most ignorant and barbarous of these barbarians carry the report abroad. None of their countrymen have a large correspondence, or sufficient credit and authority to contradict and beat down the delusion. Men's inclination to the marvellous has full opportunity to display itself. And thus a story, which is universally exploded in the place where it was first started, shall pass for certain at a thousand miles distance. But had Alexander fixed his residence at Athens, the philosophers of that renowned mart[16] of learning had immediately spread, throughout the

---

[14] Lucian (2nd century AD), Greek satirist. In *Alexander, or the False Prophet*, he exposed the fraud perpetrated by Alexander of Abonuteichos on the people of his home region of Paphlagonia (now part of northern Turkey).

[15] Marcus Aurelius (AD 121–80), Roman emperor 161–80. Stoic philosopher, author of the *Meditations*.

[16] Market or centre.

whole Roman empire, their sense of the matter; which, being supported by so great authority, and displayed by all the force of reason and eloquence, had entirely opened the eyes of mankind. It is true; Lucian, passing by chance through Paphlagonia, had an opportunity of performing this good office. But, though much to be wished, it does not always happen, that every Alexander meets with a Lucian, ready to expose and detect his impostures.

24   I may add as a *fourth* reason, which diminishes the authority of prodigies, that there is no testimony for any, even those which have not been expressly detected, that is not opposed by an infinite number of witnesses; so that not only the miracle destroys the credit of testimony, but the testimony destroys itself. To make this the better understood, let us consider, that, in matters of religion, whatever is different is contrary; and that it is impossible the religions of ancient Rome, of Turkey, of Siam,[17] and of China should, all of them, be established on any solid foundation. Every miracle, therefore, pretended to have been wrought in any of these religions (and all of them abound in miracles), as its direct scope is to establish the particular system to which it is attributed; so has it the same force, though more indirectly, to overthrow every other system. In destroying a rival system, it likewise destroys the credit of those miracles, on which that

[122] system was established; so that all the prodigies of different religions are to be regarded as contrary facts, and the evidences of these prodigies, whether weak or strong, as opposite to each other. According to this method of reasoning, when we believe any miracle of Mahomet[18] or his successors, we have for our warrant the testimony of a few barbarous Arabians: And on the other hand, we are to regard the authority of Titus Livius, Plutarch, Tacitus,[19] and, in short, of all the authors and witnesses, Grecian, Chinese, and Roman Catholic, who have related any miracle in their particular religion; I say, we are to regard their testimony in the same light as if they had mentioned that Mahometan miracle, and had in express terms contradicted it, with the same certainty as they have for the miracle they relate. This argument may appear over subtle and refined; but is not in reality different from the reasoning of a judge, who supposes, that the credit of two witnesses, maintaining a crime against any one, is destroyed by the testimony of two others, who affirm him to have been two

---

[17] Thailand.   [18] Mahomet: Muhammad. Mahometan: a Muslim.
[19] The ancient historians Titus Livius, or Livy (59 BC–AD 17), Plutarch (AD c. 46–c. 120) and Tacitus (AD c. 56–c. 120) all report marvellous or miraculous events in their histories.

hundred leagues distant, at the same instant when the crime is said to have been committed.

25   One of the best attested miracles in all profane history, is that which Tacitus reports of Vespasian,[20] who cured a blind man in Alexandria, by means of his spittle, and a lame man by the mere touch of his foot; in obedience to a vision of the god Serapis,[21] who had enjoined them to have recourse to the Emperor, for these miraculous cures. The story may be seen in that fine historian;[d] where every circumstance seems to add weight to the testimony, and might be displayed at large with all the force of argument and eloquence, if any one were now concerned to enforce the evidence of that exploded and idolatrous superstition. The gravity, solidity, [123] age, and probity of so great an emperor, who, through the whole course of his life, conversed in a familiar manner with his friends and courtiers, and never affected those extraordinary airs of divinity assumed by Alexander and Demetrius.[22] The historian, a contemporary writer, noted for candour and veracity, and withal, the greatest and most penetrating genius, perhaps, of all antiquity; and so free from any tendency to credulity, that he even lies under the contrary imputation, of atheism and profaneness: The persons, from whose authority he related the miracle, of established character for judgment and veracity, as we may well presume; eye-witnesses of the fact, and confirming their testimony, after the Flavian family was despoiled of the empire, and could no longer give any reward, as the price of a lie. "Utrumque, qui interfuere, nunc quoque memorant, postquam nullum mendacio pretium."[23] To which if we add the public nature of the facts, as related, it will appear, that no evidence can well be supposed stronger for so gross and so palpable a falsehood.

26   There is also a memorable story related by Cardinal de Retz,[24] which may well deserve our consideration. When that intriguing politician

---

[d] Hist. lib. 4. cap. 81. Suetonius gives nearly the same account, in vita Vesp. [Tacitus, *Histories*, 4.81; Suetonius, *Lives of the Caesars*,'Vespasian', 7.2–3.]
[20] Vespasian (AD 9–79), Roman emperor 69–79. The Flavian dynasty comprised himself and his two sons, Titus and Domitian.
[21] A god of Egyptian mythology. The cult of Serapis was promoted in Egypt after its conquest by Alexander the Great, in an attempt to unite Greeks and Egyptians in a common religious worship.
[22] Alexander the Great (356–323 BC) and Demetrius I of Macedonia (d. 283 BC) are both said to have claimed or been accorded divine status. See Arrian, *Anabasis of Alexander* 7.23.2; Plutarch, *Lives*, 'Demetrius', 10–3, 24–6.
[23] 'Those who were present recount both incidents even now, when there is nothing to gain from deceit.' Tacitus, *Histories*, 4.81.
[24] Cardinal de Retz (1614–79), Archbishop of Paris and politician. His *Mémoires* (pub. 1717) were translated into English in 1723.

fled into Spain, to avoid the persecution of his enemies, he passed through Saragossa, the capital of Aragon,[25] where he was shown, in the cathedral, a man, who had served seven years as a doorkeeper, and was well known to every body in town, that had ever paid his devotions at that church. He had been seen, for so long a time, wanting a leg; but recovered that limb by the rubbing of holy oil upon the stump; and the cardinal assures us that he saw him with two legs. This miracle was vouched by all the canons of the church; and the whole company in town were appealed to for a confirmation of the fact; whom the cardinal found, by their zealous devotion, to be thorough believers of the miracle. Here the relater was also contemporary to the sup-

[124] posed prodigy, of an incredulous and libertine character, as well as of great genius; the miracle of so *singular* a nature as could scarcely admit of a counterfeit, and the witnesses very numerous, and all of them, in a manner, spectators of the fact, to which they gave their testimony. And what adds mightily to the force of the evidence, and may double our surprise on this occasion, is, that the cardinal himself, who relates the story, seems not to give any credit to it, and consequently cannot be suspected of any concurrence in the holy fraud. He considered justly, that it was not requisite, in order to reject a fact of this nature, to be able accurately to disprove the testimony, and to trace its falsehood, through all the circumstances of knavery and credulity which produced it. He knew, that, as this was commonly altogether impossible at any small distance of time and place; so was it extremely difficult, even where one was immediately present, by reason of the bigotry, ignorance, cunning, and roguery of a great part of mankind. He therefore concluded, like a just reasoner, that such an evidence carried falsehood upon the very face of it, and that a miracle, supported by any human testimony, was more properly a subject of derision than of argument.

27   There surely never was a greater number of miracles ascribed to one person, than those, which were lately said to have been wrought in France upon the tomb of Abbé Paris, the famous Jansenist, with whose sanctity the people were so long deluded.[26] The curing of the sick, giving

---

[25] A formerly autonomous region in northeastern Spain.
[26] François de Paris was a Jansenist priest whose tomb became venerated as a site of miraculous cures. The Jansenists were followers of Cornelius Jansen (1585–1638), Bishop of Ypres, who promoted moral austerity and religious principles deriving from St Augustine. The Jansenists were opposed by the Jesuits, particularly by the Molinists, followers of the views of the Spanish theologian Luis de Molina (1535–1600). Jansenism flourished in France in the seventeenth century, counting among its adherents the mathematician Blaise Pascal (1623–62), the playwright Jean Racine (1639–99), and the Cartesians Antoine Arnauld (1612–94) and Pierre Nicole (1625–95). French

hearing to the deaf, and sight to the blind, were every where talked of as the usual effects of that holy sepulchre. But what is more extraordinary; many of the miracles were immediately proved upon the spot, before judges of unquestioned integrity, attested by witnesses of credit and distinction, in a learned age, and on the most eminent theatre that is now in the world. Nor is this all: A relation of them was published and dispersed everywhere; nor were the Jesuits, though a learned body, supported by the [125] civil magistrate, and determined enemies to those opinions, in whose favour the miracles were said to have been wrought, ever able distinctly to refute or detect them.^{e} Where shall we find such a number of

Jansenism was centred on the Abbey of Port-Royal in Faubourg St-Jacques, Paris; its Abbess was Angélique Arnauld, sister of Antoine. Papal Bulls condemning Jansenist doctrines led to Port-Royal's closure and eventual physical destruction in 1710. Jansenism was ultimately outlawed in France in 1730.
^{e} This book was writ by Mons. Montgeron, counsellor or judge of the parliament of Paris, a man of figure and character, who was also a martyr to the cause, and is now said to be somewhere in a dungeon on account of his book.

There is another book in three volumes (called *Recueil des Miracles de l'Abbé Paris*) giving an account of many of these miracles, and accompanied with prefatory discourses, which are very well written. There runs, however, through the whole of these a ridiculous comparison between the miracles of our Saviour and those of the Abbé; wherein it is asserted, that the evidence for the latter is equal to that for the former: As if the testimony of men could ever be put in the balance with that of God himself, who conducted the pen of the inspired writers. If these writers, indeed, were to be considered merely as human testimony, the French author is very moderate in his comparison; since he might, with some appearance of reason, pretend, that the Jansenist miracles much surpass the other in evidence and authority. The following circumstances are drawn from authentic papers, inserted in the above-mentioned book.

Many of the miracles of Abbé Paris were proved immediately by witnesses before the officiality or bishop's court at Paris, under the eye of Cardinal Noailles, whose character for integrity and capacity was never contested even by his enemies.

His successor in the archbishopric was an enemy to the Jansenists, and for that reason promoted by the see to the court. Yet 22 rectors or *curés* of Paris, with infinite earnestness, press him to examine those miracles, which they assert to be known to the whole world, and indisputably certain: but he wisely forbore.

The Molinist party had tried to discredit these miracles in one instance, that of Mademoiselle Le Franc. But, besides that their proceedings were in many respects the most irregular in the world, particularly in citing only a few of the Jansenist witnesses, whom they tampered with: Besides this, I say, they soon found themselves overwhelmed by a cloud of new witnesses, one hundred and twenty in number, most of them persons of credit and substance in Paris, who gave oath for the miracle. This was accompanied with a solemn and earnest appeal to the parliament. But the parliament were forbid by authority to meddle in the affair. It was at last observed, that where men are heated by zeal and enthusiasm, there is no degree of human testimony so strong as may not be procured for the greatest absurdity: And those who will be so silly as to examine the affair by that medium, and seek particular flaws in the testimony, are almost sure to be confounded. It must be a miserable imposture, indeed, that does not prevail in that contest. All who have been in France about that time have heard of the reputation of Mons. Herault, the *Lieutenant de Police*, whose vigilance, penetration, activity, and extensive intelligence have been much talked of. This magistrate, who by the nature of his office is almost absolute, was invested with full powers, on purpose to suppress or discredit these miracles; and he frequently seized immediately, and examined the circumstances, agreeing to the corroboration of one fact? And what have we to oppose to such a cloud of witnesses, but the absolute impossibility or miraculous nature of the events, which they relate? And this surely, in the eyes of all reasonable people, will alone be regarded as a sufficient refutation.

28   Is the consequence just, because some human testimony has the utmost force and authority in some cases, when it relates the battle of

witnesses and subjects of them: But never could reach any thing satisfactory against them. In the case of Mademoiselle Thibault he sent the famous De Sylva to examine her; whose evidence is very curious. The physician declares, that it was impossible she could have been so ill as was proved by witnesses; because it was impossible she could, in so short a time, have recovered so perfectly as he found her. He reasoned, like a man of sense, from natural causes; but the opposite party told him, that the whole was a miracle, and that his evidence was the very best proof of it.

The Molinists were in a sad dilemma. They durst not assert the absolute insufficiency of human evidence, to prove a miracle. They were obliged to say, that these miracles were wrought by witch-craft and the devil. But they were told, that this was the resource of the Jews of old.

No Jansenist was ever embarrassed to account for the cessation of miracles, when the church-yard was shut up by the king's edict. It was the touch of the tomb, which produced these extraordinary effects; and when no one could approach the tomb, no effects could be expected. God, indeed, could have thrown down the walls in a moment; but he is master of his own graces and works, and it belongs not to us to account for them. He did not throw down the walls of every city like those of Jericho, on the sounding of the rams horns, nor break up the prison of every apostle, like that of St. Paul.

No less a man, than the Duc de Chatillon, a duke and peer of France, of the highest rank and family, gives evidence of a miraculous cure, performed upon a servant of his, who had lived several years in his house with a visible and palpable infirmity.

I shall conclude with observing, that no clergy are more celebrated for strictness of life and manners than the secular clergy of France, particularly the rectors or *curés* of Paris, who bear testimony to these impostures.

The learning, genius, and probity of the gentlemen, and the austerity of the nuns of Port-Royal, have been much celebrated all over Europe. Yet they all give evidence for a miracle, wrought on the niece of the famous Pascal, whose sanctity of life, as well as extraordinary capacity, is well known. The famous Racine gives an account of this miracle in his famous history of Port-Royal, and fortifies it with all the proofs, which a multitude of nuns, priests, physicians, and men of the world, all of them of undoubted credit, could bestow upon it. Several men of letters, particularly the bishop of Tournay, thought this miracle so certain, as to employ it in the refutation of atheists and free-thinkers. The queen-regent of France, who was extremely prejudiced against the Port-Royal, sent her own physician to examine the miracle, who returned an absolute convert. In short, the super-natural cure was so incontestable, that it saved, for a time, that famous monastery from the ruin with which it was threatened by the Jesuits. Had it been a cheat, it had certainly been detected by such sagacious and powerful antagonists, and must have hastened the ruin of the contrivers. Our divines, who can build up a formidable castle from such despicable materials; what a prodigious fabric could they have reared from these and many other circumstances, which I have not mentioned! How often would the great names of Pascal, Racine, Arnauld, Nicole, have resounded in our ears? But if they be wise, they had better adopt the miracle, as being more worth, a thousand times, than all the rest of their collection. Besides, it may serve very much to their purpose. For that miracle was really performed by the touch of an authentic holy prickle of the holy thorn, which composed the holy crown, which, *etc.* [Footnote added in 1750. Much of the final paragraph ('The famous Racine' and following) was added in 1756.]

Philippi or Pharsalia[27] for instance; that therefore all kinds of testimony must, in all cases, have equal force and authority? Suppose that the Caesarean and Pompeian factions had, each of them, claimed the victory in these battles, and that the historians of each party had uniformly ascribed the advantage to their own side; how could mankind, at this distance, have been able to determine between them? The contrariety is equally strong between the miracles related by Herodotus or Plutarch, and those delivered by Mariana, Bede, or any monkish historian.[28]

29   The wise lend a very academic faith[29] to every report which favours the passion of the reporter; whether it magnifies his country, his family, or himself, or in any other way strikes in with his natural inclinations and propensities. But what greater temptation than to appear a missionary, a prophet, an ambassador from heaven? Who would not encounter many dangers and difficulties, in order to attain so sublime a character? Or if, by the help of vanity and a heated imagination, a man has first made a convert of himself, and entered seriously into the delusion; who ever scruples to make use of pious frauds, in support of so holy and meritorious a cause?

30   The smallest spark may here kindle into the greatest flame; [126] because the materials are always prepared for it. The *avidum genus auricularum*,[f] the gazing populace, receive greedily, without examination, whatever sooths superstition,[30] and promotes wonder.

31   How many stories of this nature have, in all ages, been detected and exploded in their infancy? How many more have been celebrated for a time, and have afterwards sunk into neglect and oblivion? Where such reports, therefore, fly about, the solution of the phenomenon is obvious; and we judge in conformity to regular experience and observation, when we account for it by the known and natural principles of credulity and

---

[f] Lucret. [Lucretius, *On the Nature of Things*, 4.594. Hume has adapted the passage; his version means 'the tribe greedy-eared for gossip'.]

[27] Mark Antony defeated Brutus and Cassius at Philippi in Macedonia in 42 BC. Julius Caesar defeated his great rival Pompey at the Battle of Pharsalia in Thessaly in 48 BC.

[28] Herodotus (5th century BC), Greek historian. His *Histories*, centred on the Persian invasion of Greece, includes respectful reference to oracles, omens, etc., as well as narrative history. Plutarch's *Lives* (of famous Greeks and Romans) also includes reports of marvels along with historical narrative. Juan de Mariana (1536–1624), Spanish Jesuit historian, and Bede (7th–8th century AD), English historian and monk, wrote histories in which (Christian) miracles or marvels are included.

[29] The wise adopt a Sceptical attitude, i.e. they withhold assent.

[30] Whatever verifies or justifies superstition.

delusion. And shall we, rather than have a recourse to so natural a solution, allow of a miraculous violation of the most established laws of nature?

32   I need not mention the difficulty of detecting a falsehood in any private or even public history, at the place, where it is said to happen; much more when the scene is removed to ever so small a distance. Even a court of judicature, with all the authority, accuracy, and judgment, which they can employ, find themselves often at a loss to distinguish between truth and falsehood in the most recent actions. But the matter never comes to any issue, if trusted to the common method of altercations and debate and flying rumours; especially when men's passions have taken part on either side.

33   In the infancy of new religions, the wise and learned commonly esteem the matter too inconsiderable to deserve their attention or regard. And when afterwards they would willingly detect the cheat in order to undeceive the deluded multitude, the season is now past, and the records and witnesses, which might clear up the matter, have perished beyond recovery.

[127]   34   No means of detection remain, but those which must be drawn from the very testimony itself of the reporters: And these, though always sufficient with the judicious and knowing, are commonly too fine to fall under the comprehension of the vulgar.

35   Upon the whole, then, it appears, that no testimony for any kind of miracle has ever amounted to a probability, much less to a proof; and that, even supposing it amounted to a proof, it would be opposed by another proof; derived from the very nature of the fact, which it would endeavour to establish. It is experience only, which gives authority to human testimony; and it is the same experience, which assures us of the laws of nature. When, therefore, these two kinds of experience are contrary, we have nothing to do but subtract the one from the other, and embrace an opinion, either on one side or the other, with that assurance which arises from the remainder. But according to the principle here explained, this subtraction, with regard to all popular religions, amounts to an entire annihilation; and therefore we may establish it as a maxim, that no human testimony can have such force as to prove a miracle, and make it a just foundation for any such system of religion.[31]

---

[31] In contrast to popular religion, philosophical religious views tended to ground religious belief not in miracles but in rational arguments for God's existence. See, e.g., Locke, *Essay*, 4.10.

36   I beg the limitations here made may be remarked, when I say, that a miracle can never be proved, so as to be the foundation of a system of religion. For I own,[32] that otherwise, there may possibly be miracles, or violations of the usual course of nature, of such a kind as to admit of proof from human testimony; though, perhaps, it will be impossible to find any such in all the records of history. Thus, suppose, all authors, in all languages, agree, that, from the first of January, 1600, there was a total darkness over the whole earth for eight days: Suppose that the tradition of this extraordinary event is still strong and lively among the people: That all travellers, who return from foreign countries, bring us accounts of the same tradition, without the least variation or contradiction: It is evident, [128] that our present philosophers, instead of doubting the fact, ought to receive it as certain, and ought to search for the causes whence it might be derived.[33] The decay, corruption, and dissolution of nature, is an event rendered probable by so many analogies, that any phenomenon, which seems to have a tendency towards that catastrophe, comes within the reach of human testimony, if that testimony be very extensive and uniform.[34]

37   But suppose, that all the historians who treat of England, should agree, that, on the first of January, 1600, Queen Elizabeth died; that both before and after her death she was seen by her physicians and the whole court, as is usual with persons of her rank; that her successor was acknowledged and proclaimed by the parliament; and that, after being interred a month, she again appeared, resumed the throne, and governed England for three years: I must confess that I should be surprised at the concurrence of so many odd circumstances, but should not have the least inclination to believe so miraculous an event. I should not doubt of her pretended[35] death, and of those other public circumstances that followed it: I should only assert it to have been pretended, and that it neither was, nor possibly could be real. You would in vain object to me the difficulty, and almost impossibility of deceiving the world in an affair of such consequence; the wisdom and solid judgment of that renowned queen; with the little or no advantage which she could reap from so poor an artifice: All this might astonish me; but I would still reply, that the knavery and folly of men are such common phenomena, that I should rather believe the most

---

[32] Admit.
[33] This paragraph, to this point, was originally a footnote; it was incorporated into the text in 1770.
[34] This sentence was added as a footnote in 1756, and incorporated into the text in 1770.
[35] Alleged.

extraordinary events to arise from their concurrence, than admit of so signal a violation of the laws of nature.

38   But should this miracle be ascribed to any new system of religion; men, in all ages, have been so much imposed on by ridiculous stories of that kind, that this very circumstance would be a full proof of a cheat, and sufficient, with all men of sense, not only to make them reject the fact, but even reject it without farther examination. Though the Being to whom the miracle is ascribed, be, in this case, Almighty, it does not, upon that account, become a whit more probable; since it is impossible for us to know the attributes or actions of such a Being, otherwise than from the experience which we have of his productions, in the usual course of nature.[36] This still reduces us to past observation, and obliges us to compare the instances of the violation of truth in the testimony of men, with those of the violation of the laws of nature by miracles, in order to judge which of them is most likely and probable. As the violations of truth are more common in the testimony concerning religious miracles, than in that concerning any other matter of fact; this must diminish very much the authority of the former testimony, and make us form a general resolution, never to lend any attention to it, with whatever specious pretence[37] it may be covered.[38]

39   Lord Bacon seems to have embraced the same principles of reasoning. 'We ought', says he, 'to make a collection or particular history of all monsters and prodigious births or productions, and in a word of every thing new, rare, and extraordinary in nature. But this must be done with the most severe scrutiny, lest we depart from truth. Above all, every relation must be considered as suspicious, which depends in any degree upon religion, as the prodigies of Livy: And no less so, everything that is to be found in the writers of natural magic or alchemy, or such authors, who seem, all of them, to have an unconquerable appetite for falsehood and fable.'[g]

40   I am the better pleased with the method of reasoning here delivered, as I think it may serve to confound those dangerous friends or disguised enemies to the Christian religion, who have undertaken to

---

[g] Nov. Org. lib. 2. aph. 29. [Francis Bacon, *The New Organon*, 2.29. This paragraph was added as a footnote, in Latin, in 1756. It was incorporated into the text in 1770, and translated into English in 1772.]

[36] See Section 11.   [37] Plausible appearance.

[38] Paragraphs 37 and 38 were originally a footnote; they were incorporated into the text in 1770.

defend it by the principles of human reason. Our most holy religion is founded on *faith*, not on reason;[39] and it is a sure method of exposing it to put it to such a trial as it is, by no means, fitted to endure. To make this more evident, let us examine those miracles, related in scripture; and not to lose ourselves in too wide a field, let us confine ourselves to such as we find in the *Pentateuch*,[40] which we shall examine, according to the principles of these pretended Christians, not as the word or testimony of God himself, but as the production of a mere human writer and historian. Here then we are first to consider a book, presented to us by a barbarous and ignorant people, written in an age when they were still more barbarous, and in all probability long after the facts which it relates, corroborated by no concurring testimony, and resembling those fabulous accounts, which every nation gives of its origin. Upon reading this book, we find it full of prodigies and miracles. It gives an account of a state of the world and of human nature entirely different from the present: Of our fall from that state: Of the age of man, extended to near a thousand years: Of the destruction of the world by a deluge: Of the arbitrary choice of one people, as the favourites of heaven; and that people the countrymen of the author: Of their deliverance from bondage by prodigies the most astonishing imaginable: I desire any one to lay his hand upon his heart, and after a serious consideration declare, whether he thinks that the falsehood of such a book, supported by such a testimony, would be more extraordinary and miraculous than all the miracles it relates; which is, however, necessary to make it be received, according to the measures of probability above established.[41]

41   What we have said of miracles may be applied, without any variation, to prophecies; and indeed, all prophecies are real miracles, and as such [131] only, can be admitted as proofs of any revelation. If it did not exceed the capacity of human nature to foretell future events, it would be absurd to employ any prophecy as an argument for a divine mission or authority from heaven. So that, upon the whole, we may conclude, that the Christian religion not only was at first attended with miracles, but even at this day cannot be believed by any reasonable person without one. Mere reason is insufficient to convince us of its veracity: And whoever is moved by *faith* to assent to it, is

---

[39] A prominent theme in Sceptical defences of Christianity. Thus Montaigne appeals to faith against Seneca's Stoic trust in reason: 'Apology for Raymond Sebond' (683).
[40] The first five books of the Bible, traditionally attributed to Moses.
[41] Cf. Locke, *Essay*, 4.16.13–14.

conscious of a continued miracle in his own person,[42] which subverts all the principles of his understanding, and gives him a determination to believe what is most contrary to custom and experience.

[42] A recurring theme. See Augustine, *City of God*, 22.5; Montaigne, 'Apology for Raymond Sebond' (683); and echoed in a number of seventeenth-century authors, e.g. Edward Stillingfleet (*Origines Sacrae* (1662), 2.10.5), Ralph Cudworth (*The True Intellectual System of the Universe* (1678), 709) and Jacques-Bénigne Bossuet (*Discours sur l'histoire universelle* (1681), 2.20).

11

Of a particular providence and of a future state[1]

1   I was lately engaged in conversation with a friend who loves sceptical paradoxes; where, though he advanced many principles, of which I can
by no means approve, yet as they seem to be curious, and to bear some
relation to the chain of reasoning carried on throughout this enquiry, I
shall here copy them from my memory as accurately as I can, in order to
submit them to the judgment of the reader.

2   Our conversation began with my admiring the singular good
fortune of philosophy, which, as it requires entire liberty above all other
privileges, and chiefly flourishes from the free opposition of sentiments
and argumentation, received its first birth in an age and country of freedom and toleration, and was never cramped, even in its most extravagant
principles, by any creeds, concessions, or penal statutes. For, except the
banishment of Protagoras, and the death of Socrates,[2] which last event
proceeded partly from other motives, there are scarcely any instances to
be met with, in ancient history, of this bigoted jealousy, with which the
present age is so much infested. Epicurus[3] lived at Athens to an advanced

---

[1] In the 1748 edition, this section was entitled 'Of the Practical Consequences of Natural Religion'.
Natural religion is religion based solely on arguments concerning the natural order of things.
Hume's decision to change the title was, presumably, in order to specify the consequences at
issue. Particular providence is special divine provision for individuals, e.g. special punishments
and rewards according to how one lives; it is to be contrasted with general providence, which is
the divine provision implicit in the laws of nature. The future state is, of course, one's state after
death.
[2] Protagoras of Abdera (c. 490–c. 420 BC) was banished from Athens because he denied the possibility
of knowledge of the gods. Socrates (469–399 BC) was condemned to death, according to the official
charge, for impiety (introducing new gods to worship) and for corrupting the youth.
[3] Epicurus (341–270 BC) established a philosophical school in Athens. He developed a materialist
philosophy in which indestructible atoms move in a void, unregulated by any divine providence.
The chief source for Epicurean philosophy is Lucretius, *On the Nature of Things*.

age, in peace and tranquillity: Epicureans[a] were even admitted to receive the sacerdotal character,[4] and to officiate at the altar, in the most sacred rites of the established religion: And the public encouragement[b] of pensions and salaries was afforded equally, by the wisest of all the Roman emperors,[c] to the professors of every sect of philosophy. How requisite such kind of treatment was to philosophy, in her early youth, will easily be conceived, if we reflect, that, even at present, when she may be supposed more hardy and robust, she bears with much difficulty the inclemency of the seasons, and those harsh winds of calumny and persecution, which blow upon her.

[133]

3   You admire, says my friend, as the singular good fortune of philosophy, what seems to result from the natural course of things, and to be unavoidable in every age and nation. This pertinacious bigotry, of which you complain, as so fatal to philosophy, is really her offspring, who, after allying with superstition, separates himself entirely from the interest of his parent, and becomes her most inveterate enemy and persecutor. Speculative dogmas of religion, the present occasions of such furious dispute, could not possibly be conceived or admitted in the early ages of the world; when mankind, being wholly illiterate, formed an idea of religion more suitable to their weak apprehension, and composed their sacred tenets of such tales chiefly as were the objects of traditional belief, more than of argument or disputation. After the first alarm, therefore, was over, which arose from the new paradoxes and principles of the philosophers; these teachers seem ever after, during the ages of antiquity, to have lived in great harmony with the established superstition, and to have made a fair partition of mankind between them; the former claiming all the learned and wise, the latter possessing all the vulgar and illiterate.

4   It seems then, say I, that you leave politics entirely out of the question, and never suppose, that a wise magistrate can justly be jealous[5] of certain tenets of philosophy, such as those of Epicurus, which, denying a divine existence, and consequently a providence and a future state,[6] seem

---

[a] Lucian. συμπ. ἢ Λαπίθαι. [Lucian, *The Drinking Party, or Lapithae*, 9.]
[b] Lucian. εὐνοῦχος. [Lucian, *The Eunuch*, 3, 8.]
[c] Id. & Dio. [Lucian, *The Eunuch*, 3; Dio Cassius, *Roman History*, 72.31.3.]
[4] To receive the sacerdotal character is to be ordained as a priest.
[5] Vigilant or protective (i.e. of his rights and powers).
[6] The Epicureans denied divine engagement with, and providential concern for, the world, but not divine existence itself. The denial of providence was taken to be a distinguishing mark of the

to loosen, in a great measure, the ties of morality, and may be supposed, for [134] that reason, pernicious to the peace of civil society.

5   I know, replied he, that in fact these persecutions never, in any age, proceeded from calm reason, or from experience of the pernicious consequences of philosophy; but arose entirely from passion and pre-judice. But what if I should advance farther, and assert, that if Epicurus had been accused before the people, by any of the *sycophants* or informers of those days, he could easily have defended his cause, and proved his prin-ciples of philosophy to be as salutary as those of his adversaries, who endeavoured, with such zeal, to expose him to the public hatred and jealousy?

6   I wish, said I, you would try your eloquence upon so extra-ordinary a topic, and make a speech for Epicurus, which might satisfy, not the mob of Athens, if you will allow that ancient and polite city to have contained any mob, but the more philosophical part of his audience, such as might be supposed capable of comprehending his arguments.[7]

7   The matter would not be difficult, upon such conditions, replied he: And if you please, I shall suppose myself Epicurus for a moment, and make you stand for the Athenian people, and shall deliver you such an harangue as will fill all the urn with white beans, and leave not a black one to gratify the malice of my adversaries.[8]

8   Very well: Pray proceed upon these suppositions.

9   I come hither, O ye Athenians, to justify in your assembly what I maintain in my school, and I find myself impeached by furious antago-nists, instead of reasoning with calm and dispassionate enquirers. Your deliberations, which of right should be directed to questions of public good, and the interest of the commonwealth, are diverted to the disquisi-tions of speculative philosophy; and these magnificent, but perhaps fruit-less enquiries, take place of your more familiar but more useful [135] occupations. But so far as in me lies, I will prevent this abuse. We shall not here dispute concerning the origin and government of worlds.[9] We shall

Epicurean (see e.g. Malebranche, *Search*, 2.1.4.3). Thus Hume's observation, in a letter to Gilbert Elliot of Minto (10 March 1751), that an atheist and an Epicurean are 'little or nothing different'.

[7] Pierre Bayle imagines a public debate in Athens between followers of Strato's atheist materialism and Stoics (providentialist theists) in *Continuations des pensées diverses* (1705), 106.

[8] A reference to ancient Greek voting procedures, in which voters placed a coloured bean – white for agreement or innocence, black for disagreement or guilt – in an urn.

[9] That is, of the nature of the gods and of their engagement with the world. The terminology of divine 'government' echoes Butler's discussion of natural religion (*Analogy of Religion*, Part 1).

only enquire how far such questions concern the public interest. And if I can persuade you, that they are entirely indifferent to the peace of society and security of government, I hope that you will presently send us back to our schools, there to examine, at leisure, the question the most sublime, but, at the same time, the most speculative of all philosophy.

10   The religious philosophers, not satisfied with the tradition of your forefathers, and doctrine of your priests (in which I willingly acquiesce), indulge a rash curiosity, in trying how far they can establish religion upon the principles of reason; and they thereby excite, instead of satisfying, the doubts, which naturally arise from a diligent and scrutinous enquiry. They paint, in the most magnificent colours, the order, beauty, and wise arrangement of the universe; and then ask, if such a glorious display of intelligence could proceed from the fortuitous concourse of atoms, or if chance could produce what the greatest genius can never sufficiently admire. I shall not examine the justness of this argument. I shall allow it to be as solid as my antagonists and accusers can desire. It is sufficient, if I can prove, from this very reasoning, that the question is entirely speculative, and that, when, in my philosophical disquisitions, I deny a providence and a future state, I undermine not the foundations of society, but advance principles, which they themselves, upon their own topics, if they argue consistently, must allow to be solid and satisfactory.

11   You then, who are my accusers, have acknowledged, that the chief or sole argument for a divine existence (which I never questioned) is derived from the order of nature; where there appear such marks of intelligence and design, that you think it extravagant to assign for its cause, either chance, or the blind and unguided force of matter. You allow, that [136] this is an argument drawn from effects to causes. From the order of the work, you infer, that there must have been project and forethought in the workman. If you cannot make out this point, you allow, that your conclusion fails; and you pretend not to establish the conclusion in a greater latitude than the phenomena of nature will justify. These are your concessions. I desire you to mark the consequences.

12   When we infer any particular cause from an effect, we must proportion the one to the other, and can never be allowed to ascribe to the cause any qualities, but what are exactly sufficient to produce the effect. A body of ten ounces raised in any scale may serve as a proof, that the counterbalancing weight exceeds ten ounces; but can never afford a reason that it exceeds a hundred. If the cause, assigned for any effect, be not sufficient

to produce it, we must either reject that cause, or add to it such qualities as will give it a just proportion to the effect. But if we ascribe to it farther qualities, or affirm it capable of producing other effects, we can only indulge the licence of conjecture, and arbitrarily suppose the existence of qualities and energies, without reason or authority.

13   The same rule holds, whether the cause assigned be brute unconscious matter, or a rational intelligent being. If the cause be known only by the effect, we never ought to ascribe to it any qualities, beyond what are precisely requisite to produce the effect: Nor can we, by any rules of just reasoning, return back from the cause, and infer other effects from it, beyond those by which alone it is known to us. No one, merely from the sight of one of Zeuxis's pictures, could know, that he was also a statuary or architect,[10] and was an artist no less skilful in stone and marble than in colours. The talents and taste, displayed in the particular work before us; these we may safely conclude the workman to be possessed of. The cause must be proportioned to the effect; and if we exactly and precisely pro- [137] portion it, we shall never find in it any qualities, that point farther, or afford an inference concerning any other design or performance. Such qualities must be somewhat beyond what is merely requisite for producing the effect, which we examine.

14   Allowing, therefore, the gods to be the authors of the existence or order of the universe; it follows, that they possess that precise degree of power, intelligence, and benevolence, which appears in their workman-ship; but nothing farther can ever be proved, except we call in the assis-tance of exaggeration and flattery to supply the defects of argument and reasoning. So far as the traces of any attributes, at present, appear, so far may we conclude these attributes to exist. The supposition of farther attributes is mere hypothesis; much more the supposition, that, in distant regions of space or periods of time, there has been, or will be, a more magnificent display of these attributes, and a scheme of administration more suitable to such imaginary virtues. We can never be allowed to mount up from the universe, the effect, to Jupiter,[11] the cause; and then descend downwards, to infer any new effect from that cause; as if the present effects alone were not entirely worthy of the glorious attributes, which we ascribe to that deity. The knowledge of the cause being derived solely from the

---

[10] Zeuxis of Heraclea (fl. 420–390 BC), Greek painter and sculptor. (A statuary is a sculptor.)
[11] Jupiter (or Jove): the chief god of Roman religion, the equivalent of Greek Zeus. (Given that the imagined audience is Greek, not Roman, this is a slip on Hume's part.)

effect, they must be exactly adjusted to each other; and the one can never refer to anything farther, or be the foundation of any new inference and conclusion.

15   You find certain phenomena in nature. You seek a cause or author. You imagine that you have found him. You afterwards become so enamoured of this offspring of your brain, that you imagine it impossible, but he must produce something greater and more perfect than the present scene of things, which is so full of ill and disorder. You forget, that this superlative intelligence and benevolence are entirely imaginary, or, at least, [138] without any foundation in reason; and that you have no ground to ascribe to him any qualities, but what you see he has actually exerted and displayed in his productions. Let your gods, therefore, O philosophers, be suited to the present appearances of nature: And presume not to alter these appearances by arbitrary suppositions, in order to suit them to the attributes, which you so fondly ascribe to your deities.

16   When priests and poets, supported by your authority, O Athenians, talk of a golden or silver age, which preceded the present state of vice and misery,[12] I hear them with attention and with reverence. But when philosophers, who pretend to neglect authority, and to cultivate reason, hold the same discourse, I pay them not, I own, the same obsequious submission and pious deference. I ask; who carried them into the celestial regions, who admitted them into the councils of the gods, who opened to them the book of fate, that they thus rashly affirm, that their deities have executed, or will execute, any purpose beyond what has actually appeared? If they tell me, that they have mounted on the steps or by the gradual ascent of reason, and by drawing inferences from effects to causes, I still insist, that they have aided the ascent of reason by the wings of imagination; otherwise they could not thus change their manner of inference, and argue from causes to effects; presuming, that a more perfect production than the present world would be more suitable to such perfect beings as the gods, and forgetting that they have no reason to ascribe to these celestial beings any perfection or any attribute, but what can be found in the present world.

---

[12] In Greek and Roman mythology, the golden age was the earliest age of human (mortal) beings, a period of untroubled happiness. The subsequent silver age was less happy, but still better than the more recent bronze and heroic ages, and the present iron age, an age of 'toil and misery'. See Hesiod, *Works and Days*, 109–202; Ovid, *Metamorphoses*, 1.76–150.

17   Hence all the fruitless industry to account for the ill appearances of nature, and save the honour of the gods; while we must acknowledge the reality of that evil and disorder, with which the world so much
abounds. The obstinate and intractable qualities of matter, we are told, or [139]
the observance of general laws, or some such reason,[13] is the sole cause,
which controlled the power and benevolence of Jupiter, and obliged him to
create mankind and every sensible creature so imperfect and so unhappy.
These attributes then, are, it seems, beforehand, taken for granted, in their
greatest latitude. And upon that supposition, I own that such conjectures
may, perhaps, be admitted as plausible solutions of the ill phenomena. But
still I ask; Why take these attributes for granted, or why ascribe to the cause
any qualities but what actually appear in the effect? Why torture your brain
to justify the course of nature upon suppositions, which, for aught you
know, may be entirely imaginary, and of which there are to be found no
traces in the course of nature?

18   The religious hypothesis,[14] therefore, must be considered only
as a particular method of accounting for the visible phenomena of the
universe: But no just reasoner will ever presume to infer from it any single
fact, and alter or add to the phenomena, in any single particular. If you
think, that the appearances of things prove such causes, it is allowable for
you to draw an inference concerning the existence of these causes. In such
complicated and sublime subjects, every one should be indulged in the
liberty of conjecture and argument. But here you ought to rest. If you come
backward, and arguing from your inferred causes, conclude, that any other
fact has existed, or will exist, in the course of nature, which may serve as a
fuller display of particular attributes; I must admonish you, that you have
departed from the method of reasoning, attached to the present subject,
and have certainly added something to the attributes of the cause, beyond
what appears in the effect; otherwise you could never, with tolerable sense
or propriety, add anything to the effect, in order to render it more worthy of
the cause.

19   Where, then, is the odiousness of that doctrine, which I teach [140]
in my school, or rather, which I examine in my gardens?[15] Or what do

[13] The Platonists, in particular, emphasized the intractability of matter, the Stoics the limitations
imposed by general laws.
[14] A Newtonian echo. A hypothesis is an explanatory principle 'not deduced from phenomena', but
imposed on them: *Principia*, General Scholium (92).
[15] Epicurus taught in his garden; 'The Garden' was a synonym for Epicurean philosophy.

you find in this whole question, wherein the security of good morals, or the peace and order of society, is in the least concerned?

20   I deny a providence, you say, and supreme governor of the world, who guides the course of events, and punishes the vicious with infamy and disappointment, and rewards the virtuous with honour and success, in all their undertakings. But surely, I deny not the course itself of events, which lies open to every one's enquiry and examination. I acknowledge, that, in the present order of things, virtue is attended with more peace of mind than vice, and meets with a more favourable reception from the world. I am sensible, that, according to the past experience of mankind, friendship is the chief joy of human life, and moderation the only source of tranquillity and happiness. I never balance between the virtuous and the vicious course of life; but am sensible, that, to a well-disposed mind, every advantage is on the side of the former. And what can you say more, allowing all your suppositions and reasonings? You tell me, indeed, that this disposition of things proceeds from intelligence and design. But whatever it proceeds from, the disposition itself, on which depends our happiness or misery, and consequently our conduct and deportment in life, is still the same. It is still open for me, as well as you, to regulate my behaviour, by my experience of past events. And if you affirm, that, while a divine providence is allowed, and a supreme distributive justice in the universe, I ought to expect some more particular reward of the good, and punishment of the bad, beyond the ordinary course of events; I here find the same fallacy, which I have before endeavoured to detect. You persist in imagining, that, if we grant that divine existence, for which you so earnestly contend, you may safely infer consequences from it, and add [141] something to the experienced order of nature, by arguing from the attributes which you ascribe to your gods. You seem not to remember, that all your reasonings on this subject can only be drawn from effects to causes; and that every argument, deduced from causes to effects, must of necessity be a gross sophism;[16] since it is impossible for you to know anything of the cause, but what you have antecedently, not inferred, but discovered to the full, in the effect.

21   But what must a philosopher think of those vain reasoners, who instead of regarding the present scene of things as the sole object of their contemplation, so far reverse the whole course of nature, as to render this

---

[16] A fallacious argument.

life merely a passage to something farther; a porch, which leads to a greater, and vastly different building; a prologue, which serves only to introduce the piece, and give it more grace and propriety? Whence, do you think, can such philosophers derive their idea of the gods? From their own conceit and imagination surely. For if they derived it from the present phenomena, it would never point to anything farther, but must be exactly adjusted to them. That the divinity may *possibly* be endowed with attributes, which we have never seen exerted; may be governed by principles of action, which we cannot discover to be satisfied: All this will freely be allowed. But still this is mere *possibility* and hypothesis. We never can have reason to *infer* any attributes, or any principles of action in him, but so far as we know them to have been exerted and satisfied.

22 *Are there any marks of a distributive justice in the world?* If you answer in the affirmative, I conclude, that, since justice here exerts itself, it is satisfied. If you reply in the negative, I conclude, that you have then no reason to ascribe justice, in our sense of it, to the gods. If you hold a medium between affirmation and negation, by saying, that the justice of [142] the gods, at present, exerts itself in part, but not in its full extent; I answer, that you have no reason to give it any particular extent, but only so far as you see it, *at present*, exert itself.

23 Thus I bring the dispute, O Athenians, to a short issue with my antagonists. The course of nature lies open to my contemplation as well as to theirs. The experienced train of events is the great standard, by which we all regulate our conduct. Nothing else can be appealed to in the field, or in the senate. Nothing else ought ever to be heard of in the school, or in the closet. In vain would our limited understanding break through those boundaries, which are too narrow for our fond imagination. While we argue from the course of nature, and infer a particular intelligent cause, which first bestowed, and still preserves order in the universe, we embrace a principle, which is both uncertain and useless. It is uncertain; because the subject lies entirely beyond the reach of human experience. It is useless; because our knowledge of this cause being derived entirely from the course of nature, we can never, according to the rules of just reasoning, return back from the cause with any new inference, or making additions to the common and experienced course of nature, establish any new principles of conduct and behaviour.

24 I observe (said I, finding he had finished his harangue) that you neglect not the artifice of the demagogues of old; and as you were pleased

to make me stand for the people, you insinuate yourself into my favour by embracing those principles, to which, you know, I have always expressed a particular attachment. But allowing you to make experience (as indeed I think you ought) the only standard of our judgment concerning this, and all other questions of fact; I doubt not but, from the very same experience, [143] to which you appeal, it may be possible to refute this reasoning, which you have put into the mouth of Epicurus. If you saw, for instance, a half-finished building, surrounded with heaps of brick and stone and mortar, and all the instruments of masonry; could you not *infer* from the effect, that it was a work of design and contrivance? And could you not return again, from this inferred cause, to infer new additions to the effect, and conclude, that the building would soon be finished, and receive all the further improvements, which art could bestow upon it? If you saw upon the seashore the print of one human foot, you would conclude, that a man had passed that way, and that he had also left the traces of the other foot, though effaced by the rolling of the sands or inundation of the waters. Why then do you refuse to admit the same method of reasoning with regard to the order of nature? Consider the world and the present life only as an imperfect building, from which you can infer a superior intelligence; and arguing from that superior intelligence, which can leave nothing imperfect; why may you not infer a more finished scheme or plan, which will receive its completion in some distant point of space or time? Are not these methods of reasoning exactly similar? And under what pretence can you embrace the one, while you reject the other?

25   The infinite difference of the subjects, replied he, is a sufficient foundation for this difference in my conclusions. In works of *human* art and contrivance, it is allowable to advance from the effect to the cause, and returning back from the cause, to form new inferences concerning the effect, and examine the alterations, which it has probably undergone, or may still undergo. But what is the foundation of this method of reasoning? Plainly this; that man is a being, whom we know by experience, whose motives and designs we are acquainted with, and whose projects and [144] inclinations have a certain connexion and coherence, according to the laws which nature has established for the government of such a creature. When, therefore, we find, that any work has proceeded from the skill and industry of man; as we are otherwise acquainted with the nature of the animal, we can draw a hundred inferences concerning what may be expected from him; and these inferences will all be founded in experience

and observation. But did we know man only from the single work or production which we examine, it were impossible for us to argue in this manner; because our knowledge of all the qualities, which we ascribe to him,
being in that case derived from the production, it is impossible they could
point to anything farther, or be the foundation of any new inference. The
print of a foot in the sand can only prove, when considered alone, that
there was some figure adapted to it, by which it was produced: But the
print of a human foot proves likewise, from our other experience, that
there was probably another foot, which also left its impression, though
effaced by time or other accidents. Here we mount from the effect to the
cause; and descending again from the cause, infer alterations in the effect;
but this is not a continuation of the same simple chain of reasoning. We
comprehend in this case a hundred other experiences and observations,
concerning the *usual* figure and members of that species of animal, without which this method of argument must be considered as fallacious and
sophistical.

26   The case is not the same with our reasonings from the works of
nature. The Deity is known to us only by his productions, and is a single
being in the universe, not comprehended under any species or genus,
from whose experienced attributes or qualities, we can, by analogy, infer
any attribute or quality in him. As the universe shows wisdom and goodness, we infer wisdom and goodness. As it shows a particular degree of
these perfections, we infer a particular degree of them, precisely adapted [145]
to the effect which we examine. But farther attributes or farther degrees of
the same attributes, we can never be authorised to infer or suppose, by any
rules of just reasoning. Now, without some such licence of supposition, it
is impossible for us to argue from the cause, or infer any alteration in the
effect, beyond what has immediately fallen under our observation. Greater
good produced by this Being must still prove a greater degree of goodness: A more impartial distribution of rewards and punishments must
proceed from a greater regard to justice and equity. Every supposed addition to the works of nature makes an addition to the attributes of the
Author of nature; and consequently, being entirely unsupported by any
reason or argument, can never be admitted but as mere conjecture and
hypothesis.[d]

---

[d] In general, it may, I think, be established as a maxim, that where any cause is known only by
its particular effects, it must be impossible to infer any new effects from that cause; since the
qualities, which are requisite to produce these new effects along with the former, must either be

27   The great source of our mistake in this subject, and of the unbounded licence of conjecture, which we indulge, is, that we tacitly consider ourselves, as in the place of the Supreme Being, and conclude, [146] that he will, on every occasion, observe the same conduct, which we ourselves, in his situation, would have embraced as reasonable and eligible. But, besides that the ordinary course of nature may convince us, that almost everything is regulated by principles and maxims very different from ours; besides this, I say, it must evidently appear contrary to all rules of analogy to reason, from the intentions and projects of men, to those of a Being so different, and so much superior. In human nature, there is a certain experienced coherence of designs and inclinations; so that when, from any fact, we have discovered one intention of any man, it may often be reasonable, from experience, to infer another, and draw a long chain of conclusions concerning his past or future conduct. But this method of reasoning can never have place with regard to a Being, so remote and incomprehensible, who bears much less analogy to any other being in the universe than the sun to a waxen taper,[17] and who discovers[18] himself only by some faint traces or outlines, beyond which we have no authority to ascribe to him any attribute or perfection. What we imagine to be a superior perfection, may really be a defect. Or were it ever so much a perfection, the ascribing of it to the Supreme Being, where it appears not to have been really exerted, to the full, in his works, savours more of flattery and panegyric,[19] than of just reasoning and sound philosophy. All the philosophy, therefore, in the world, and all the religion, which is nothing but a species of philosophy, will never be able to carry us beyond the usual course of experience, or give us measures of conduct and behaviour different from those which are furnished by reflections on common life. No new fact can

---

different, or superior, or of more extensive operation, than those which simply produced the effect, whence alone the cause is supposed to be known to us. We can never, therefore, have any reason to suppose the existence of these qualities. To say, that the new effects proceed only from a continuation of the same energy, which is already known from the first effects, will not remove the difficulty. For even granting this to be the case (which can seldom be supposed), the very continuation and exertion of a like energy (for it is impossible it can be absolutely the same), I say, this exertion of a like energy, in a different period of space and time, is a very arbitrary supposition, and what there cannot possibly be any traces of in the effects, from which all our knowledge of the cause is originally derived. Let the *inferred* cause be exactly proportioned (as it should be) to the known effect; and it is impossible that it can possess any qualities, from which new or different effects can be *inferred*. [Transferred from text to footnote in 1756. Implicitly at issue here are arguments for the existence of God: see e.g. Locke, *Essay*, 4.10; Clarke, *A Demonstration of the Being and Attributes of God*, VIII; and *A Letter from a Gentleman*.]

[17] A candle.   [18] Reveals or discloses.   [19] A speech of praise; eulogy.

ever be inferred from the religious hypothesis; no event foreseen or fore-told; no reward or punishment expected or dreaded, beyond what is already known by practice and observation. So that my apology for[20] Epicurus will still appear solid and satisfactory; nor have the political interests of society [147] any connexion with the philosophical disputes concerning metaphysics and religion.

28   There is still one circumstance, replied I, which you seem to have overlooked. Though I should allow your premises, I must deny your conclusion. You conclude, that religious doctrines and reasonings *can* have no influence on life, because they *ought* to have no influence; never con-sidering, that men reason not in the same manner you do, but draw many consequences from the belief of a divine existence, and suppose that the Deity will inflict punishments on vice, and bestow rewards on virtue, beyond what appear in the ordinary course of nature. Whether this rea-soning of theirs be just or not, is no matter. Its influence on their life and conduct must still be the same. And those, who attempt to disabuse them of such prejudices, may, for aught I know, be good reasoners, but I cannot allow them to be good citizens and politicians; since they free men from one restraint upon their passions, and make the infringement of the laws of society, in one respect, more easy and secure.

29   After all, I may, perhaps, agree to your general conclusion in favour of liberty, though upon different premises from those, on which you endeavour to found it. I think, that the state ought to tolerate every prin-ciple of philosophy; nor is there an instance, that any government has suffered in its political interests by such indulgence. There is no enthu-siasm[21] among philosophers; their doctrines are not very alluring to the people; and no restraint can be put upon their reasonings, but what must be of dangerous consequence to the sciences, and even to the state, by paving the way for persecution and oppression in points, where the gen-erality of mankind are more deeply interested and concerned.

30   But there occurs to me (continued I) with regard to your [148] main topic, a difficulty, which I shall just propose to you without insisting on it; lest it lead into reasonings of too nice[22] and delicate a nature. In a word, I much doubt whether it be possible for a cause to be known only by its effect (as you have all along supposed) or to be of so singular and

[20] Defence of.   [21] Fervour characteristic of intense religious belief.
[22] Subtle.

129

particular a nature as to have no parallel and no similarity with any other cause or object, that has ever fallen under our observation. It is only when two *species* of objects are found to be constantly conjoined, that we can infer the one from the other; and were an effect presented, which was entirely singular, and could not be comprehended under any known *species*, I do not see, that we could form any conjecture or inference at all concerning its cause. If experience and observation and analogy be, indeed, the only guides which we can reasonably follow in inferences of this nature; both the effect and cause must bear a similarity and resemblance to other effects and causes, which we know, and which we have found, in many instances, to be conjoined with each other. I leave it to your own reflection to pursue the consequences of this principle. I shall just observe, that, as the antagonists of Epicurus always suppose the universe, an effect quite singular and unparalleled, to be the proof of a Deity, a cause no less singular and unparalleled; your reasonings, upon that supposition, seem, at least, to merit our attention. There is, I own, some difficulty, how we can ever return from the cause to the effect, and, reasoning from our ideas of the former, infer any alteration on the latter, or any addition to it.

12

Of the academical or sceptical philosophy

Part 1

1   There is not a greater number of philosophical reasonings, displayed upon any subject, than those, which prove the existence of a Deity,
and refute the fallacies of *atheists*; and yet the most religious philosophers
still dispute whether any man can be so blinded as to be a speculative
atheist.[1] How shall we reconcile these contradictions? The knights-errant,
who wandered about to clear the world of dragons and giants, never
entertained the least doubt with regard to the existence of these monsters.

2   The *Sceptic* is another enemy of religion, who naturally provokes
the indignation of all divines and graver philosophers; though it is certain,
that no man ever met with any such absurd creature, or conversed with a
man, who had no opinion or principle concerning any subject, either of
action or speculation. This begets a very natural question; What is meant
by a sceptic? And how far it is possible to push these philosophical principles of doubt and uncertainty?

3   There is a species of scepticism, *antecedent* to all study and philosophy, which is much inculcated by Descartes and others, as a sovereign
preservative against error and precipitate judgment. It recommends an
universal doubt, not only of all our former opinions and principles, but
also of our very faculties; of whose veracity, say they, we must assure our-   [150]
selves, by a chain of reasoning, deduced from some original principle,

---

[1]   In eighteenth-century usage, atheists could be theoretical ('speculative') or practical. The former
denied the existence of God; the latter denied, or by their actions implicitly denied, divine providence or an afterlife. For evidence that doubts concerning the existence of speculative atheists were
widespread, see Berkeley, *Alciphron*, Advertisement.

which cannot possibly be fallacious or deceitful.[2] But neither is there any such original principle, which has a prerogative above others, that are self-evident and convincing: Or if there were, could we advance a step beyond it, but by the use of those very faculties, of which we are supposed to be already diffident. The Cartesian doubt, therefore, were it ever possible to be attained by any human creature (as it plainly is not) would be entirely incurable; and no reasoning could ever bring us to a state of assurance and conviction upon any subject.

4   It must, however, be confessed, that this species of scepticism, when more moderate, may be understood in a very reasonable sense, and is a necessary preparative to the study of philosophy, by preserving a proper impartiality in our judgments, and weaning our mind from all those prejudices, which we may have imbibed from education or rash opinion. To begin with clear and self-evident principles, to advance by timorous[3] and sure steps, to review frequently our conclusions, and examine accurately all their consequences; though by these means we shall make both a slow and a short progress in our systems; are the only methods, by which we can ever hope to reach truth, and attain a proper stability and certainty in our determinations.

5   There is another species of scepticism, *consequent* to science and enquiry, when men are supposed to have discovered, either the absolute fallaciousness of their mental faculties, or their unfitness to reach any fixed determination in all those curious subjects of speculation, about which they are commonly employed. Even our very senses are brought into dispute, by a certain species of philosophers; and the maxims of common life are subjected to the same doubt as the most profound principles or con-
[151] clusions of metaphysics and theology. As these paradoxical tenets (if they may be called tenets)[4] are to be met with in some philosophers, and the refutation of them in several, they naturally excite our curiosity, and make us enquire into the arguments, on which they may be founded.

6   I need not insist upon the more trite topics, employed by the sceptics in all ages, against the evidence of *sense*; such as those which are

---

[2] Descartes, *Meditations*, First and Second Meditations; *Principles of Philosophy*, Part I (2.12–23, 1.193–222).
[3] Diffident or cautious.
[4] A tenet is a basic principle; the point is that universal doubt must doubt that its own methods or recommendations can be such principles.

derived from the imperfection and fallaciousness of our organs, on num-
berless occasions; the crooked appearance of an oar in water; the various
aspects of objects, according to their different distances; the double images
which arise from the pressing one eye; with many other appearances of a
like nature.[5] These sceptical topics, indeed, are only sufficient to prove,
that the senses alone are not implicitly to be depended on; but that we
must correct their evidence by reason, and by considerations, derived from
the nature of the medium, the distance of the object, and the disposition of
the organ, in order to render them, within their sphere, the proper *criteria*
of truth and falsehood.[6] There are other more profound arguments against
the senses, which admit not of so easy a solution.

7   It seems evident, that men are carried, by a natural instinct or
prepossession, to repose faith in their senses; and that, without any reasoning, or even almost before the use of reason, we always suppose an
external universe, which depends not on our perception, but would exist,
though we and every sensible creature were absent or annihilated. Even the
animal creation are governed by a like opinion, and preserve this belief of
external objects, in all their thoughts, designs, and actions.

8   It seems also evident, that, when men follow this blind and
powerful instinct of nature, they always suppose the very images, presented by the senses, to be the external objects, and never entertain any
suspicion, that the one are nothing but representations of the other. This
very table, which we see white, and which we feel hard, is believed to
exist, independent of our perception, and to be something external to [152]
our mind, which perceives it. Our presence bestows not being on it: Our
absence does not annihilate it. It preserves its existence uniform and
entire, independent of the situation of intelligent beings, who perceive
or contemplate it.

9   But this universal and primary opinion of all men is soon
destroyed by the slightest philosophy,[7] which teaches us, that nothing can
ever be present to the mind but an image or perception, and that the senses are only the inlets, through which these images are conveyed, without

---

[5] See e.g. Sextus Empiricus, *Outlines of Scepticism*, 1.36–94; Montaigne, 'Apology for Raymond
Sebond' (660–80); also Descartes, *Meditations*, First Meditation, and Third Set of Objections and
Replies (Hobbes's objections) (2.12–13, 121).
[6] In Stoic philosophy, the criterion is the standard for judging the truth of a perception or thought.
See Epictetus, *Discourses*, 2.11, 'What is the beginning of philosophy?'
[7] Natural science.

being able to produce any immediate intercourse between the mind and the object. The table, which we see, seems to diminish, as we remove farther from it: But the real table, which exists independent of us, suffers no alteration: It was, therefore, nothing but its image, which was present to the mind. These are the obvious dictates of reason; and no man, who reflects, ever doubted, that the existences, which we consider, when we say, *this house* and *that tree*, are nothing but perceptions in the mind, and fleeting copies or representations of other existences, which remain uniform and independent.

10   So far, then, are we necessitated by reasoning to contradict or depart from the primary instincts of nature, and to embrace a new system with regard to the evidence of our senses. But here philosophy finds herself extremely embarrassed, when she would justify this new system, and obviate the cavils[8] and objections of the sceptics. She can no longer plead the infallible and irresistible instinct of nature: For that led us to a quite different system, which is acknowledged fallible and even erroneous. And to justify this pretended philosophical system, by a chain of clear and convincing argument, or even any appearance of argument, exceeds the power of all human capacity.

[153]   11   By what argument can it be proved, that the perceptions of the mind must be caused by external objects, entirely different from them, though resembling them (if that be possible) and could not arise either from the energy of the mind itself, or from the suggestion of some invisible and unknown spirit, or from some other cause still more unknown to us? It is acknowledged, that, in fact, many of these perceptions arise not from anything external, as in dreams, madness, and other diseases.[9] And nothing can be more inexplicable than the manner, in which body should so operate upon mind as ever to convey an image of itself to a substance, supposed of so different, and even contrary a nature.

12   It is a question of fact, whether the perceptions of the senses be produced by external objects, resembling them: How shall this question be determined? By experience surely; as all other questions of a like nature. But here experience is, and must be entirely silent. The mind has never anything present to it but the perceptions, and cannot possibly reach any

---

[8] Quibbling arguments.
[9] Montaigne, 'Apology for Raymond Sebond' (674–9); Descartes, *Meditations*, First Meditation (2.13).

experience of their connexion with objects. The supposition of such a connexion is, therefore, without any foundation in reasoning.

13   To have recourse to the veracity of the Supreme Being, in order to prove the veracity of our senses, is surely making a very unexpected circuit.[10] If his veracity were at all concerned in this matter, our senses would be entirely infallible; because it is not possible that he can ever deceive. Not to mention, that, if the external world be once called in question, we shall be at a loss to find arguments, by which we may prove the existence of that Being or any of his attributes.

14   This is a topic, therefore, in which the profounder and more philosophical sceptics will always triumph, when they endeavour to introduce an universal doubt into all subjects of human knowledge and enquiry. Do you follow the instincts and propensities of nature, may they say, in assenting to the veracity of sense? But these lead you to believe that [154] the very perception or sensible image is the external object. Do you disclaim this principle, in order to embrace a more rational opinion, that the perceptions are only representations of something external? You here depart from your natural propensities and more obvious sentiments; and yet are not able to satisfy your reason, which can never find any convincing argument from experience to prove, that the perceptions are connected with any external objects.

15   There is another sceptical topic of a like nature, derived from the most profound philosophy; which might merit our attention, were it requisite to dive so deep, in order to discover arguments and reasonings, which can so little serve to any serious purpose. It is universally allowed by modern enquirers, that all the sensible qualities of objects, such as hard, soft, hot, cold, white, black, etc, are merely secondary, and exist not in the objects themselves, but are perceptions of the mind, without any external archetype or model, which they represent. If this be allowed, with regard to secondary qualities, it must also follow, with regard to the supposed primary qualities of extension and solidity; nor can the latter be any more entitled to that denomination than the former. The idea of extension is entirely acquired from the senses of sight and feeling; and if all the qualities, perceived by the senses, be in the mind, not in the object, the same conclusion must reach the idea of extension, which is wholly dependent on the sensible ideas or the ideas of secondary qualities. Nothing can save us

---

[10] This is Descartes's procedure in the *Meditations*.

from this conclusion, but the asserting, that the ideas of those primary qualities are attained by abstraction, an opinion, which, if we examine it accurately, we shall find to be unintelligible, and even absurd. An extension, that is neither tangible nor visible, cannot possibly be conceived: And [155] a tangible or visible extension, which is neither hard nor soft, black nor white, is equally beyond the reach of human conception. Let any man try to conceive a triangle in general, which is neither *Isosceles* nor *Scalenum*, nor has any particular length or proportion of sides; and he will soon perceive the absurdity of all the scholastic notions with regard to abstraction and general ideas.[a]

16   Thus the first philosophical objection to the evidence of sense or to the opinion of external existence consists in this, that such an opinion, if rested on natural instinct, is contrary to reason, and if referred to reason, is contrary to natural instinct, and at the same time carries no rational evidence with it, to convince an impartial enquirer. The second objection goes farther, and represents this opinion as contrary to reason; at least, if it be a principle of reason, that all sensible qualities are in the mind, not in the object. Bereave matter of all its intelligible qualities, both primary and secondary, you in a manner annihilate it, and leave only a certain unknown, inexplicable *something*, as the cause of our perceptions;[11] a notion so imperfect, that no sceptic will think it worth while to contend against it.

Part 2

17   It may seem a very extravagant attempt of the sceptics to destroy *reason* by argument and ratiocination; yet is this the grand scope of all [156] their enquiries and disputes. They endeavour to find objections, both to

---

[a] This argument is drawn from Dr. Berkeley; and indeed most of the writings of that very ingenious author form the best lessons of scepticism, which are to be found either among the ancient or modern philosophers, Bayle not excepted. He professes, however, in his title-page (and undoubtedly with great truth) to have composed his book against the sceptics as well as against the atheists and free-thinkers. But that all his arguments, though otherwise intended, are, in reality, merely sceptical, appears from this, *that they admit of no answer and produce no conviction.* Their only effect is to cause that momentary amazement and irresolution and confusion, which is the result of scepticism. [See Berkeley (*Principles*, 1.9–25), and Bayle (*Dictionary*,'Zeno of Elea', Note H) for criticism of the distinction between primary and secondary qualities. The 'scholastic notions with regard to abstraction and general ideas' include Locke's account (*Essay*, 2.11.9, 4.7.9).]
[11] Cf. Locke, *Essay*, 2.23.2.

our abstract reasonings, and to those which regard matter of fact and existence.

18   The chief objection against all *abstract* reasonings is derived from the ideas of space and time; ideas, which, in common life and to a careless view, are very clear and intelligible, but when they pass through the scrutiny of the profound sciences (and they are the chief object of these sciences) afford principles, which seem full of absurdity and contradiction.[12] No priestly *dogmas*, invented on purpose to tame and subdue the rebellious reason of mankind, ever shocked common sense more than the doctrine of the infinite divisibility of extension, with its consequences; as they are pompously displayed by all geometricians and metaphysicians, with a kind of triumph and exultation. A real quantity, infinitely less than any finite quantity, containing quantities infinitely less than itself, and so on, *in infinitum*; this is an edifice so bold and prodigious, that it is too weighty for any pretended demonstration to support, because it shocks the clearest and most natural principles of human reason.[b] But what renders the matter more extraordinary, is, that these seemingly absurd opinions are supported by a chain of reasoning, the clearest and most natural; nor is it possible for us to allow the premises without admitting the consequences. Nothing can be more convincing and satisfactory than all the conclusions concerning the properties of circles and triangles; and yet, when these are [**157**] once received, how can we deny, that the angle of contact between a circle and its tangent is infinitely less than any rectilineal angle, that as you may increase the diameter of the circle *in infinitum*, this angle of contact becomes still less, even *in infinitum*, and that the angle of contact between other curves and their tangents may be infinitely less than those between any circle and its tangent, and so on, *in infinitum?* The demonstration of these principles seems as unexceptionable as that which proves the three angles of a triangle to be equal to two right ones, though the latter opinion be natural and easy, and the former big with contradiction and

---

[b] Whatever disputes there may be about the mathematical points, we must allow that there are physical points; that is, parts of extension, which cannot be divided or lessened, either by the eye or imagination. These images, then, which are present to the fancy or senses, are absolutely indivisible, and consequently must be allowed by mathematicians to be infinitely less than any real part of extension; and yet nothing appears more certain to reason, than that an infinite number of them composes an infinite extension. How much more an infinite number of those infinitely small parts of extension, which are still supposed infinitely divisible. [Mathematical points are points as defined in geometry, i.e. indivisible points of no magnitude.]

[12] The following paradoxes concerning space and time are discussed by Bayle, *Dictionary*, 'Zeno of Elea', Notes F, G and I.

absurdity. Reason here seems to be thrown into a kind of amazement and suspense, which, without the suggestions of any sceptic, gives her a diffidence of herself, and of the ground on which she treads. She sees a full light, which illuminates certain places; but that light borders upon the most profound darkness. And between these she is so dazzled and confounded, that she scarcely can pronounce with certainty and assurance concerning any one object.

19   The absurdity of these bold determinations of the abstract sciences seems to become, if possible, still more palpable with regard to time than extension. An infinite number of real parts of time, passing in succession, and exhausted one after another, appears so evident a contradiction, that no man, one should think, whose judgment is not corrupted, instead of being improved, by the sciences, would ever be able to admit of it.

20   Yet still reason must remain restless, and unquiet, even with regard to that scepticism, to which she is driven by these seeming absurdities and contradictions. How any clear, distinct idea can contain circumstances, contradictory to itself, or to any other clear, distinct idea, is absolutely incomprehensible; and is, perhaps, as absurd as any [158] proposition, which can be formed. So that nothing can be more sceptical, or more full of doubt and hesitation, than this scepticism itself, which arises from some of the paradoxical conclusions of geometry or the science of quantity.[c]

21   The sceptical objections to *moral* evidence, or to the reasonings concerning matter of fact, are either *popular* or *philosophical*. The popular objections are derived from the natural weakness of human understanding; the contradictory opinions, which have been entertained in

---

[c] It seems to be not impossible to avoid these absurdities and contradictions, if it be admitted, that there is no such thing as abstract or general ideas, properly speaking; but that all general ideas are, in reality, particular ones, attached to a general term, which recalls, upon occasion, other particular ones, that resemble, in certain circumstances, the idea, present to the mind. Thus when the term *horse* is pronounced, we immediately figure to ourselves the idea of a black or a white animal, of a particular size or figure: But as that term is also usually applied to animals of other colours, figures and sizes, these ideas, though not actually present to the imagination, are easily recalled; and our reasoning and conclusion proceed in the same way, as if they were actually present. If this be admitted (as seems reasonable) it follows that all the ideas of quantity, upon which mathematicians reason, are nothing but particular, and such as are suggested by the senses and imagination, and consequently, cannot be infinitely divisible. It is sufficient to have dropped this hint at present, without prosecuting it any farther. It certainly concerns all lovers of science not to expose themselves to the ridicule and contempt of the ignorant by their conclusions; and this seems the readiest solution of these difficulties. [See Berkeley, *Principles*, Introduction, 6–20.]

different ages and nations; the variations of our judgment in sickness and health, youth and old age, prosperity and adversity; the perpetual contradiction of each particular man's opinions and sentiments; with many other topics of that kind.[13] It is needless to insist farther on this head. These objections are but weak. For as, in common life, we reason every moment concerning fact and existence, and cannot possibly subsist, without continually employing this species of argument, any popular objections, derived from thence, must be insufficient to destroy that evidence. The great subverter of Pyrrhonism or the excessive principles of scepticism is [159] action, and employment, and the occupations of common life. These principles may flourish and triumph in the schools; where it is, indeed, difficult, if not impossible, to refute them. But as soon as they leave the shade, and by the presence of the real objects, which actuate our passions and sentiments, are put in opposition to the more powerful principles of our nature, they vanish like smoke, and leave the most determined sceptic in the same condition as other mortals.

22   The sceptic, therefore, had better keep within his proper sphere, and display those *philosophical* objections, which arise from more profound researches. Here he seems to have ample matter of triumph; while he justly insists, that all our evidence for any matter of fact, which lies beyond the testimony of sense or memory, is derived entirely from the relation of cause and effect; that we have no other idea of this relation than that of two objects, which have been frequently *conjoined* together; that we have no argument to convince us, that objects, which have, in our experience, been frequently conjoined, will likewise, in other instances, be conjoined in the same manner; and that nothing leads us to this inference but custom or a certain instinct of our nature; which it is indeed difficult to resist, but which, like other instincts, may be fallacious and deceitful. While the sceptic insists upon these topics, he shows his force, or rather, indeed, his own and our weakness; and seems, for the time at least, to destroy all assurance and conviction. These arguments might be displayed at greater length, if any durable good or benefit to society could ever be expected to result from them.

23   For here is the chief and most confounding objection to *excessive* scepticism, that no durable good can ever result from it; while it remains in its full force and vigour. We need only ask such a sceptic, *What his meaning is? And what he proposes by all these curious researches?* He is immediately [160]

---

[13] See e.g. Sextus Empiricus, *Outlines of Scepticism*, 1.79–163.

at a loss, and knows not what to answer. A Copernican or Ptolemaic,[14] who supports each his different system of astronomy, may hope to produce a conviction, which will remain constant and durable, with his audience. A Stoic or Epicurean displays principles, which may not be durable, but which have an effect on conduct and behaviour. But a Pyrrhonian[15] cannot expect, that his philosophy will have any constant influence on the mind: Or if it had, that its influence would be beneficial to society. On the contrary, he must acknowledge, if he will acknowledge anything, that all human life must perish, were his principles universally and steadily to prevail. All discourse, all action would immediately cease; and men remain in a total lethargy, till the necessities of nature, unsatisfied, put an end to their miserable existence. It is true; so fatal an event is very little to be dreaded. Nature is always too strong for principle. And though a Pyrrhonian may throw himself or others into a momentary amazement and confusion by his profound reasonings; the first and most trivial event in life will put to flight all his doubts and scruples, and leave him the same, in every point of action and speculation, with the philosophers of every other sect, or with those who never concerned themselves in any philosophical researches. When he awakes from his dream, he will be the first to join in the laugh against himself, and to confess, that all his objections are mere amusement, and can have no other tendency than to show the whimsical condition of mankind, who must act and reason and believe; though they are not able, by their most diligent enquiry, to satisfy themselves concerning the foundation of these operations, or to remove the objections, which may be raised against them.

[161]   Part 3

24   There is, indeed, a more *mitigated* scepticism, or *Academical* philosophy,[16] which may be both durable and useful, and which may, in part,

---

[14] Followers of the two rival systems of cosmology. Ptolemy (2nd century AD) produced a modified version of Aristotle's cosmology, with the earth at the centre, and the complex motions of the planets explained by a series of epicycles. The Polish astronomer Nicolaus Copernicus (1473–1543) advanced the sun-centred system, in which the earth is one of a group of planets following elliptical orbits around the sun.

[15] A member of an ancient school of Scepticism noted for its extreme stance. The Pyrrhonians sought to resist assent to any proposition; they traced their descent from Pyrrho of Elis (c. 360–c. 270 BC).

[16] The more moderate school of ancient Scepticism that developed in Plato's Academy from about 270 BC, under the leadership of Arcesilaus (c. 315–240 BC) and Carneades (214–129 BC).

be the result of this *Pyrrhonism*, or *excessive* scepticism, when its undistinguished doubts are, in some measure, corrected by common sense and reflection. The greater part of mankind are naturally apt to be affirmative and dogmatical in their opinions; and while they see objects only on one side, and have no idea of any counterpoising argument, they throw themselves precipitately into the principles, to which they are inclined; nor have they any indulgence for those who entertain opposite sentiments. To hesitate or balance perplexes their understanding, checks their passion, and suspends their action. They are, therefore, impatient till they escape from a state, which to them is so uneasy; and they think, that they could never remove themselves far enough from it, by the violence of their affirmations and obstinacy of their belief. But could such dogmatical reasoners become sensible of the strange infirmities of human understanding, even in its most perfect state, and when most accurate and cautious in its determinations; such a reflection would naturally inspire them with more modesty and reserve, and diminish their fond opinion of themselves, and their prejudice against antagonists. The illiterate may reflect on the disposition of the learned, who, amidst all the advantages of study and reflection, are commonly still diffident in their determinations: And if any of the learned be inclined, from their natural temper, to haughtiness and obstinacy, a small tincture of Pyrrhonism might abate their pride, by showing them, that the few advantages, which they may have attained over their fellows, are but inconsiderable, if compared with the universal perplexity and confusion, which is inherent in human nature. In general, there is a degree of doubt, and caution, and [162] modesty, which, in all kinds of scrutiny and decision, ought for ever to accompany a just reasoner.

25   Another species of *mitigated* scepticism, which may be of advantage to mankind, and which may be the natural result of the Pyrrhonian doubts and scruples, is the limitation of our enquiries to such subjects as are best adapted to the narrow capacity of human understanding. The *imagination* of man is naturally sublime, delighted with whatever is remote and extraordinary, and running, without control, into the most distant parts of space and time in order to avoid the objects, which custom has rendered too familiar to it. A correct *judgment* observes a contrary method, and avoiding all distant and high enquiries, confines itself to common life, and to such subjects as fall under daily practice and experience; leaving the more sublime topics to the embellishment of poets

and orators, or to the arts of priests and politicians. To bring us to so salutary a determination, nothing can be more serviceable, than to be once thoroughly convinced of the force of the Pyrrhonian doubt, and of the impossibility, that anything, but the strong power of natural instinct, could free us from it. Those who have a propensity to philosophy, will still continue their researches; because they reflect, that, besides the immediate pleasure attending such an occupation, philosophical decisions are nothing but the reflections of common life, methodized and corrected. But they will never be tempted to go beyond common life, so long as they consider the imperfection of those faculties which they employ, their narrow reach, and their inaccurate operations. While we cannot give a satisfactory reason, why we believe, after a thousand experiments, that a stone will fall, or fire burn; can we ever satisfy ourselves concerning any determination, which we may form, with regard to the origin of worlds, and the situation of nature, from, and to eternity?

[163]   26   This narrow limitation, indeed, of our enquiries, is, in every respect, so reasonable, that it suffices to make the slightest examination into the natural powers of the human mind and to compare them with their objects, in order to recommend it to us. We shall then find what are the proper subjects of science and enquiry.

27   It seems to me, that the only objects of the abstract science or of demonstration are quantity and number, and that all attempts to extend this more perfect species of knowledge beyond these bounds are mere sophistry and illusion. As the component parts of quantity and number are entirely similar, their relations become intricate and involved; and nothing can be more curious, as well as useful, than to trace, by a variety of mediums, their equality or inequality, through their different appearances. But as all other ideas are clearly distinct and different from each other, we can never advance farther, by our utmost scrutiny, than to observe this diversity, and, by an obvious reflection, pronounce one thing not to be another. Or if there be any difficulty in these decisions, it proceeds entirely from the indeterminate meaning of words, which is corrected by juster definitions. That *the square of the hypotenuse is equal to the squares of the other two sides*, cannot be known, let the terms be ever so exactly defined, without a train of reasoning and enquiry. But to convince us of this proposition, *that where there is no property, there can be no injustice*, it is only necessary to define the terms, and explain injustice to be a violation of property. This proposition is, indeed, nothing but a more imperfect

definition.[17] It is the same case with all those pretended syllogistical reasonings,[18] which may be found in every other branch of learning, except the sciences of quantity and number; and these may safely, I think, be pronounced the only proper objects of knowledge and demonstration.

28   All other enquiries of men regard only matter of fact and [164] existence; and these are evidently incapable of demonstration. Whatever *is* may *not be*. No negation of a fact can involve a contradiction. The non-existence of any being, without exception, is as clear and distinct an idea as its existence. The proposition, which affirms it not to be, however false, is no less conceivable and intelligible, than that which affirms it to be. The case is different with the sciences, properly so called.[19] Every proposition, which is not true, is there confused and unintelligible. That the cube root of 64 is equal to the half of 10, is a false proposition, and can never be distinctly conceived. But that Caesar, or the angel Gabriel, or any being never existed, may be a false proposition, but still is perfectly conceivable, and implies no contradiction.

29   The existence, therefore, of any being can only be proved by arguments from its cause or its effect; and these arguments are founded entirely on experience. If we reason *a priori*, anything may appear able to produce anything. The falling of a pebble may, for aught we know, extinguish the sun; or the wish of a man control the planets in their orbits. It is only experience, which teaches us the nature and bounds of cause and effect, and enables us to infer the existence of one object from that of another.[d] Such is the foundation of moral reasoning, which forms the greater part of human knowledge, and is the source of all human action and behaviour.

30   Moral reasonings are either concerning particular or general facts. All deliberations in life regard the former; as also all disquisitions in history, chronology, geography, and astronomy.

---

[d] That impious maxim of the ancient philosophy, *Ex nihilo, nihil fit*, by which the creation of matter was excluded, ceases to be a maxim, according to this philosophy. Not only the will of the Supreme Being may create matter; but, for aught we know *a priori*, the will of any other being might create it, or any other cause, that the most whimsical imagination can assign. [The Latin phrase means 'out of nothing comes nothing'. The point, if not the precise phrase, occurs in Lucretius (*Nature of Things*, 1.149–58); but this 'impious maxim' is also the starting-point of many contemporary arguments for God's existence (e.g. Locke, *Essay*, 4.10.3ff; Clarke, *Demonstration*, I).]

[17] In eighteenth-century usage, 'injustice' means legal injustice, i.e. invasion of another's right or property.

[18] Cf. Locke, *Essay*, 4.17.4–8.   [19] That is, properly so called according to paragraph 27 above.

[165]   31   The sciences, which treat of general facts, are politics, natural philosophy, physic,[20] chemistry, etc., where the qualities, causes and effects of a whole species of objects are enquired into.

32   Divinity or theology, as it proves the existence of a Deity, and the immortality of souls, is composed partly of reasonings concerning particular, partly concerning general facts. It has a foundation in *reason*, so far as it is supported by experience. But its best and most solid foundation is *faith* and divine revelation.

33   Morals and criticism are not so properly objects of the understanding as of taste and sentiment. Beauty, whether moral or natural, is felt, more properly than perceived. Or if we reason concerning it, and endeavour to fix its standard, we regard a new fact, to wit, the general taste of mankind, or some such fact, which may be the object of reasoning and enquiry.

34   When we run over libraries, persuaded of these principles, what havoc must we make? If we take in our hand any volume; of divinity or school metaphysics, for instance; let us ask, *Does it contain any abstract reasoning concerning quantity or number?* No. *Does it contain any experimental reasoning concerning matter of fact and existence?* No. Commit it then to the flames: For it can contain nothing but sophistry and illusion.

[20] Medicine.

144

Other writings

A Letter from a Gentleman to his Friend in Edinburgh[1]

Sir,

I have read over the *Specimen of the Principles concerning Religion and Morality,*[2] said to be maintained in a book lately published, entitled, *A Treatise of Human Nature*; being an attempt to introduce the experimental method of reasoning into moral subjects. I have also read over what is called the *Sum of the Charge*. Which papers, as you inform me, have been industriously spread about, and were put into your hands some few days ago.

I was persuaded that the clamour of *scepticism, atheism,* etc., had been so often employed by the worst of men against the best, that it had now lost all its influence; and should never have thought of making any remarks on these *maimed excerpts*, if you had not laid your commands on me, as a piece of common justice to the author, and for undeceiving some well-meaning people, on whom it seems the enormous charge has made impression.

I shall insert the accusation at full length, and then go regularly through what is called the *Sum of the Charge*; because it is intended,

---

[1] The origins of the *Letter* are set out in the Introduction. It was edited and published by Henry Home; so, although the main thread is probably Hume's own, the details cannot all be attributed to him.
[2] The author was probably the Revd William Wishart (1692–1753), Principal of Edinburgh University, 1737–53.

I suppose, to contain the substance of the whole. I shall also take notice of the *Specimen* as I go along.

Specimen of the Principles concerning *Religion* and *Morality*, etc.

The author puts on his title-page (Vol. 1) a passage of Tacitus to this purpose: 'Rare happiness of our times, that you may think as you will, and speak as you think.'[3]

He expresses his deference to the public in these words (Advertisement): 'The approbation of the public I consider as the *greatest* reward of my labours; but am determined to regard its judgment, *whatever it be*, as my *best* instruction.'

He gives us the summary view of his philosophy,[4] 'I am confounded with that forlorn solitude, in which I am placed in my philosophy. – I have exposed my self to the enmity of all metaphysicians, logicians, mathematicians, and even theologians. – I have declared my disapprobations of their systems. – When I turn my eye inward, I find nothing but doubt and ignorance. All the world conspires to oppose and contradict me; though such is my weakness, that I feel all my opinions loosen and fall of themselves, when unsupported by the approbation of others. – Can I be sure, that, in leaving all established opinions, I am following truth? And by what criterion shall I distinguish her, even if Fortune should at last guide me on her footsteps? After the most accurate and exact of my reasonings, I can give no reason why I should assent to it, and feel nothing but a strong propensity to consider objects strongly in that view under which they appear to me. – The memory, senses, and understanding, are all of them founded on the *imagination*. – No wonder a principle so inconstant and fallacious should lead us into errors, when implicitly followed (as it must be) in all its variations. – I have already shown, that the understanding, when it acts alone, and according to its most general principles, *entirely* subverts itself, and leaves not the *lowest degree* of evidence in any proposition either in philosophy or common life. – We have no choice left, but betwixt a *false reason* and *none at all*. – Where am I, or what? From what

---

[3] Tacitus, *Histories*, I.I.

[4] The following paragraph is all excerpted from *Treatise*, 1.4.7. (In these and the following quotations, Hume's actual words in the *Treatise* are not always accurately reproduced.)

causes do I derive my existence, and to what condition shall I return? Whose favour shall I court, and whose anger must I dread? What beings surround me? On whom have I any influence, or who have any influence on me? I am confounded with all these questions, and begin to fancy myself in the most deplorable condition imaginable, environed with the deepest darkness, and utterly deprived of the use of every member and faculty. – If I must be *a fool*, as all those who reason or believe any thing certainly are, my follies shall at least be natural and agreeable. – In all the incidents of life, we ought still to preserve our scepticism: If we believe that *fire warms*, or *water refreshes*, 'tis only because it costs us *too much pains* to think otherwise; nay, if we are philosophers, *it ought only* to be on sceptical principles. – I cannot forebear having a curiosity to be acquainted with the principles of moral good and evil, etc. I am concerned for the condition of the *learned world*, which lies under such a deplorable ignorance in all these particulars. I feel an ambition arise in me of contributing to the instruction of mankind, and of acquiring *a name by my inventions and discoveries*. – Should I endeavour to banish these sentiments, I feel I should be a loser in point of pleasure; and this is the origin of my philosophy.'

Agreeable to this summary view, he tells us, 'Let us fix our attention *out of ourselves* as much as possible. – We never really advance a step *beyond ourselves*; nor can conceive any kind of existence, but these perceptions which have appeared in that narrow compass: This is the universe of the imagination, nor have we any idea but what is there produced.' – Accordingly, 'An opinion or belief may be most accurately defined, *a lively idea related or associated with a present impression*; and is more properly an act of the sensitive than of the cogitative part of our natures'. And, 'Belief in general consists in nothing but the vivacity of an idea. Again, the idea of *existence* is the very same with the idea of what we conceive to be existent. – Any idea we please to form is the idea of a being; and the idea of a being is any idea we please to form. And as to the notion of an external existence, when taken for something specifically different from our perceptions, we have shown its absurdity: And what we call a mind is nothing but a heap or collection of different perceptions united together by certain relations, and supposed, though falsely, to be endowed with a perfect simplicity.' And, 'The only existence, of which we are certain, are perceptions. When I enter most intimately into what I call *myself*, I always stumble on some particular perception or other. – I never can catch *myself* at any time without a perception, and never can observe *any thing but the perception*. – If any one think he has a different notion of himself, I must confess I can reason no longer with him. – I may venture to affirm of the rest of mankind, that they are nothing but a bundle of perceptions, which succeed each other with an inconceivable rapidity, and are in a perpetual flux and movement.' – And lest the reader should forget to apply all this to the Supreme Mind, and the existence of the first cause, he has a long disquisition concerning *causes* and *effects*, the sum of which amounts to this, that all our reasoning concerning causes and effects are derived from *nothing* but *custom*: That,'If any pretend to define a cause by saying it is something productive of another, 'tis evident he would say nothing; for what does he mean by production? That we may define a cause to be *an object precedent and contiguous to another, and where all the objects resembling the former are placed in like relations of precedence and contiguity to these objects that resemble the latter*; or, *a cause is an object precedent and contiguous to another, and so united with it, that the idea of the one determines the mind to form the idea of the other, and the impression of the one to form a more lively idea of the other.*' From these clear and plain definitions he infers, 'That all causes are of the same kind; and there is no foundation for the distinction between efficient causes, and causes *sine qua non*; or betwixt *efficient* causes and formal and material, and exemplary, and final causes: And that there is but one kind of necessity, and the common distinction betwixt moral and physical is without any foundation in nature: And that the distinction we often make betwixt power, and the exercise of it, is equally without foundation: And that the necessity of a cause to every beginning of existence, is not founded on any arguments demonstrative or intuitive: And in fine, that *any thing* may produce *any thing*; creation, annihilation, motion, reason, volition; all these may arise from one another, or from any other object we can imagine.' This curious *nostrum*[5] he often repeats. Again he tells us,'That when we talk of any being, whether of a superior or inferior nature, as endowed with a power or force proportioned to any effect, – we have really no distinct meaning, and make use only of common words, without any clear and determinate ideas. And if we have really no idea of power or efficacy in any object, or of any real connection betwixt causes and effects, 'twill be to little purpose to prove that an efficacy is necessary in all operations. We do not understand our own meaning in talking so, but ignorantly confound ideas which are entirely distinct from each other.' Again he says, 'The efficacy or energy of causes is

---

[5] A doctrine of the author's own invention.

neither placed in the causes themselves, nor in the Deity, nor in the concurrence of these two principles, but belongs entirely to the soul (*or the bundle of perceptions*) which considers the union of two or more objects in all past instances: 'Tis here that the real power of causes is placed, along with their connection and necessity. And in fine, we may observe a conjunction or a relation of cause *and effect between different perceptions*, but can never observe it between perceptions and objects.' 'Tis impossible therefore, that, from the existence or any of the qualities of the former, we can ever form any conclusion concerning the existence of the latter, or ever satisfy our reason in this particular with regard to the Supreme Being. 'Tis well known that this principle, *whatever begins to exist must have a cause of existence*, is the first step in the argument for the being of a Supreme Cause; and that, without it, 'tis impossible to go one step further in that argument. Now this maxim he is at great pains to explode, and to show, 'That it is neither intuitively nor demonstratively certain'; and he says, 'Reason can never satisfy us that the existence of any object does ever imply that of another. So that, when we pass from the impression of one to the idea and belief of another, we are not determined by reason, but by custom.' In a marginal note on the preceding page he says, 'In that proposition, *God is*, or indeed in any other which regards existence, the idea of existence is no distinct idea which we unite with that of the object, and which is capable of forming a compound idea by the union.' Concerning this principle, *That the Deity is the prime mover of the universe, who first created matter, and gave its original impulse, and likewise supports its existence, and successively bestows on it its motions*; he says, 'This opinion is certainly very curious, but it will appear superfluous to examine it in this place. – For, if the very idea be derived from an impression, the idea of a Deity proceeds from the same origin; and, if no impression implies any force or efficacy, 'tis equally impossible to discover, or even imagine, any such active principle in the Deity. – Since philosophers therefore have concluded, that matter cannot be endowed with any efficacious principle, because it is impossible to discover in it such a principle; the same course of reasoning should determine them to exclude it from the Supreme Being: Or if they esteem that opinion absurd and impious, as it really is, I shall tell them how they may avoid it, and that is, by *concluding from the very first*, that they have no adequate idea of power or efficacy in any object; since neither in body nor spirit, neither in superior nor inferior natures, are they able to discover one single instance of it.' And says he, 'We have no idea of a being endowed with any power, much less of one endowed with infinite power.'

Concerning *the immateriality of the soul* (from which the argument is taken for its natural immortality, or that it cannot perish by dissolution as the body) he says, 'We certainly may conclude that motion may be and actually is the cause of thought and perception: And no wonder, for any thing may be the cause or effect of *any thing*; which evidently gives the advantage to the materialists above their adversaries.' But yet more plainly, 'I assert', says he, 'that the doctrine of the immateriality, simplicity, and indivisibility of a thinking substance, *is a true atheism*, and will serve to justify *all* these sentiments for which Spinoza is so universally infamous.' This hideous hypothesis is almost the same with that of the immateriality of the soul, which has become so popular. And again he endeavours to prove, that all the absurdities which have been found in the systems of Spinoza, may likewise be discovered in that of the theologians: And he concludes, that 'We cannot advance one step towards the establishing the simplicity and immateriality of the soul, without preparing the way for a dangerous and irrecoverable atheism.'

The author's sentiments in morality we have in Vol. 3. He there tells us, that 'Reason has no influence on our passions and actions: Actions may be laudable or blameable, but they cannot be *reasonable* or *unreasonable*. That all beings in the universe, considered in themselves, appear entirely loose and independent of each other; 'tis only by experience we learn their influence and connection, and this influence we ought *never* to extend beyond *experience*.'

He takes great pains to prove that justice is not a natural, but an artificial virtue; and gives one pretty odd reason for it: 'We may conclude, that the laws of justice, being universal and perfectly inflexible, can never be derived from nature. I suppose (says he) a person to have lent me a sum of money, on condition that it be restored in a few days; and also suppose, that, after expiration of the term agreed on, he demands the sum: I ask, *What reason or motive have I to return the money?* Public interest is not naturally attached to the observation of the rules of justice, but is only connected with it, after an artificial convention, for the establishment of these rules. Unless we will allow that nature has established a *sophistry*, and rendered it necessary and unavoidable; we must allow that the sense of justice and injustice is not derived from nature, but arises artificially, though necessarily, from education and human conventions. Here is a proposition which I think may be regarded as certain, *That it is only from the selfishness and confined generosity of men, along with the scanty provision nature has made for his wants, that justice derives its origin.* These impressions, which give rise to this sense of justice, are not natural to the mind of man, but arise from artifice and human conventions. Without such a convention, no one would ever have dreamed that there was such a virtue as justice, or have been induced to conform his actions to it. Taking any single act, my justice may be pernicious in every respect: And 'tis only upon the supposition that others are to imitate my example, that I can be induced to embrace that virtue; since nothing but the combination can render justice advantageous, or afford me any motive to conform myself to its rules. And in general it may be affirmed, that there is no such passion in human minds, *as the love of mankind* merely as such, independent of personal qualities, of service, or of relations to ourself.'

Mr. Hobbes, who was at pains to shake loose all other natural obligations, yet found it necessary to leave, or pretended to leave, the obligation of promises or pacts; but our author strikes a bolder stroke: 'That the rule of morality (says he) which enjoins the performance of *promises*, is not natural, will sufficiently appear from these two propositions, which I proceed to prove, *viz. That a promise would not be intelligible before human conventions had established it; and that, even if it were intelligible, it would not be attended with any moral obligation.*' And he concludes, 'That promises impose no natural obligation'. And, 'I shall further observe, that since every new promise imposes a new obligation of morality upon the person who promises, and since this new obligation arises from his will, it is one of the most mysterious and incomprehensible operations that can possibly be imagined, and may even be compared to transubstantiation[6] or *holy orders*,[7] where a certain form of words, along with a certain intention, changes entirely the nature of an external object, and even of a human creature. In fine (says he) as force is supposed to invalidate all contracts, such a principle is a proof that promises have no natural obligation, and are mere artificial contrivances, for the convenience and advantage of society.'

---

[6] The Catholic doctrine that, in the sacrament of the Eucharist, the substance (but not the appearance) of the bread and wine becomes, at its consecration, the body and blood of Christ. (It is also known as the doctrine of the real presence.)
[7] The sacrament or rite of ordination as a member of the clergy.

Sum of the Charge

From the preceding Specimen it will appear, that the author maintains,

1　Universal scepticism. See his assertions where he doubts of every thing (his own existence excepted) and maintains the folly of pretending to believe any thing with certainty.[8]

2　Principles leading to downright atheism, by denying the doctrine of causes and effects, where he maintains, that the necessity of a cause to every beginning of existence is not founded on any arguments demonstrative or intuitive.[9]

3　Errors concerning the very being and existence of a God. For instance, as to that proposition, *God is*, he says (or indeed as to any other thing which regards existence) 'the idea of existence is no distinct idea which we unite with that of the object, and which is capable of forming a compound idea by union'.[10]

4　Errors concerning God's being the first cause, and prime mover of the universe: For as to this principle, that the Deity first created matter, and gave it its original impulse, and likewise supports its existence, he says, 'this opinion is certainly very curious, but it will appear superfluous to examine it in this place, etc.'[11]

5　He is chargeable with denying the immateriality of the soul, and the consequences flowing from this denial.[12]

6　With sapping the foundations of morality, by denying the natural and essential difference between right and wrong, good and evil, justice and injustice; making the difference only artificial, and to arise from human conventions and compacts.[13]

You see, *Dear Sir*, that I have concealed no part of the accusation, but have inserted the *Specimen* and *Charge*, as transmitted to me, without the smallest variation. I shall now go regularly through what is called the *Sum of the Charge*, because it is intended, I suppose, to contain the substance of the whole; and shall take notice of the *Specimen* as I go along.

　　1.　　As to the *scepticism* with which the author is charged, I must observe, that the doctrines of the Pyrrhonians or Sceptics have been regarded in all ages as principles of mere curiosity, or a kind of *jeux*

---

[8] *Treatise*, 1.4.7.　[9] *Treatise*, 1.3.3.　[10] *Treatise*, 1.3.7.　[11] *Treatise*, 1.3.14.　[12] *Treatise*, 1.4.5.
[13] *Treatise*, 3.1–2.

d'esprit,[14] without any influence on a man's steady principles or conduct in life. In reality, a philosopher who affects to doubt of the maxims of *common reason*, and even of his *senses*, declares sufficiently that he is not in earnest, and that he intends not to advance an opinion which he would recommend as standards of judgment and action. All he means by these scruples is to abate the pride of *mere human reasoners*, by showing them, that even with regard to principles which seem the clearest, and which they are necessitated from the strongest instincts of nature to embrace, they are not able to attain a full consistency and absolute certainty. *Modesty* then, and *humility*, with regard to the operations of our natural faculties, is the result of scepticism; not a universal doubt, which it is impossible for any man to support, and which the first and most trivial accident in life must immediately disconcert and destroy.

How is such a frame of mind prejudicial to piety? And must not a man be ridiculous to assert that our author denies the principles of religion, when he looks upon them as equally certain with the objects of his senses? If I be as much assured of these principles, as that this table at which I now write is before me; can any thing further be desired by the most rigorous antagonist? It is evident, that so extravagant a doubt as that which scepticism may seem to recommend, by destroying *every thing*, really affects *nothing*, and was never intended to be understood *seriously*, but was meant as a *mere* philosophical amusement, or trial of *wit* and *subtlety*.

This is a construction suggested by the very nature of the subject; but he has not been contented with that, but expressly declared it. And all those principles, cited in the *Specimen as* proofs of his scepticism, are positively renounced in a few pages afterwards, and called the effects of *philosophical melancholy* and *delusion*. These are his very words; and his accuser's overlooking them may be thought very prudent, but is a degree of unfairness which appears to me altogether astonishing.

Were authorities proper to be employed in any philosophical reasoning, I could cite you that of Socrates the wisest and most religious of the Greek philosophers, as well as Cicero among the Romans, who both of them carried their philosophical doubts to the highest degree of scepticism. All the ancient fathers, as well as our first Reformers, are copious in representing the weakness and uncertainty of *mere* human reason. And Monsieur Huet the learned Bishop of Avaranches (so celebrated for his

---

[14] Literally, a 'mind game'; a light-hearted exercise in cleverness. Cf. *Enquiry*, 12.23.

Demonstration Evangelique which contains all the great proofs of the Christian religion) wrote also a book on this very topic, wherein he endeavours to revive all the doctrines of the ancient Sceptics or Pyrrhonians.[15]

In reality, whence come all the various tribes of heretics, the Arians, Socinians and Deists,[16] but from too great a confidence in mere human reason, which they regard as the *standard* of every thing, and which they will not submit to the superior light of revelation? And can one do a more essential service to piety, than by showing them that this boasted reason of theirs, so far from accounting for the great mysteries of the Trinity and Incarnation, is not able fully to satisfy itself with regard to its own operations, and must in some measure fall into a kind of implicit faith, even in the most obvious and familiar principles?

2.   The author is charged with opinions leading to *downright atheism*, chiefly by denying this principle, *that whatever begins to exist must have a cause of existence*. To give you a notion of the extravagance of this charge, I must enter into a little detail. It is common for philosophers to distinguish the kinds of evidence into *intuitive, demonstrative, sensible*, and *moral*; by which they intend *only* to mark a difference between them, not to denote a superiority of one above another. *Moral certainty* may reach as *high* a degree of assurance as *mathematical*; and our senses are surely to be comprised amongst the clearest and most convincing of all evidences. Now, it being the author's purpose, in the pages cited in the Specimen, to examine the grounds of that proposition; he used the freedom of disputing the common opinion, that it was founded on *demonstrative* or *intuitive certainty*; but asserts, that it is supported by *moral evidence*, and is followed by a conviction of the same kind with these truths, *that all men must die*, and that *the sun will rise tomorrow*. Is this any thing like denying the truth of that proposition, which indeed *a man must have lost all common sense to doubt of*?

But, granting that he had denied it, how is this a principle that leads to atheism? It would be no difficult matter to show, that the arguments

---

[15] Pierre-Daniel Huet (1630–1721), *Traité philosophique de la foiblesse de l'esprit humain* [An Essay concerning the Weakness of the Human Understanding] (1723).

[16] Arians (after Arius (c. 250–c. 336), a priest of Alexandria) and Socinians (after Laelius Socinus (1525–62) and his nephew Faustus Socinus (1539–1604), Italian theologians) were Christian heretics who denied the divinity of Christ, and thus the doctrine of the Trinity. Deists accepted that human reason established the existence of a creator or designer of the world, but rejected appeals to revelation. They thus denied the existence of the God of the monotheistic religions: a supernatural being who cares for, and interacts with, human beings.

a posteriori from the order and course of nature, these arguments so sensible, so convincing, and so obvious, remain still in their full force; and that nothing is affected by it but the *metaphysical* argument *a priori*, which many men of learning cannot comprehend, and which many men both of piety and learning show no great value for. Bishop Tillotson has used a degree of freedom on this head, which I would not willingly allow myself; it is in his excellent sermon *concerning the wisdom of being religious*, where he says, *that the being of a God is not capable of demonstration, but of moral evidence.* I hope none will pretend that that pious prelate intended by these assertions to weaken the evidences for a divine existence, but only to distinguish accurately its species of evidence.

I say further, that even the metaphysical arguments for a Deity are not affected by a denial of the proposition above-mentioned. It is only Dr. Clarke's argument which can be supposed to be any way concerned.[17] Many other arguments of the same kind still remain; Descartes's for instance, which has always been esteemed as solid and convincing as the other. I shall add, that a great distinction ought always to be made between a man's positive and avowed opinions, and the inferences which it may please others to draw from them. Had the author really denied the truth of the foregoing proposition, (which the most superficial reader cannot think ever entered his head) still he could not properly be charged as designing to invalidate any one argument that any philosopher has employed for a *divine existence*; that is only an inference and construction of others, which he may refuse if he thinks proper.

Thus you may judge of the candour of the whole charge, when you see the assigning of *one kind of evidence* for a proposition, instead of *another*, is called denying that proposition; that the invalidating only *one kind* of argument for the divine existence is called *positive atheism*; nay, that the weakening only of *one individual argument* of that kind is called rejecting that *whole species of argument*, and the inferences of others are ascribed to the author as his real opinion.

'Tis impossible ever to satisfy a captious adversary, but it would be easy for me to convince the severest judge, that all the solid arguments for natural religion retain their full force upon the author's principles concerning causes and effects, and that there is no necessity even for altering

---

[17] Samuel Clarke argued, in *A Demonstration of the Being and Attributes of God*, that God's existence could be proved from the premise that everything that exists has a cause.

the common methods of expressing or conceiving these arguments. The author has indeed asserted, that we can judge only of the operations of causes by experience, and that, reasoning *a priori*, any thing might appear able to produce any thing. We could not know that stones would descend, or fire burn, had we not experience of these effects; and indeed, without such experience, we could not certainly infer the existence of one thing from that of another. This is no great paradox, but seems to have been the opinion of several philosophers, and seems the most obvious and familiar sentiment on that subject; but, though all inferences concerning matter of fact be thus resolved into experience, these inferences are no way weakened by such an assertion, but on the contrary will be found to acquire more force, as long as men are disposed to trust to their experience rather than to mere human reasoning. Wherever I see order, I infer from experience that *there*, there has been design and contrivance. And the same principle which leads me into this inference, when I contemplate a building, regular and beautiful in its whole frame and structure; the same principle obliges me to infer an infinitely perfect Architect, from the infinite art and contrivance which is displayed in the whole fabric of the universe. Is not this the light in which this argument hath been placed by all writers concerning natural religion?

    3.   The next proof of atheism is so unaccountable, that I know not what to make of it. Our author indeed asserts, after the present pious and learned Bishop of Cloyne,[18] that we have no *abstract* or *general ideas*, properly so speaking; and that those ideas, which are called general, are nothing but particular ideas affixed to general terms. Thus, when I think of a horse in general, I must always conceive that horse as black or white, fat or lean, etc. and can form no notion of a horse that is not of some particular colour or size.[19] In prosecution of the same topic, the author has said, that we have no general idea of existence, distinct from every particular existence. But a man must have strange sagacity, that could discover atheism in so harmless a proposition. This, in my opinion, might be justified before the University of Salamanca, or a Spanish Inquisition. I do indeed believe, that, when we assert the existence of a Deity, we do not form a general abstract idea of existence, which we unite with the idea of God, and which is capable of forming a compound idea by union; but this is the case with regard to every proposition concerning existence. So that, by this course of

[18] Bishop Berkeley.   [19] Cf. *Enquiry*, 12.20n.

reasoning, we must deny the existence of every thing, even of ourselves, of which at least even the accuser himself will admit our author is persuaded.

4.   Before answering the fourth charge, I must use the freedom to deliver a short history of a particular opinion in philosophy. When men considered the several effects and operations of nature, they were led to examine into the force or power by which they were performed; and they divided into several opinions upon this head, according as their *other* principles were more or less favourable to religion. The followers of Epicurus and Strato[20] asserted, that this force was original and inherent in matter, and, operating blindly, produced all the various effects which we behold. The Platonic and Peripatetic[21] schools, perceiving the absurdity of this proposition, ascribed the origin of all force to one primary efficient cause, who first bestowed it on matter, and successively guided it in all its operations. But all the ancient philosophers agreed, that there was a real force in matter, either original or derived; and that it was really fire which burnt, and food that nourished, when we observed any of these effects to follow upon the operations of these bodies: The Schoolmen supposed also a real power in matter, to whose operations however the continual concurrence of the Deity was requisite, as well as to the support of that existence which had been bestowed on matter, and which they considered as a perpetual creation. No one, till Descartes and Malebranche, ever entertained an opinion that matter had no force either *primary* or *secondary*, and *independent* or *concurrent*, and could not so much as properly be called an *instrument* in the hands of the Deity, to serve any of the purposes of providence. These philosophers last mentioned substituted the notion of *occasional causes*, by which it was asserted that a billiard ball did not move another by its impulse, but was only the occasion why the Deity, in pursuance of general laws, bestowed motion on the second ball.[22] But, though this opinion be very innocent, it never gained great credit, especially in England, where it was considered as too much contrary to received popular opinions, and too little supported by philosophical arguments, ever to be admitted as any thing but a *mere hypothesis*. Cudworth,[23] Locke, and Clarke

---

[20] Strato of Lampsacus (c. 340–c. 270 BC) was, like Epicurus, a philosophical materialist. He formulated a cosmology in which the universe is composed of matter which is self-organizing, and so wholly unreliant on any deities. He was thus the first philosophical atheist.

[21] Aristotelians.   [22] Malebranche, *Search after Truth*, 3.2.3.

[23] Ralph Cudworth (1617–88), the leading Cambridge Platonist philosopher. He admired Descartes and adopted some of his principles, but not the occasionalism which became a mark of the Cartesian school.

make little or no mention of it. Sir Isaac Newton (though some of his followers have taken a different turn of thinking) plainly rejects it, by substituting the hypothesis of an etherial fluid, not the immediate volition of the Deity, as the cause of attraction.[24] And, in short, this has been a dispute left entirely to the arguments of philosophers, and in which religion has never been supposed to be in the least concerned.

Now it is evidently concerning this Cartesian doctrine, of *secondary causes*, the author is treating, when he says, (in the passage referred to in the Charge) *that it was a curious opinion, but which it would appear superfluous to examine in that place.*

The topic there handled is somewhat abstract: But I believe any reader will easily perceive the truth of this assertion, and that the author is far from pretending to deny (as asserted in the Charge) God's *being the first cause and prime mover of the universe.* That the author's words could have no such meaning as they stand connected, is to me so evident, that I could pledge on this head, not only my small credit as a philosopher, but even all my pretensions to trust or belief in the common affairs of life.

V.   As to the fifth article; the author has not anywhere that I remember denied the immateriality of the soul in the common sense of the word. He only says, that that question did not admit of any distinct meaning; because we had no distinct idea of substance. This opinion may be found everywhere in Mr. Locke, as well as in Bishop Berkeley.

VI.   I come now to the last charge, which, according to the prevalent opinion of philosophers in this age, will certainly be regarded as the severest, *viz.* the author's destroying all the foundations of morality.

He has indeed denied the eternal difference of right and wrong in the sense in which Clarke and Wollaston[25] maintained them, *viz.* that the propositions of morality were of the same nature with the truths of mathematics and the abstract sciences, the objects *merely* of reason, not the *feelings* of our internal *tastes* and *sentiments*. In this opinion he concurs with all the ancient moralists, as well as with Mr. Hutcheson,[26] Professor of Moral Philosophy in the University of Glasgow, who, with others, has

---

[24] Newton posited the ether, a rarefied and elastic substance which permeated all space, and all objects within it, in order to explain gravitation and the transmission of light. See, e.g., the Correspondence with Robert Boyle and *Principia*, General Scholium (1–11, 93). Cf. *Enquiry*, 7.25n.

[25] William Wollaston (1659–1724), English rationalist philosopher. He held that all moral wrongs are violations of moral truth, and so forms of lying.

[26] See the Introduction for Hutcheson's role in the Edinburgh affair.

revived the ancient philosophy in this particular. How poor the artifice, to cite a *broken passage* of a philosophical discourse, in order to throw an odium on the author!

When the author asserts that justice is an *artificial* not a *natural virtue*, he seems sensible that he employed words that admit of an invidious construction; and therefore makes use of all proper expedients, by *definitions* and *explanations*, to prevent it. But of these his accuser takes no notice. By the *natural virtues* he plainly understands *compassion* and *generosity*, and such as we are immediately carried to by a *natural instinct*; and by the *artificial virtues* he means *justice, loyalty*, and such as require, along with a *natural instinct*, a certain reflection on the general interests of human society, and a combination with others. In the same sense, sucking is an action natural to man, and speech is artificial. But what is there in this doctrine that can be supposed in the least pernicious? Has he not expressly asserted, that justice, in another sense of the word, is so natural to man, that no society of men, and even no individual member of any society, was ever entirely devoid of all sense of it? Some persons (although without any reason, in my opinion) are displeased with Mr. Hutcheson's philosophy, in founding all the virtues so much on *instinct*, and admitting so little of *reason* and *reflection*. Those should be pleased to find that so considerable a branch of the moral duties are founded on that principle.

The author has likewise taken care in positive terms to assert, that he does not maintain that men lie under no obligation to observe contracts, independent of society; but only, that they never would have formed contracts, and even would not have understood the meaning of them, independent of society. And whereas it is observed in the Specimen, that our author offers further to prove, that, suppose a promise was intelligible before human conventions had established it, it would not be attended with any moral obligation. The most careless reader must perceive that he does not understand *moral* in such an extended sense, as to deny the obligation of promises, independent of society; feeling he not only asserts what is above represented, but likewise that the laws of justice are universal, and perfectly inflexible. It is evident, that suppose mankind, in some primitive unconnected state, should by some means come to the knowledge of the nature of those things which we call contracts and promises; that this knowledge would have laid them under no such actual obligation, if not placed in such circumstances as give rise to these contracts.

I am sorry I should be obliged to cite from my memory, and cannot mention page and chapter so accurately as the accuser. I came hither by post, and brought no books along with me, and cannot now provide myself in the country with the book referred to.[27]

This long letter, with which I have troubled you, was composed in one morning, that I might gratify your demand of an immediate answer to the heavy charge brought against your friend; and this, I hope, will excuse any inaccuracies that may have crept into it. I am indeed of opinion, that the author had better delayed the publishing of that book; not on account of any dangerous principles contained in it, but because on more mature consideration he might have rendered it much less imperfect by further corrections and revisals. I must not at the same time omit observing, that nothing can be wrote so accurately or innocently, which may not be perverted by such arts as have been employed on this occasion. No man would undertake so invidious a task as that of our author's accuser, who was not actuated by particular interests; and you know how easy it is, by broken and partial citations, to pervert any discourse, much more one of so abstract a nature, where it is difficult, or almost impossible, to justify one's self to the public. The words which have been carefully picked out from a large volume will no doubt have a dangerous aspect to careless readers; and the author, in my apprehension, cannot fully defend himself without a particular detail, which it is impossible for a careless reader to enter into. This advantage of the ground has been trusted to by his accuser, and surely never more abused than on the present occasion. But he has one advantage, I trust, which is worth a hundred of what his opposers can boast of, viz. *that of innocence*; and I hope he has also another advantage, viz. *that of favour*, if we really live in a country of freedom, where informers and inquisitors are so deservedly held in universal detestation, where liberty, at least of philosophy, is so highly valued and esteemed. I am,

Sir,

Your most obedient
humble servant.

May *8th* 1745.

---

[27] The *Treatise*: Hume wrote the *Letter* when in England, after becoming tutor to the Marquess of Annandale at Weldehall, near St Albans in Hertfordshire.

The Sceptic[1]

I have long entertained a suspicion, with regard to the decisions of philosophers upon all subjects, and found in myself a greater inclination to dispute, than assent to their conclusions. There is one mistake, to which they seem liable, almost without exception; they confine too much their principles, and make no account of that vast variety, which nature has so much affected in all her operations. When a philosopher has once laid hold of a favourite principle, which perhaps accounts for many natural effects, he extends the same principle over the whole creation, and reduces to it every phenomenon, though by the most violent and absurd reasoning. Our own mind being narrow and contracted, we cannot extend our conception to the variety and extent of nature; but imagine, that she is as much bounded in her operations, as we are in our speculation.

But if ever this infirmity of philosophers is to be suspected on any occasion, it is in their reasonings concerning human life, and the methods of attaining happiness. In that case, they are led astray, not only by the narrowness of their understandings, but by that also of their passions. Almost every one has a predominant inclination, to which his other desires and affections submit, and which governs him, though, perhaps, with

---

[1] This is one of four related essays – the others being 'The Epicurean', 'The Stoic', and 'The Platonist' – the purpose of which Hume describes as follows: 'The intention of this and the three [companion] essays is not so much to explain accurately the sentiments of the ancient sects of philosophy, as to deliver the sentiments of sects, that naturally form themselves in the world, and entertain different ideas of human life and of happiness. I have given each of them the name of the philosophical sect, to which it bears the greatest affinity.' (Footnote to 'The Epicurean', *Essays Moral, Political and Literary*.) Its content cannot therefore be simply identified with Hume's philosophical outlook. It does, however, show what Hume takes the marks of a practical Scepticism to be, and therefore also what it is that a *mitigated* Scepticism mitigates.

some intervals, through the whole course of his life. It is difficult for him to apprehend, that any thing, which appears totally indifferent to him, can ever give enjoyment to any person, or can possess charms, which altogether escape his observation. His own pursuits are always, in his account, the most engaging: The objects of his passion, the most valuable: And the road, which he pursues, the only one that leads to happiness.

But would these prejudiced reasoners reflect a moment, there are many obvious instances and arguments, sufficient to undeceive them, and make them enlarge their maxims and principles. Do they not see the vast variety of inclinations and pursuits among our species; where each man seems fully satisfied with his own course of life, and would esteem it the greatest unhappiness to be confined to that of his neighbour? Do they not feel in themselves, that what pleases at one time, displeases at another, by the change of inclination; and that it is not in their power, by their utmost efforts, to recall that taste or appetite, which formerly bestowed charms on what now appears indifferent or disagreeable? What is the meaning therefore of those general preferences of the town or country life, of a life of action or one of pleasure, of retirement or society; when besides the different inclinations of different men, every one's experience may convince him, that each of these kinds of life is agreeable in its turn, and that their variety or their judicious mixture chiefly contributes to the rendering all of them agreeable.

But shall this business be allowed to go altogether at adventures? And must a man consult only his humour and inclination, in order to determine his course of life, without employing his reason to inform him what road is preferable, and leads most surely to happiness? Is there no difference then between one man's conduct and another?

I answer, there is a great difference. One man, following his inclination, in choosing his course of life, may employ much surer means for succeeding than another, who is led by his inclination into the same course of life, and pursues the same object. *Are riches the chief object of your desires?* Acquire skill in your profession; be diligent in the exercise of it; enlarge the circle of your friends and acquaintance; avoid pleasure and expense; and never be generous, but with a view of gaining more than you could save by frugality. *Would you acquire the public esteem?* Guard equally against the extremes of arrogance and fawning. Let it appear that you set a value upon yourself, but without despising others. If you fall into either of the extremes, you either provoke men's pride by your insolence, or teach them to despise you by your timorous submission, and by the mean opinion which you seem to entertain of yourself.

These, you say, are the maxims of common prudence, and discretion; what every parent inculcates on his child, and what every man of sense pursues in the course of life, which he has chosen. – What is it then you desire more? Do you come to a philosopher as to a *cunning man*, to learn something by magic or witchcraft, beyond what can be known by common prudence and discretion? – Yes; we come to a philosopher to be instructed, how we shall choose our ends, more than the means for attaining these ends: We want to know what desire we shall gratify, what passion we shall comply with, what appetite we shall indulge. As to the rest, we trust to common sense, and the general maxims of the world for our instruction.

I am sorry then, I have pretended to be a philosopher: For I find your questions very perplexing; and am in danger, if my answer be too rigid and severe, of passing for a pedant and scholastic; if it be too easy and free, of being taken for a preacher of vice and immorality. However, to satisfy you, I shall deliver my opinion upon the matter, and shall only desire you to esteem it of as little consequence as I do myself. By that means you will neither think it worthy of your ridicule nor your anger.

If we can depend upon any principle, which we learn from philosophy, this, I think, may be considered as certain and undoubted, that there is nothing, in itself, valuable or despicable, desirable or hateful, beautiful or deformed; but that these attributes arise from the particular constitution and fabric of human sentiment and affection. What seems the most delicious food to one animal, appears loathsome to another: What affects the feeling of one with delight, produces uneasiness in another. This is confessedly the case with regard to all the bodily senses: But if we examine the matter more accurately, we shall find, that the same observation holds even where the mind concurs with the body, and mingles its sentiment with the exterior appetite.

Desire this passionate lover to give you a character of his mistress: He will tell you, that he is at a loss for words to describe her charms, and will ask you very seriously if ever you were acquainted with a goddess or an angel? If you answer that you never were: He will then say, that it is impossible for you to form a conception of such divine beauties as those which his charmer possesses; so complete a shape; such well-proportioned features; so engaging an air; such sweetness of disposition; such gaiety of humour. You can infer nothing, however, from all this discourse, but that the poor man is in love; and that the general appetite between the sexes, which nature has infused into all animals, is in him determined to a particular object by some qualities, which give him pleasure. The same divine creature, not only to a different animal, but also to a different man, appears a mere mortal being, and is beheld with the utmost indifference.

Nature has given all animals a like prejudice in favour of their offspring. As soon as the helpless infant sees the light, though in every other eye it appears a despicable and a miserable creature, it is regarded by its fond parent with the utmost affection, and is preferred to every other object, however perfect and accomplished. The passion alone, arising from the original structure and formation of human nature, bestows a value on the most insignificant object.

We may push the same observation further, and may conclude, that, even when the mind operates alone, and feeling the sentiment of blame or approbation, pronounces one object deformed and odious, another beautiful and amiable; I say, that, even in this case, those qualities are not really in the objects, but belong entirely to the sentiment of that mind which blames or praises. I grant, that it will be more difficult to make this proposition evident, and as it were, palpable,[2] to negligent thinkers; because nature is more uniform in the sentiments of the mind than in most feelings of the body, and produces a nearer resemblance in the inward than in the outward part of human kind. There is something approaching to principles in mental taste; and critics can reason and dispute more plausibly than cooks or perfumers. We may observe, however, that this uniformity among human kind, hinders not, but that there is a considerable diversity in the sentiments of beauty and worth, and that education, custom, prejudice, caprice, and humour, frequently vary our taste of this kind. You will never convince a man, who is not accustomed to Italian music, and has not an ear to follow its intricacies, that a Scotch tune is not preferable. You have not even any single argument, beyond your own taste, which you can employ in your behalf: And to your antagonist, his particular taste will always appear a more convincing argument to the contrary. If you be wise, each of you will allow, that the other may be in the right; and having many other instances of this diversity of taste, you will both confess, that beauty and worth are merely of a relative nature, and consist in an agreeable

---

[2] Perceptible by touch; plain and obvious.

sentiment, produced by an object in a particular mind, according to the peculiar structure and constitution of that mind.

By this diversity of sentiment, observable in human kind, nature has, perhaps, intended to make us sensible[3] of her authority, and let us see what surprising changes she could produce on the passions and desires of mankind, merely by the change of their inward fabric, without any alteration on the objects. The vulgar[4] may even be convinced by this argument: But men, accustomed to thinking, may draw a more convincing, at least a more general argument, from the very nature of the subject.

In the operation of reasoning, the mind does nothing but run over its objects, as they are supposed to stand in reality, without adding any thing to them, or diminishing any thing from them. If I examine the Ptolemaic and Copernican systems, I endeavour only, by my enquiries, to know the real situation of the planets; that is in other words, I endeavour to give them, in my conception, the same relations, that they bear towards each other in the heavens. To this operation of the mind, therefore, there seems to be always a real, though often an unknown standard, in the nature of things; nor is truth or falsehood variable by the various apprehensions of mankind. Though all human race should for ever conclude, that the sun moves, and the earth remains at rest, the sun stirs not an inch from his place for all these reasonings; and such conclusions are eternally false and erroneous.

But the case is not the same with the qualities of *beautiful and deformed, desirable and odious*, as with truth and falsehood. In the former case, the mind is not content with merely surveying its objects, as they stand in themselves: It also feels a sentiment of delight or uneasiness, approbation or blame, consequent to that survey; and this sentiment determines it to affix the epithet *beautiful or deformed, desirable or odious*. Now, it is evident, that this sentiment must depend upon the particular fabric or structure of the mind, which enables such particular forms to operate in such a particular manner, and produces a sympathy or conformity between the mind and its objects. Vary the structure of the mind or inward organs, the sentiment no longer follows, though the form remains the same. The sentiment being different from the object, and arising from its operation upon the organs of the mind, an alteration upon the latter must vary the effect, nor

[3] Aware.   [4] The masses.

can the same object, presented to a mind totally different, produce the same sentiment.

This conclusion every one is apt to draw of himself, without much philosophy, where the sentiment is evidently distinguishable from the object. Who is not sensible, that power, and glory, and vengeance, are not desirable of themselves, but derive all their value from the structure of human passions, which begets a desire towards such particular pursuits? But with regard to beauty, either natural or moral, the case is commonly supposed to be different. The agreeable quality is thought to lie in the object, not in the sentiment; and that merely because the sentiment is not so turbulent and violent as to distinguish itself, in an evident manner, from the perception of the object.

But a little reflection suffices to distinguish them. A man may know exactly all the circles and ellipses of the Copernican system, and all the irregular spirals of the Ptolemaic, without perceiving that the former is more beautiful than the latter. Euclid has fully explained every quality of the circle, but has not, in any proposition, said a word of its beauty. The reason is evident. Beauty is not a quality of the circle. It lies not in any part of the line *whose* parts are all equally distant from a common centre. It is only the effect, which that figure produces upon a mind, whose particular fabric or structure renders it susceptible of such sentiments. In vain would you look for it in the circle, or seek it, either by your senses, or by mathematical reasonings, in all the properties of that figure.[5]

The mathematician, who took no other pleasure in reading Virgil,[6] but that of examining Aeneas's voyage by the map, might perfectly understand the meaning of every Latin word, employed by that divine author; and consequently, might have a distinct idea of the whole narration. He would even have a more distinct idea of it, than they could attain who had not studied so exactly the geography of the poem. He knew, therefore, every thing in the poem: But he was ignorant of its beauty; because the beauty, properly speaking, lies not in the poem, but in the sentiment or taste of the reader. And where a man has no such delicacy of temper, as to make him

---

[5] This paragraph reappears in *An Enquiry concerning the Principles of Morals*, Appendix 1.14.

[6] Virgil (70–19 BC), Roman poet. The author of *The Aeneid*, the tale of Aeneas's wanderings after the fall of Troy, and his foundation of the city of Rome.

feel this sentiment, he must be ignorant of the beauty, though possessed of the science and understanding of an angel.[a]

The inference upon the whole is, that it is not from the value or worth of the object, which any person pursues, that we can determine his enjoyment, but merely from the passion with which he pursues it, and the success which he meets with in his pursuit. Objects have absolutely no worth or value in themselves. They derive their worth merely from the passion. If that be strong, and steady, and successful, the person is happy. It cannot reasonably be doubted, but a little miss, dressed in a new gown for a dancing-school ball, receives as complete enjoyment as the greatest orator, who triumphs in the splendour of his eloquence, while he governs the passions and resolutions of a numerous assembly.

All the difference, therefore, between one man and another, with regard to life, consists either in the *passion*, or in the *enjoyment*: And these differences are sufficient to produce the wide extremes of happiness and misery.

To be happy, the *passion* must neither be too violent nor too remiss. In the first case, the mind is in a perpetual hurry and tumult; in the second, it sinks into a disagreeable indolence and lethargy.

To be happy, the passion must be benign and social; not rough or fierce. The affections of the latter kind are not near so agreeable to the feeling, as those of the former. Who will compare rancour and animosity, envy and revenge, to friendship, benignity, clemency, and gratitude?

To be happy, the passion must be cheerful and gay, not gloomy and melancholy. A propensity to hope and joy is real riches: One to fear and sorrow, real poverty.

Some passions or inclinations, in the *enjoyment* of their object, are not so steady or constant as others, nor convey such durable pleasure and satisfaction. *Philosophical devotion*, for instance, like the enthusiasm of a poet, is the transitory effect of high spirits, great leisure, a fine genius, and a habit of study and contemplation: But notwithstanding all these

---

[a] Were I not afraid of appearing too philosophical, I should remind my reader of that famous doctrine, supposed to be fully proved in modern times,'That tastes and colours, and all other sensible qualities, lie not in the bodies, but merely in the senses.' The case is the same with beauty and deformity, virtue and vice. This doctrine, however, takes off no more from the reality of the latter qualities, than from that of the former; nor need it give any umbrage either to critics or moralists. Though colours were allowed to lie only in the eye, would dyers or painters ever be less regarded or esteemed? There is a sufficient uniformity in the senses and feelings of mankind, to make all these qualities the objects of art and reasoning, and to have the greatest influence on life and manners. And as it is certain, that the discovery above-mentioned in natural philosophy, makes no alteration on action and conduct; why should a like discovery in moral philosophy make any alteration?

circumstances, an abstract, invisible object, like that which *natural* religion alone presents to us, cannot long actuate the mind, or be of any moment in life. To render the passion of continuance, we must find some method of affecting the senses and imagination, and must embrace some *historical*, as well as *philosophical* account of the Divinity. Popular superstitions and observances are even found to be of use in this particular.

Though the tempers of men be very different, yet we may safely pronounce in general, that a life of pleasure cannot support itself so long as one of business, but is much more subject to satiety and disgust. The amusements, which are the most durable, have all a mixture of application and attention in them; such as gaming and hunting. And in general, business and action fill up all the great vacancies in human life.

But where the temper is the best disposed for any *enjoyment*, the object is often wanting: And in this respect, the passions, which pursue external objects, contribute not so much to happiness, as those which rest in ourselves; since we are neither so certain of attaining such objects, nor so secure in possessing them. A passion for learning is preferable, with regard to happiness, to one for riches.

Some men are possessed of great strength of mind; and even when they pursue *external* objects, are not much affected by a disappointment, but renew their application and industry with the greatest cheerfulness. Nothing contributes more to happiness than such a turn of mind.

According to this short and imperfect sketch of human life, the happiest disposition of mind is the *virtuous*; or, in other words, that which leads to action and employment, renders us sensible to the social passions, steels the heart against the assaults of fortune, reduces the affections to a just moderation, makes our own thoughts an entertainment to us, and inclines us rather to the pleasures of society and conversation, than to those of the senses. This, in the mean time, must be obvious to the most careless reasoner, that all dispositions of mind are not alike favourable to happiness, and that one passion or humour may be extremely desirable, while another is equally disagreeable. And indeed, all the difference between the conditions of life depends upon the mind; nor is there any one situation of affairs, in itself, preferable to another. Good and ill, both natural and moral, are entirely relative to human sentiment and affection. No man would ever be unhappy, could he alter his feelings.

Proteus-like,[7] he would elude all attacks, by the continual alterations of his shape and form.

But of this resource nature has, in a great measure, deprived us. The fabric and constitution of our mind no more depends on our choice, than that of our body. The generality of men have not even the smallest notion, that any alteration in this respect can ever be desirable. As a stream necessarily follows the several inclinations of the ground, on which it runs; so are the ignorant and thoughtless part of mankind actuated by their natural propensities. Such are effectually excluded from all pretensions to philosophy, and the *medicine of the mind*, so much boasted. But even upon the wise and thoughtful, nature has a prodigious influence; nor is it always in a man's power, by the utmost art and industry, to correct his temper, and attain that virtuous character, to which he aspires. The empire of philosophy extends over a few; and with regard to these too, her authority is very weak and limited. Men may well be sensible of the value of virtue, and may desire to attain it; but it is not always certain, that they will be successful in their wishes.

Whoever considers, without prejudice, the course of human actions, will find, that mankind are almost entirely guided by constitution and temper, and that general maxims have little influence, but so far as they affect our taste or sentiment. If a man have a lively sense of honour and virtue, with moderate passions, his conduct will always be conformable to the rules of morality; or if he depart from them, his return will be easy and expeditious. On the other hand, where one is born of so perverse a frame of mind, of so callous and insensible a disposition, as to have no relish for virtue and humanity, no sympathy with his fellow-creatures, no desire of esteem and applause; such a one must be allowed entirely incurable, nor is there any remedy in philosophy. He reaps no satisfaction but from low and sensual objects, or from the indulgence of malignant passions: He feels no remorse to control his vicious inclinations: He has not even that sense or taste, which is requisite to make him desire a better character: For my part, I know not how I should address myself to such a one, or by what arguments I should endeavour to reform him. Should I tell him of the inward satisfaction which results from laudable and humane actions, the delicate pleasure of disinterested love and friendship, the lasting enjoyments of a

---

[7] In Greek mythology, Proteus is a sea god with the power of prophecy who assumes different shapes to avoid answering questions.

good name and an established character, he might still reply, that these were, perhaps, pleasures to such as were susceptible of them; but that, for his part, he finds himself of a quite different turn and disposition. I must repeat it; my philosophy affords no remedy in such a case, nor could I do any thing but lament this person's unhappy condition. But then I ask, If any other philosophy can afford a remedy; or if it be possible, by any system, to render all mankind virtuous, however perverse may be their natural frame of mind? Experience will soon convince us of the contrary; and I will venture to affirm, that, perhaps, the chief benefit, which results from philosophy, arises in an indirect manner, and proceeds more from its secret, insensible influence, than from its immediate application.

It is certain, that a serious attention to the sciences and liberal arts softens and humanizes the temper, and cherishes those fine emotions, in which true virtue and honour consists. It rarely, very rarely happens, that a man of taste and learning is not, at least, an honest man, whatever frailties may attend him. The bent of his mind to speculative studies must mortify[8] in him the passions of interest and ambition, and must, at the same time, give him a greater sensibility of all the decencies and duties of life. He feels more fully a moral distinction in characters and manners; nor is his sense of this kind diminished, but, on the contrary, it is much increased, by speculation.

Besides such insensible changes upon the temper and disposition, it is highly probable, that others may be produced by study and application. The prodigious effects of education may convince us, that the mind is not altogether stubborn and inflexible, but will admit of many alterations from its original make and structure. Let a man propose to himself the model of a character, which he approves: Let him be well acquainted with those particulars, in which his own character deviates from this model: Let him keep a constant watch over himself, and bend his mind, by a continual effort, from the vices, towards the virtues; and I doubt not but, in time, he will find, in his temper, an alteration for the better.

Habit is another powerful means of reforming the mind, and implanting in it good dispositions and inclinations. A man, who continues in a course of sobriety and temperance, will hate riot and disorder: If he engage in business or study, indolence will seem a punishment to him: If he constrain himself to practise beneficence and affability, he will soon abhor all

---

[8] To subdue or overcome bodily desires.

instances of pride and violence. Where one is thoroughly convinced that the virtuous course of life is preferable; if he have but resolution enough, for some time, to impose a violence on himself; his reformation need not be despaired of. The misfortune is, that this conviction and this resolution never can have place, unless a man be, before-hand, tolerably virtuous.

Here then is the chief triumph of art and philosophy: It insensibly refines the temper, and it points out to us those dispositions which we should endeavour to attain, by a constant *bent* of mind, and by repeated *habit*. Beyond this I cannot acknowledge it to have great influence; and I must entertain doubts concerning all those exhortations and consolations, which are in such vogue among speculative reasoners.

We have already observed, that no objects are, in themselves, desirable or odious, valuable or despicable; but that objects acquire these qualities from the particular character and constitution of the mind, which surveys them. To diminish therefore, or augment any person's value for an object, to excite or moderate his passions, there are no direct arguments or reasons, which can be employed with any force or influence. The catching of flies, like Domitian, if it give more pleasure, is preferable to the hunting of wild beasts, like William Rufus, or conquering of kingdoms, like Alexander.[9]

But though the value of every object can be determined only by the sentiment or passion of every individual, we may observe, that the passion, in pronouncing its verdict, considers not the object simply, as it is in itself, but surveys it with all the circumstances, which attend it. A man transported with joy, on account of his possessing a diamond, confines not his view to the glistering stone before him: He also considers its rarity, and thence chiefly arises his pleasure and exultation. Here therefore a philosopher may step in, and suggest particular views, and considerations, and circumstances, which otherwise would have escaped us; and, by that means, he may either moderate or excite any particular passion.

It may seem unreasonable absolutely to deny the authority of philosophy in this respect: But it must be confessed, that there lies this strong presumption against it, that, if these views be natural and obvious, they would

---

[9] Domitian (AD 51–96, Roman emperor 81–96) would spend hours each day doing nothing but catching flies and stabbing them with his knife (Suetonius, *Lives of the Caesars*, 'Domitian', 3). William Rufus (c. 1060–1100, William II of England, 1087–1100) devoted himself to hunting. He was killed by a stray arrow during a hunt. Alexander the Great (356–323 BC, King of Macedon 336–323) devoted his kingship to military adventure, conquering territory from Greece east to India.

have occurred of themselves, without the assistance of philosophy; if they be not natural, they never can have any influence on the affections. *These are of a very delicate nature, and cannot be forced or constrained by the utmost art or industry.* A consideration, which we seek for on purpose, which we enter into with difficulty, which we cannot retain without care and attention, will never produce those genuine and durable movements of passion, which are the result of nature, and the constitution of the mind. A man may as well pretend to cure himself of love, by viewing his mistress through the *artificial* medium of a microscope or prospect,[10] and beholding there the coarseness of her skin, and monstrous disproportion of her features, as hope to excite or moderate any passion by the *artificial* arguments of a Seneca or an Epictetus.[11] The remembrance of the natural aspect and situation of the object, will, in both cases, still recur upon him. The reflections of philosophy are too subtle and distant to take place in common life, or eradicate any affection. The air is too fine to breathe in, where it is above the winds and clouds of the atmosphere.

Another defect of those refined reflections, which philosophy suggests to us, is, that commonly they cannot diminish or extinguish our vicious passions, without diminishing or extinguishing such as are virtuous, and rendering the mind totally indifferent and inactive. They are, for the most part, general, and are applicable to all our affections. In vain do we hope to direct their influence only to one side. If by incessant study and meditation we have rendered them intimate and present to us, they will operate throughout, and spread an universal insensibility over the mind. When we destroy the nerves, we extinguish the sense of pleasure, together with that of pain, in the human body.

It will be easy, by one glance of the eye, to find one or other of these defects in most of those philosophical reflections, so much celebrated both in ancient and modern times. *Let not the injuries or violence of men*, say the philosophers,[b] *ever discompose you by anger or hatred. Would you be angry at the ape for its malice, or the tiger for its ferocity?* This reflection leads us into a bad opinion of human nature, and must extinguish the social affections. It tends also to prevent all remorse for a man's own crimes; when he considers, that vice is as natural to mankind, as the particular instincts to brute creatures.

[b] Plut. *De ira cohibenda*. [Plutarch, 'On the Control of Anger', *Moralia*.]
[10] Telescope or magnifying lens.
[11] Seneca (c. 4 BC–AD 65) and Epictetus (AD c. 55–c. 135) were both Stoic philosophers.

All ills arise from the order of the universe, which is absolutely perfect. Would you wish to disturb so divine an order for the sake of your own particular interest? What if the ills I suffer arise from malice or oppression? *But the vices and imperfections of men are also comprehended in the order of the universe:*

> *If plagues and earthquakes break not heaven's design,*
> *Why then a Borgia or a Catiline?*[12]

Let this be allowed; and my own vices will also be a part of the same order.

To one who said, that none were happy, who were not above opinion, a Spartan replied, *then none are happy but knaves and robbers.*[c]

Man is born to be miserable; and is he surprised at any particular misfortune? And can he give way to sorrow and lamentation upon account of any disaster? Yes: He very reasonably laments, that he should be born to be miserable. Your consolation presents a hundred ills for one, of which you pretend to ease him.

You should always have before your eyes death, disease, poverty, blindness, exile, calumny, and infamy, as ills which are incident to human nature. If any one of these ills falls to your lot, you will bear it the better, when you have reckoned upon it. I answer, if we confine ourselves to a general and distant reflection on the ills of human life, *that* can have no effect to prepare us for them. If by close and intense meditation we render them present and intimate to us, *that* is the true secret for poisoning all our pleasures, and rendering us perpetually miserable.

Your sorrow is fruitless, and will not change the course of destiny. Very true: And for that very reason I am sorry.

Cicero's consolation for deafness is somewhat curious. *How many languages are there*, says he, *which you do not understand? The* Punic, Spanish, Gallic, Egyptian, etc. *With regard to all these, you are as if you were deaf, yet you are indifferent about the matter. Is it then so great a misfortune to be deaf to one language more?*[d]

I like better the repartee of Antipater the Cyrenaic, when some women were condoling with him for his blindness: *What!* says he, *Do you think there are no pleasures in the dark?*[13]

[c] Plut. *Lacon. Apophtheg.* [Plutarch, 'Spartan Sayings', *Moralia.*]
[d] Tusc. *Quest.* lib. v. [Cicero, *Tusculan Disputations*, 5.40.]
[12] Pope, *An Essay on Man*, 1.155–6. The Italian Renaissance family of the Borgias were masters of political intrigue and ruthlessness. If Pope has a particular Borgia in mind, it would probably be Cesare Borgia (1475–1507), whose career was treated as an object lesson by Machiavelli (*The Prince*, 7). Catiline (c. 108–62 BC), a Roman nobleman and conspirator who planned an unsuccessful uprising in 63 BC.
[13] *Tusculan Disputations*, 5.38.

Nothing can be more destructive, says Fontenelle,[14] *to ambition, and the passion for conquest, than the true system of astronomy. What a poor thing is even the whole globe in comparison of the infinite extent of nature?* This consideration is evidently too distant ever to have any effect. Or, if it had any, would it not destroy patriotism as well as ambition? The same gallant author adds with some reason, that the bright eyes of the ladies are the only objects, which lose nothing of their lustre or value from the most extensive views of astronomy, but stand proof against every system. Would philosophers advise us to limit our affection to them?

Exile, says Plutarch to a friend in banishment, *is no evil: Mathematicians tell us, that the whole earth is but a point, compared to the heavens. To change one's country then is little more than to remove from one street to another. Man is not a plant, rooted to a certain spot of earth: All soils and all climates are alike suited to him.*[e] These topics are admirable, could they fall only into the hands of banished persons. But what if they come also to the knowledge of those who are employed in public affairs, and destroy all their attachment to their native country? Or will they operate like the quack's medicine, which is equally good for a diabetes and a dropsy?[15]

It is certain, were a superior being thrust into a human body, that the whole of life would to him appear so mean, contemptible, and puerile,[16] that he never could be induced to take part in any thing, and would scarcely give attention to what passes around him. To engage him to such a condescension as to play even the part of a Philip[17] with zeal and alacrity, would be much more difficult, than to constrain the same Philip, after having been a king and a conqueror during fifty years, to mend old shoes with proper care and attention; the occupation which Lucian assigns him in the infernal regions.[18] Now all the same topics of disdain towards human affairs, which could operate on this supposed being, occur also to a philosopher; but being, in some measure, disproportioned to human capacity, and not being fortified by the experience of any thing better, they make not a full impression on him. He sees, but he feels not sufficiently their truth; and is always a sublime philosopher, when he needs not; that

---

[e] *De exilio.* [Plutarch, 'On Exile', *Moralia.*]
[14] Bernard le Bouvier de Fontenelle (1657–1757), *Conversations on the Plurality of Worlds* (1686).
[15] An excess of watery fluid in cavities and tissues of the body.   [16] Childish or trivial.
[17] Philip II of Macedon (382–336 BC), conqueror of Greece and father of Alexander the Great.
[18] Lucian (AD c. 120–c. 180), *Menippus, or the Descent into Hades*, 17.

is, as long as nothing disturbs him, or rouses his affections. While others play, he wonders at their keenness and ardour; but he no sooner puts in his own stake, than he is commonly transported with the same passions, that he had so much condemned, while he remained a simple spectator.

There are two considerations chiefly, to be met with in books of philosophy, from which any important effect is to be expected, and that because these considerations are drawn from common life, and occur upon the most superficial view of human affairs. When we reflect on the shortness and uncertainty of life, how despicable seem all our pursuits of happiness? And even, if we would extend our concern beyond our own life, how frivolous appear our most enlarged and most generous projects; when we consider the incessant changes and revolutions of human affairs, by which laws and learning, books and governments are hurried away by time, as by a rapid stream, and are lost in the immense ocean of matter? Such a reflection certainly tends to mortify all our passions: But does it not thereby counterwork the artifice of nature, who has happily deceived us into an opinion, that human life is of some importance? And may not such a reflection be employed with success by voluptuous reasoners,[19] in order to lead us, from the paths of action and virtue, into the flowery fields of indolence and pleasure?

We are informed by Thucydides,[20] that, during the famous plague of Athens, when death seemed present to every one, a dissolute mirth and gaiety prevailed among the people, who exhorted one another to make the most of life as long as it endured. The same observation is made by Boccace[21] with regard to the plague of Florence. A like principle makes soldiers, during war, be more addicted to riot and expense, than any other race of men. Present pleasure is always of importance; and whatever diminishes the importance of all other objects must bestow on it an additional influence and value.

The *second* philosophical consideration, which may often have an influence on the affections, is derived from a comparison of our own condition with the condition of others. This comparison we are continually making, even in common life; but the misfortune is, that we are rather apt to compare our situation with that of our superiors, than with that of our inferiors. A philosopher corrects this natural infirmity, by turning his view to

---

[19] Those whose thinking is swayed by considerations of luxury or sensual pleasure.
[20] Thucydides (c. 455–c. 400 BC), *The Peloponnesian War*, 2.53.
[21] Giovanni Boccaccio (1313–75), *Decameron*, Introduction.

the other side, in order to render himself easy in the situation, to which fortune has confined him. There are few people, who are not susceptible of some consolation from this reflection, though, to a very good-natured man, the view of human miseries should rather produce sorrow than comfort, and add, to his lamentations for his own misfortunes, a deep compassion for those of others. Such is the imperfection, even of the best of these philosophical topics of consolation.^f

---

^f The Sceptic, perhaps, carries the matter too far, when he limits all philosophical topics and reflections to these two. There seem to be others, whose truth is undeniable, and whose natural tendency is to tranquillize and soften all the passions. Philosophy greedily seizes these, studies them, weighs them, commits them to the memory, and familiarizes them to the mind: And their influence on tempers, which are thoughtful, gentle, and moderate, may be considerable. But what is their influence, you will say, if the temper be antecedently disposed after the same manner as that to which they pretend to form it? They may, at least, fortify that temper, and furnish it with views, by which it may entertain and nourish itself. Here are a few examples of such philosophical reflections.

1. Is it not certain, that every condition has concealed ills? Then why envy any body?
2. Every one has known ills; and there is a compensation throughout. Why not be contented with the present?
3. Custom deadens the sense both of the good and the ill, and levels every thing.
4. Health and humour all. The rest of little consequence, except these be affected.
5. How many other good things have I? Then why be vexed for one ill?
6. How many are happy in the condition of which I complain? How many envy me?
7. Every good must be paid for: Fortune by labour, favour by flattery. Would I keep the price, yet have the commodity?
8. Expect not too great happiness in life. Human nature admits it not.
9. Propose not a happiness too complicated. But does that depend on me? Yes: The first choice does. Life is like a game: One may choose the game: And passion, by degrees, seizes the proper object.
10. Anticipate by your hopes and fancy future consolation, which time infallibly brings to every affliction.
11. I desire to be rich. Why? That I may possess many fine objects; houses, gardens, equipage, etc. How many fine objects does nature offer to every one without expense? If enjoyed, sufficient. If not: See the effect of custom or of temper, which would soon take off the relish of the riches.
12. I desire fame. Let this occur: If I act well, I shall have the esteem of all my acquaintance. And what is all the rest to me?

These reflections are so obvious, that it is a wonder they occur not to every man: So convincing, that it is a wonder they persuade not every man. But perhaps they do occur to and persuade most men; when they consider human life, by a general and calm survey: But where any real, affecting incident happens; when passion is awakened, fancy agitated, example draws, and counsel urges; the philosopher is lost in the man, and he seeks in vain for that persuasion which before seemed so firm and unshaken. What remedy for this inconvenience? Assist yourself by a frequent perusal of the entertaining moralists: Have recourse to the learning of Plutarch, the imagination of Lucian, the eloquence of Cicero, the wit of Seneca, the gaiety of Montaigne, the sublimity of Shaftesbury. Moral precepts, so couched, strike deep, and fortify the mind against the illusions of passion. But trust not altogether to external aid: By habit and study acquire that philosophical temper which both gives force to reflection, and by rendering a great part of your happiness independent, takes off the edge from all disorderly passions, and tranquillizes the mind. Despise not these helps; but confide not too much in them neither; unless nature has been favourable in the temper, with which she has endowed you.

I shall conclude this subject with observing, that, though virtue be undoubtedly the best choice, when it is attainable; yet such is the disorder and confusion of human affairs, that no perfect or regular distribution of happiness and misery is ever, in this life, to be expected. Not only the goods of fortune, and the endowments of the body (both of which are important), not only these advantages, I say, are unequally divided between the virtuous and vicious, but even the mind itself partakes, in some degree, of this disorder, and the most worthy character, by the very constitution of the passions, enjoys not always the highest felicity.

It is observable, that, though every bodily pain proceeds from some disorder in the part or organ, yet the pain is not always proportioned to the disorder; but is greater or less, according to the greater or less sensibility of the part, upon which the noxious humours exert their influence. A *toothache* produces more violent convulsions of pain than a *phthisis*[22] or a *dropsy*. In like manner, with regard to the economy of the mind, we may observe, that all vice is indeed pernicious; yet the disturbance or pain is not measured out by nature with exact proportion to the degree of vice, nor is the man of highest virtue, even abstracting from external accidents, always the most happy. A gloomy and melancholy disposition is certainly, *to our sentiments*, a vice or imperfection; but as it may be accompanied with great sense of honour and great integrity, it may be found in very worthy characters; though it is sufficient alone to embitter life, and render the person affected with it completely miserable. On the other hand, a selfish villain may possess a spring and alacrity of temper, a certain *gaiety of heart*, which is indeed a good quality, but which is rewarded much beyond its merit, and when attended with good fortune, will compensate for the uneasiness and remorse arising from all the other vices.

I shall add, as an observation to the same purpose, that, if a man be liable to a vice or imperfection, it may often happen, that a good quality, which he possesses along with it, will render him more miserable, than if he were completely vicious. A person of such imbecility[23] of temper as to be easily broken by affliction, is more unhappy for being endowed with a generous and friendly disposition, which gives him a lively concern for others, and exposes him the more to fortune and accidents. A sense of shame, in an imperfect character, is certainly a virtue; but produces great

---

[22] Pulmonary tuberculosis or a similar progressive wasting disease.
[23] Weakness. The modern sense of the term – stupidity – dates from the nineteenth century.

uneasiness and remorse, from which the abandoned villain is entirely free. A very amorous complexion,[24] with a heart incapable of friendship, is happier than the same excess in love, with a generosity of temper, which transports a man beyond himself, and renders him a total slave to the object of his passion.

In a word, human life is more governed by fortune than by reason; is to be regarded more as a dull pastime than as a serious occupation; and is more influenced by particular humour, than by general principles. Shall we engage ourselves in it with passion and anxiety? It is not worthy of so much concern. Shall we be indifferent about what happens? We lose all the pleasure of the game by our phlegm[25] and carelessness. While we are reasoning concerning life, life is gone; and death, though *perhaps* they receive him differently, yet treats alike the fool and the philosopher. To reduce life to exact rule and method, is commonly a painful, oft a fruitless occupation: And is it not also a proof, that we overvalue the prize for which we contend? Even to reason so carefully concerning it, and to fix with accuracy its just idea, would be overvaluing it, were it not that, to some tempers, this occupation is one of the most amusing, in which life could possibly be employed.

[24] Temperament or character.
[25] In medieval science, one of the four bodily humours; a calm, stolid or apathetic temperament.

Of Suicide

One considerable advantage, that arises from philosophy, consists in the sovereign antidote, which it affords to superstition and false religion. All other remedies against that pestilent distemper are vain, or, at least, uncertain. Plain good sense, and the practice of the world, which alone serve most purposes of life, are here found ineffectual: History, as well as daily experience, affords instances of men, endowed with the strongest capacity for business and affairs, who have all their lives crouched under slavery to the grossest superstition. Even gaiety and sweetness of temper, which infuse a balm into every other wound, afford no remedy to so virulent a poison; as we may particularly observe of the fair sex, who, though commonly possessed of these rich presents of nature, feel many of their joys blasted by this importunate intruder. But when sound philosophy has once gained possession of the mind, superstition is effectually excluded; and one may safely affirm, that her triumph over this enemy is more complete than over most of the vices and imperfections, incident to human nature. Love or anger, ambition or avarice, have their root in the temper and affections, which the soundest reason is scarce ever able fully to correct. But superstition, being founded on false opinion, must immediately vanish, when true philosophy has inspired juster sentiments of superior powers. The contest is here more equal between the distemper and the medicine: And nothing can hinder the latter from proving effectual, but its being false and sophisticated.[1]

It will here be superfluous to magnify the merits of philosophy, by displaying the pernicious tendency of that vice, of which it cures the human

[1] Misleading or corrupted; the effect of sophistry.

mind. The superstitious man, says *Tully*,[a] is miserable in every scene, in every incident of life. Even sleep itself, which banishes all other cares of unhappy mortals, affords to him matter of new terror; while he examines his dreams, and finds in those visions of the night, prognostications of future calamities. I may add, that, though death alone can put a full period to his misery, he dares not fly to this refuge, but still prolongs a miserable existence, from a vain fear, lest he offend his maker, by using the power, with which that beneficent being has endowed him. The presents of God and Nature are ravished from us by this cruel enemy; and notwithstanding that one step would remove us from the regions of pain and sorrow, her menaces still chain us down to a hated being, which she herself chiefly contributes to render miserable.

It is observed of such as have been reduced by the calamities of life to the necessity of employing this fatal remedy, that, if the unseasonable care of their friends deprive them of that species of death, which they proposed to themselves, they seldom venture upon any other, or can summon up so much resolution, a second time, as to execute their purpose. So great is our horror of death, that when it presents itself under any form, besides that to which a man has endeavoured to reconcile his imagination, it acquires new terrors, and overcomes his feeble courage. But when the menaces of superstition are joined to this natural timidity, no wonder it quite deprives men of all power over their lives; since even many pleasures and enjoyments, to which we are carried by a strong propensity, are torn from us by this inhuman tyrant. Let us here endeavour to restore men to their native liberty, by examining all the common arguments against suicide, and showing, that that action may be free from every imputation of guilt or blame; according to the sentiments of all the ancient philosophers.

If suicide be criminal, it must be a transgression of our duty, either to God, our neighbour, or ourselves.

To prove, that suicide is no transgression of our duty to God, the following considerations may perhaps suffice. In order to govern the material world, the almighty Creator has established general and immutable laws, by which all bodies, from the greatest planet to the smallest particle of matter, are maintained in their proper sphere and function. To govern the animal world, he has endowed all living creatures with bodily and mental powers; with senses, passions, appetites, memory, and judgment; by

---

[a] *De Divin.* lib. ii. [Cicero, *On Divination*, 2.72.]

which they are impelled or regulated in that course of life, to which they are destined. These two distinct principles of the material and animal world continually encroach upon each other, and mutually retard or forward each other's operation. The powers of men and of all other animals are restrained and directed by the nature and qualities of the surrounding bodies; and the modifications and actions of these bodies are incessantly altered by the operation of all animals. Man is stopped by rivers in his passage over the surface of the earth; and rivers, when properly directed, lend their force to the motion of machines, which serve to the use of man. But though the provinces of the material and animal powers are not kept entirely separate, there result from thence no discord or disorder in the Creation: On the contrary, from the mixture, union, and contrast of all the various powers of inanimate bodies and living creatures, arises that surprising harmony and proportion, which affords the surest argument of supreme wisdom.

The Providence of the Deity appears not immediately in any operation, but governs every thing by those general and immutable laws, which have been established from the beginning of time. All events, in one sense, may be pronounced the action of the Almighty: They all proceed from those powers, with which he has endowed his creatures. A house, which falls by its own weight, is not brought to ruin by his Providence more than one destroyed by the hands of men; nor are the human faculties less his workmanship than the laws of motion and gravitation. When the passions play, when the judgment dictates, when the limbs obey; this is all the operation of God; and upon these animate principles, as well as upon the inanimate, has he established the government of the universe.

Every event is alike important in the eyes of that infinite being, who takes in, at one glance, the most distant regions of space and remotest periods of time. There is no one event, however important to us, which he has exempted from the general laws that govern the universe, or which he has peculiarly reserved for his own immediate action and operation. The revolutions of states and empires depend upon the smallest caprice or passion of single men; and the lives of men are shortened or extended by the smallest accident of air or diet, sunshine or tempest. Nature still continues her progress and operation; and if general laws be ever broken by particular volitions of the Deity, 'tis after a manner which entirely escapes human observation. As on the one hand, the elements and other inanimate parts of the Creation carry on their action without regard to the particular interest and situation of men; so men are entrusted to their own judgment and discretion in the various shocks of matter, and may employ every faculty, with which they are endowed, in order to provide for their ease, happiness, or preservation.

What is the meaning, then, of that principle, that a man, who, tired of life, and hunted by pain and misery, bravely overcomes all the natural terrors of death, and makes his escape from this cruel scene; that such a man, I say, has incurred the indignation of his Creator, by encroaching on the office of divine Providence, and disturbing the order of the universe? Shall we assert, that the Almighty has reserved to himself, in any peculiar manner, the disposal of the lives of men, and has not submitted that event, in common with others, to the general laws, by which the universe is governed? This is plainly false. The lives of men depend upon the same laws as the lives of all other animals; and these are subjected to the general laws of matter and motion. The fall of a tower or the infusion of a poison will destroy a man equally with the meanest creature: An inundation sweeps away every thing, without distinction, that comes within the reach of its fury. Since therefore the lives of men are for ever dependent on the general laws of matter and motion; is a man's disposing of his life criminal, because, in every case, it is criminal to encroach upon these laws, or disturb their operation? But this seems absurd. All animals are entrusted to their own prudence and skill for their conduct in the world, and have full authority, as far as their power extends, to alter all the operations of nature. Without the exercise of this authority, they could not subsist a moment. Every action, every motion of a man innovates in the order of some parts of matter, and diverts, from their ordinary course, the general laws of motion. Putting together, therefore, these conclusions, we find, *that* human life depends upon the general laws of matter and motion, and *that* 'tis no encroachment on the office of Providence to disturb or alter these general laws. Has not every one, of consequence, the free disposal of his own life? And may he not lawfully employ that power with which nature has endowed him?

In order to destroy the evidence of this conclusion, we must show a reason, why this particular case is excepted. Is it because human life is of so great importance, that it is a presumption for human prudence to dispose of it? But the life of man is of no greater importance to the universe than that of an oyster. And were it of ever so great importance, the order of nature has actually submitted it to human prudence, and reduced us to a necessity, in every incident, of determining concerning it.

Were the disposal of human life so much reserved as the peculiar province of the Almighty that it were an encroachment on his right for men to dispose of their own lives; it would be equally criminal to act for the preservation of life as for its destruction. If I turn aside a stone, which is falling upon my head, I disturb the course of nature, and I invade the peculiar province of the Almighty, by lengthening out my life, beyond the period, which, by the general laws of matter and motion, he had assigned to it.

A hair, a fly, an insect is able to destroy this mighty being, whose life is of such importance. Is it an absurdity to suppose, that human prudence may lawfully dispose of what depends on such insignificant causes?

It would be no crime in me to divert the *Nile* or *Danube* from its course, were I able to effect such purposes. Where then is the crime of turning a few ounces of blood from their natural channels!

Do you imagine that I repine[2] at Providence, or curse my creation, because I go out of life, and put a period to a being, which, were it to continue, would render me miserable? Far be such sentiments from me. I am only convinced of a matter of fact, which you yourself acknowledge possible, that human life may be unhappy, and that my existence, if farther prolonged, would become uneligible. But I thank Providence, both for the good, which I have already enjoyed, and for the power, with which I am endowed, of escaping the ill that threatens me.[b] To you it belongs to repine at Providence, who foolishly imagine that you have no such power, and who must still prolong a hated being, though loaded with pain and sickness, with shame and poverty.

Do you not teach, that when any ill befalls me, though by the malice of my enemies, I ought to be resigned to Providence; and that the actions of men are the operations of the Almighty as much as the actions of inanimate beings? When I fall upon my own sword, therefore, I receive my death equally from the hands of the Deity, as if it had proceeded from a lion, a precipice, or a fever.

The submission, which you require to Providence, in every calamity, that befalls me, excludes not human skill and industry; if possibly, by their

[b] *Agamus Deo gratias, quod nemo in vita teneri potest.* Seneca, *Epist.* xii. ['And let us thank God that no man can be kept in life.' Seneca, *Epistles*, 'On Old Age' (12.10).]
[2] Feel or express discontent.

means, I can avoid or escape the calamity. And why may I not employ one remedy as well as another?

If my life be not my own, it were criminal for me to put it in danger, as well as to dispose of it: Nor could one man deserve the appellation of *hero*, whom glory or friendship transports into the greatest dangers, and another merit the reproach of *wretch* or *miscreant*, who puts a period to his life, from the same or like motives.

There is no being, which possesses any power or faculty, that it receives not from its Creator; nor is there any one, which, by ever so irregular an action, can encroach upon the plan of his Providence, or disorder the universe. Its operations are his work equally with that chain of events, which it invades; and which ever principle prevails, we may, for that very reason, conclude it to be most favoured by him. Be it animate or inanimate, rational or irrational, 'tis all a case: Its power is still derived from the supreme Creator, and is alike comprehended in the order of his Providence. When the horror of pain prevails over the love of life: When a voluntary action anticipates the effect of blind causes; it is only in consequence of those powers and principles, which he has implanted in his creatures. Divine Providence is still inviolate, and placed far beyond the reach of human injuries.

It is impious, says the old Roman superstition,[c] to divert rivers from their course, or invade the prerogatives of nature. 'Tis impious, says the French superstition, to inoculate for the small-pox, or usurp the business of Providence, by voluntarily producing distempers and maladies. 'Tis impious, says the modern European superstition, to put a period to our own life, and thereby rebel against our Creator. And why not impious, say I, to build houses, cultivate the ground, and sail upon the ocean? In all these actions, we employ our powers of mind and body to produce some innovation in the course of nature; and in none of them do we any more. They are all of them, therefore, equally innocent or equally criminal.

But you are placed by Providence, like a sentinel, in a particular station; and when you desert it without being recalled, you are guilty of rebellion against your Almighty Sovereign, and have incurred his displeasure. I ask, why do you conclude, that Providence has placed me in this station? For my part, I find, that I owe my birth to a long chain of causes, of which many and even the principal, depended upon voluntary actions of men. *But Providence guided*

---

[c] *Tacit. Ann.* lib. i. [Tacitus, *Annals*, 1.79.]

all these causes, and nothing happens in the universe without its consent and co-operation. If so, then neither does my death, however voluntary, happen without its consent; and whenever pain and sorrow so far overcome my patience as to make me tired of life, I may conclude, that I am recalled from my station, in the clearest and most express terms.

It is Providence, surely, that has placed me at present in this chamber:[3] But may I not leave it, when I think proper, without being liable to the imputation of having deserted my post or station? When I shall be dead, the principles, of which I am composed, will still perform their part in the universe, and will be equally useful in the grand fabric, as when they composed this individual creature. The difference to the whole will be no greater than between my being in a chamber and in the open air. The one change is of more importance to me than the other; but not more so to the universe.

It is a kind of blasphemy to imagine, that any created being can disturb the order of the world, or invade the business of Providence. It supposes, that that being possesses powers and faculties, which it received not from its Creator, and which are not subordinate to his government and authority. A man may disturb society, no doubt; and thereby incur the displeasure of the Almighty: But the government of the world is placed far beyond his reach and violence. And how does it appear, that the Almighty is displeased with those actions, that disturb society? By the principles which he has implanted in human nature, and which inspire us with a sentiment of remorse, if we ourselves have been guilty of such actions, and with that of blame and disapprobation, if we ever observe them in others. Let us now examine, according to the method proposed, whether suicide be of this kind of actions, and be a breach of our duty to our *neighbour* and to society.

A man, who retires from life, does no harm to society. He only ceases to do good; which, if it be an injury, is of the lowest kind.

All our obligations to do good to society seem to imply something reciprocal. I receive the benefits of society, and therefore ought to promote its interest. But when I withdraw myself altogether from society, can I be bound any longer?

But allowing, that our obligations to do good were perpetual, they have certainly some bounds. I am not obliged to do a small good to society, at the expense of a great harm to myself. Why then should I prolong a miserable

---

[3] The body.

existence, because of some frivolous advantage, which the public may, perhaps, receive from me? If upon account of age and infirmities, I may lawfully resign any office, and employ my time altogether in fencing against these calamities, and alleviating, as much as possible, the miseries of my future life: Why may I not cut short these miseries at once by an action, which is no more prejudicial to society?

But suppose, that it is no longer in my power to promote the interest of the public: Suppose, that I am a burden to it: Suppose, that my life hinders some person from being much more useful to the public. In such cases my resignation of life must not only be innocent but laudable. And most people, who lie under any temptation to abandon existence, are in some such situation. Those, who have health, or power, or authority, have commonly better reason to be in humour with the world.

A man is engaged in a conspiracy for the public interest; is seized upon suspicion; is threatened with the rack; and knows, from his own weakness, that the secret will be extorted from him: Could such a one consult the public interest better than by putting a quick period to a miserable life? This was the case of the famous and brave Strozzi of Florence.[4]

Again, suppose a malefactor justly condemned to a shameful death; can any reason be imagined, why he may not anticipate his punishment, and save himself all the anguish of thinking on its dreadful approaches? He invades the business of Providence no more than the magistrate did, who ordered his execution; and his voluntary death is equally advantageous to society, by ridding it of a pernicious member.

That suicide may often be consistent with interest and with our duty to *ourselves*, no one can question, who allows, that age, sickness, or misfortune may render life a burden, and make it worse even than annihilation. I believe that no man ever threw away life, while it was worth keeping. For such is our natural horror of death, that small motives will never be able to reconcile us to it. And though perhaps the situation of a man's health or fortune did not seem to require this remedy, we may at least be assured, that any one, who, without apparent reason, has had recourse to it, was cursed with such an incurable depravity or gloominess of temper, as must poison all enjoyment, and render him equally miserable as if he had been loaded with the most grievous misfortunes.

---

[4] Filippo Strozzi (1489–1538), a Florentine exile who led an army against the Medici. He was captured and tortured, and subsequently took his own life. He portrayed his suicide as done for the sake of Florence.

If suicide be supposed a crime, 'tis only cowardice can impel us to it. If it be no crime, both prudence and courage should engage us to rid ourselves at once of existence, when it becomes a burden. 'Tis the only way, that we can then be useful to society, by setting an example, which, if imitated, would preserve to every one his chance for happiness in life, and would effectually free him from all danger of misery.[d]

---

[d] It would be easy to prove, that suicide is as lawful under the Christian dispensation as it was to the heathens. There is not a single text of scripture, which prohibits it. That great and infallible rule of faith and practice, which must control all philosophy and human reasoning, has left us, in this particular, to our natural liberty. Resignation to Providence is, indeed, recommended in scripture; but that implies only submission to ills, which are unavoidable, not to such as may be remedied by prudence or courage. *Thou shalt not kill* is evidently meant to exclude only the killing of others, over whose life we have no authority. That this precept like most of the scripture precepts, must be modified by reason and common sense, is plain from the practice of magistrates, who punish criminals capitally, notwithstanding the letter of this law. But were this commandment ever so express against suicide, it could now have no authority. For all the law of Moses is abolished, except so far as it is established by the law of nature; and we have already endeavoured to prove, that suicide is not prohibited by that law. In all cases, Christians and Heathens are precisely upon the same footing; and if Cato and Brutus, Arria and Portia acted heroically, those who now imitate their example ought to receive the same praises from posterity. The power of committing suicide is regarded by Pliny as an advantage which men possess even above the Deity himself. *Deus non sibi potest mortem consciscere, si velit, quod homini dedit optimum in tantis vitae poenis.* Lib. ii. Cap. 7. ['God cannot, even if he wishes, commit suicide, the supreme boon that he has bestowed on man among all the penalties of life.' Pliny (the Elder), *Natural History*, 2.5.27.]

Of the Immortality of the Soul

By the mere light of reason it seems difficult to prove the immortality of the soul. The arguments for it are commonly derived either from *meta-physical* topics, or *moral* or *physical*. But in reality, it is the gospel, and the gospel alone, that has brought life and immortality to light.

I.   Metaphysical topics are founded on the supposition that the soul is immaterial, and that it is impossible for thought to belong to a material substance.

But just metaphysics teach us, that the notion of substance is wholly confused and imperfect, and that we have no other idea of any substance than as an aggregate of particular qualities, inhering in an unknown something. Matter, therefore, and spirit are at bottom equally unknown; and we cannot determine what qualities may inhere in the one or in the other.

They likewise teach us, that nothing can be decided *a priori* concerning any cause or effect; and that experience being the only source of our judgments of this nature, we cannot know from any other principle, whether matter, by its structure or arrangement, may not be the cause of thought. Abstract reasonings cannot decide any question of fact or existence.

But admitting a spiritual substance to be dispersed throughout the universe, like the etherial fire of the Stoics,[1] and to be the only inherent subject of thought; we have reason to conclude from *analogy*, that nature uses it after the same manner she does the other substance, matter. She

---

[1] The Stoics held that fire or heat was a vital force that pervaded the universe. See Cicero, *On the Nature of the Gods*, 2.23–4.

employs it as a kind of paste or clay; modifies it into a variety of forms and existences; dissolves after a time each modification; and from its substance erects a new form. As the same material substance may successively compose the body of all animals, the same spiritual substance may compose their minds: Their consciousness, or that system of thought, which they formed during life, may be continually dissolved by death; and nothing interest them in the new modification. The most positive asserters of the mortality of the soul, never denied the immortality of its substance. And that an immaterial substance, as well as a material, may lose its memory or consciousness appears, in part, from experience, if the soul be immaterial.

Reasoning from the common course of nature, and without supposing any *new* interposition of the supreme cause, which ought always to be excluded from philosophy; what is incorruptible must also be ingenerable. The soul, therefore, if immortal, existed before our birth: And if the former state of existence no wise concerned us, neither will the latter.[2]

Animals undoubtedly feel, think, love, hate, will, and even reason, though in a more imperfect manner than man. Are their souls also immaterial and immortal?

II.   Let us now consider the *moral* arguments, chiefly those arguments derived from the justice of God, which is supposed to be farther interested in the farther punishment of the vicious, and reward of the virtuous.

But these arguments are grounded on the supposition, that God has attributes beyond what he has exerted in this universe, with which alone we are acquainted. Whence do we infer the existence of these attributes?

It is very safe for us to affirm, that, whatever we know the Deity to have actually done, is best; but it is very dangerous to affirm, that he must always do what to us seems best. In how many instances would this reasoning fail us with regard to the present world?

But if any purpose of nature be clear, we may affirm, that the whole scope and intention of man's creation, so far as we can judge by natural reason, is limited to the present life. With how weak a concern, from the original, inherent structure of the mind and passions, does he ever look farther? What comparison, either for steadiness or efficacy, between so floating an idea, and the most doubtful persuasion of any matter of fact, that occurs in common life.

---

[2] See Lucretius, *On the Nature of Things*, 3.670–8; 830–42.

There arise, indeed, in some minds, some unaccountable terrors with regard to futurity: But these would quickly vanish, were they not artificially fostered by precept and education. And those, who foster them; what is their motive? Only to gain a livelihood, and to acquire power and riches in this world. Their very zeal and industry, therefore, are an argument against them.

What cruelty, what iniquity, what injustice in nature, to confine thus all our concern, as well as all our knowledge, to the present life, if there be another scene still awaiting us, of infinitely greater consequence? Ought this barbarous deceit to be ascribed to a beneficent and wise being?

Observe with what exact proportion the task to be performed and the performing powers are adjusted throughout all nature. If the reason of man gives him a great superiority above other animals, his necessities are proportionably multiplied upon him. His whole time, his whole capacity, activity, courage, passion, find sufficient employment, in fencing against the miseries of his present condition. And frequently, nay almost always, are too slender for the business assigned them.

A pair of shoes, perhaps, was never yet wrought to the highest degree of perfection, which that commodity is capable of attaining. Yet is it necessary, at least very useful, that there should be some politicians and moralists, even some geometers, historians, poets, and philosophers among mankind.

The powers of men are no more superior to their wants, considered merely in this life, than those of foxes and hares are, compared to *their* wants and to *their* period of existence. The inference from parity of reason is therefore obvious.

On the theory of the soul's mortality, the inferiority of women's capacity is easily accounted for: Their domestic life requires no higher faculties either of mind or body. This circumstance vanishes and becomes absolutely insignificant, on the religious theory: The one sex has an equal task to perform with the other: Their powers of reason and resolution ought also to have been equal, and both of them infinitely greater than at present.

As every effect implies a cause, and that another, till we reach the first cause of all, which is the Deity; every thing that happens is ordained by him; and nothing can be the object of his punishment or vengeance.

By what rule are punishments and rewards distributed? What is the divine standard of merit and demerit? Shall we suppose, that human sentiments have place in the Deity? However bold that hypothesis, we have no conception of any other sentiments.

According to human sentiments, sense, courage, good manners, industry, prudence, genius, etc. are essential parts of personal merit. Shall we therefore erect an elysium for poets and heroes, like that of the ancient mythology?[3] Why confine all rewards to one species of virtue?

Punishment, without any proper end or purpose, is inconsistent with *our* ideas of goodness and justice; and no end can be served by it after the whole scene is closed.

Punishment, according to *our* conceptions, should bear some proportion to the offence. Why then eternal punishment for the temporary offences of so frail a creature as man? Can any one approve of Alexander's rage, who intended to exterminate a whole nation, because they had seized his favourite horse, Bucephalus?[a]

Heaven and hell suppose two distinct species of men, the good and the bad. But the greatest part of mankind float between vice and virtue.

Were one to go round the world with an intention of giving a good supper to the righteous and a sound drubbing to the wicked, he would frequently be embarrassed in his choice, and would find, that the merits and demerits of most men and women scarcely amount to the value of either.

To suppose measures of approbation and blame, different from the human, confounds every thing. Whence do we learn, that there is such a thing as moral distinctions but from our own sentiments?

What man, who has not met with personal provocation (or what good natured man who has) could inflict on crimes, from the sense of blame alone, even the common, legal, frivolous punishments? And does any thing steel the breast of judges and juries against the sentiments of humanity but reflections on necessity and public interest?

By the Roman law, those who had been guilty of parricide and confessed their crime, were put into a sack, along with an ape, a dog, and a serpent; and thrown into the river: Death alone was the punishment of those, who denied their guilt, however fully proved. A criminal was tried before Augustus, and condemned after full conviction: But the humane emperor, when he put the last interrogatory, gave it such a turn as to lead the wretch

---

[a] Quint. Curtius, lib. vi. cap. 5. [Quintus Curtius Rufus, *The History of Alexander*, 6.5.]

[3] Elysium, or the Elysian Fields, was, in ancient Greek mythology, the home of those who escaped death through being specially favoured by the gods.

into a denial of his guilt. *You surely*, said the prince, *did not kill your father.*[b] This lenity suits our natural ideas of Right,[4] even towards the greatest of all criminals, and even though it prevents so inconsiderable a sufferance. Nay, even the most bigoted priest would naturally, without reflection, approve of it; provided the crime was not heresy or infidelity. For as these crimes hurt himself in his *temporal* interests and advantages; perhaps he may not be altogether so indulgent to them.

The chief source of moral ideas is the reflection on the interests of human society. Ought these interests, so short, so frivolous, to be guarded by punishments, eternal and infinite? The damnation of one man is an infinitely greater evil in the universe, than the subversion of a thousand million of kingdoms.

Nature has rendered human infancy peculiarly frail and mortal; as it were on purpose to refute the notion of a probationary state. The half of mankind die before they are rational creatures.

III. The *physical* arguments from the analogy of nature are strong for the mortality of the soul; and these are really the only philosophical arguments, which ought to be admitted with regard to this question, or indeed any question of fact.

Where any two objects are so closely connected, that all alterations, which we have ever seen in the one, are attended with proportionable alterations in the other; we ought to conclude, by all rules of analogy, that, when there are still greater alterations produced in the former, and it is totally dissolved, there follows a total dissolution of the latter.

Sleep, a very small effect on the body, is attended with a temporary extinction; at least, a great confusion in the soul.

The weakness of the body and that of the mind in infancy are exactly proportioned; their vigour in manhood; their sympathetic disorder in sickness; their common gradual decay in old age. The step farther seems unavoidable; their common dissolution in death.[5]

The last symptoms, which the mind discovers, are disorder, weakness, insensibility, stupidity, the forerunners of its annihilation. The farther progress of the same causes, increasing the same effects, totally extinguish it.

---

[b] Sueton. August. cap. 3. [Suetonius, *Lives of the Caesars*, 'Augustus', 3.]
[4] Legal justice.   [5] See Lucretius, *On the Nature of Things*, 3.445–58.

Judging by the usual analogy of nature, no form can continue, when transferred to a condition of life very different from the original one, in which it was placed. Trees perish in the water; fishes in the air; animals in the earth. Even so small a difference as that of climate is often fatal. What reason then to imagine, that an immense alteration, such as is made on the soul by the dissolution of its body and all its organs of thought and sensation, can be effected without the dissolution of the whole?

Every thing is in common between soul and body. The organs of the one are all of them the organs of the other. The existence therefore of the one must be dependent on that of the other.

The souls of animals are allowed to be mortal; and these bear so near a resemblance to the souls of men, that the analogy from one to the other forms a very strong argument. Their bodies are not more resembling; yet no one rejects the arguments drawn from comparative anatomy. The *metempsychosis* is therefore the only system of this kind, that philosophy can so much as hearken to.[6]

Nothing in this world is perpetual. Every being, however seemingly firm, is in continual flux and change: The world itself gives symptoms of frailty and dissolution: How contrary to analogy, therefore, to imagine, that one single form, seemingly the frailest of any, and from the slightest causes, subject to the greatest disorders, is immortal and indissoluble? What a daring theory is that! How lightly, not to say, how rashly entertained!

How to dispose of the infinite number of posthumous existences ought also to embarrass the religious theory. Every planet, in every solar system, we are at liberty to imagine peopled with intelligent, mortal beings: At least, we can fix on no other supposition. For these, then, a new universe must, every generation, be created, beyond the bounds of the present universe; or one must have been created at first so prodigiously wide as to admit of this continual influx of beings.[7] Ought such bold suppositions to be received by any philosophy; and that merely on pretence of a bare possibility?

When it is asked, whether Agamemnon, Thersites, Hannibal, Nero,[8] and every stupid clown, that ever existed in Italy, Scythia, Bactria, or

---

[6] The transmigration at death of the soul from one body to another; reincarnation. See Bayle's objection to Leibniz, *Historical and Critical Dictionary*, 'Rorarius', Note H.

[7] See Lucretius, *On the Nature of Things*, 3.776–83.

[8] In Homer, *The Iliad*, Agamemnon is 'lord of men', king of Mycenae and leader of the Greek army, Thersites the 'ugliest man who ever came to Troy', a cowardly soldier who questions Agamemnon's

Guinea,[9] are now alive; can any man think, that a scrutiny of nature will furnish arguments strong enough to answer so strange a question in the affirmative? The want of arguments, without revelation, sufficiently establishes the negative.

Quanto facilius, says Pliny,[c] *certiusque sibi quemque credere, ac specimen securitatis antigenitali sumere experimento.* Our insensibility, before the composition of the body, seems to natural reason a proof of a like state after its dissolution.

Were our horror of annihilation an original passion, not the effect of our general love of happiness, it would rather prove the mortality of the soul. For as nature does nothing in vain,[10] she would never give us a horror against an impossible event. She may give us a horror against an unavoidable event, provided our endeavours, as in the present case, may often remove it to some distance. Death is in the end unavoidable; yet the human species could not be preserved, had not nature inspired us with an aversion towards it.

All doctrines are to be suspected, which are favoured by our passions. And the hopes and fears which give rise to this doctrine, are very obvious.

It is an infinite advantage in every controversy, to defend the negative. If the question be out of the common experienced course of nature, this circumstance is almost, if not altogether, decisive. By what arguments or analogies can we prove any state of existence, which no one ever saw, and which no wise resembles any that ever was seen? Who will repose such trust in any pretended philosophy, as to admit upon its testimony the reality of so marvellous a scene? Some new species of logic is requisite for that

---

authority. Hannibal (247–182 BC) was a Carthaginian general who inflicted several defeats on the Romans in the second Punic War (218–201 BC). Nero (AD 37–68, Roman emperor, 54–68); he was notorious for his cruelty and for fiddling (or singing) while Rome burned in 64 (Tacitus, *Annals*, 5.38; Suetonius, *Lives of the Caesars*, 'Nero', 38).

[c] Lib. vii. cap. 55. ['How much easier and safer for each to trust in himself, and for us to derive our idea of future tranquillity from our experience of it before birth!' Pliny (the Elder), *Natural History*, 7.55.]

[9] Scythia was an ancient empire centred on the northern shores of the Black Sea. Bactria was an ancient country in what is now northern Afghanistan. Guinea was an early modern European term for sub-Saharan west Africa. The point is that these are all well off the beaten track.

[10] A maxim of natural teleology deriving from Aristotle (*On the Heavens*, 271a33; *Parts of Animals*, 658a9; *Politics*, 1253a9; etc.), and affirmed by Newton, *Principia*, Rules for the Study of Natural Philosophy, Rule 1 (87).

purpose; and some new faculties of the mind, which may enable us to comprehend that logic.

Nothing could set in a fuller light the infinite obligations, which mankind have to divine revelation; since we find, that no other medium could ascertain this great and important truth.

Thumbnail biographies
from *The History of England*

Francis Bacon, Baron Verulam and Viscount St Albans (1561–1626)

The great glory of literature in this island, during the reign of James,[1] was Lord Bacon. Most of his performances were composed in Latin; though he possessed neither the elegance of that, nor of his native tongue. If we consider the variety of talents displayed by this man; as a public speaker, a man of business, a wit, a courtier, a companion, an author, a philosopher; he is justly the object of great admiration. If we consider him merely as an author and philosopher, the light in which we view him at present, though very estimable, he was yet inferior to his contemporary Galileo,[2] perhaps even to Kepler.[3] Bacon pointed out at a distance the road to true philosophy: Galileo both pointed it out to others, and made himself considerable advances in it. The Englishman was ignorant of geometry: The Florentine revived that science, excelled in it, and was the first that applied it, together with experiment, to natural philosophy. The former rejected, with the most positive disdain, the system of Copernicus: The latter fortified it with new proofs, derived both from reason and the senses. Bacon's style is stiff and rigid: His wit, though often brilliant, is also often unnatural and

---

[1] James VI and I (1566–1625), reigned in Scotland 1567–1625, and in England 1603–25.

[2] Galileo Galilei (1564–1642), Italian astronomer and physicist. He applied the telescope to astronomy, and used his discoveries (most notably, craters on the moon, the moons of Jupiter and the phases of Venus) to champion Copernicus's astronomy and to oppose Aristotle's physics.

[3] Johannes Kepler (1571–1630), German astronomer whose three laws of orbital motion established principles governing the movements of the planets.

far-fetched; and he seems to be the original of those pointed similes and long-spun allegories, which so much distinguish the English authors: Galileo is a lively and agreeable, though somewhat a prolix writer. But Italy, not united in any single government, and perhaps satiated with that literary glory, which it has possessed both in ancient and modern times, has too much neglected the renown which it has acquired by giving birth to so great a man. That national spirit, which prevails among the English, and which forms their great happiness, is the cause why they bestow on all their eminent writers, and on Bacon among the rest, such praises and acclamations, as may often appear partial and excessive. He died in 1626, in the 66th year of his age. [V, 153–4]

Thomas Hobbes (1588–1679)

No English author in that age was more celebrated both abroad and at home than Hobbes: In our time, he is much neglected: A lively instance how precarious all reputations, founded on reasoning and philosophy! A pleasant comedy, which paints the manners of the age, and exposes a faithful picture of nature, is a durable work, and is transmitted to the latest posterity. But a system, whether physical or metaphysical, commonly owes its success to its novelty; and is no sooner canvassed with impartiality than its weakness is discovered. Hobbes's politics are fitted only to promote tyranny, and his ethics to encourage licentiousness. Though an enemy to religion, he partakes nothing of the spirit of scepticism; but is as positive and dogmatical as if human reason, and his reason in particular, could attain a thorough conviction in these subjects. Clearness and propriety of style are the chief excellences of Hobbes's writings. In his own person he is represented to have been a man of virtue; a character no wise surprising, notwithstanding his libertine system of ethics. Timidity is the principal fault, with which he is reproached: He lived to an extreme old age, yet could never reconcile himself to the thoughts of death. The boldness of his opinions and sentiments form a remarkable contrast to this part of his character. He died in 1679, aged 91. [VI, 153]

William Harvey (1578–1657)

Harvey is entitled to the glory of having made, by reasoning alone, without any mixture of accident, a capital discovery in one of the most important branches of science. He had also the happiness of establishing at once his theory on the most solid and convincing proofs; and posterity has added little to the arguments suggested by his industry and ingenuity. His treatise of the circulation of the blood is farther embellished by that warmth and spirit, which so naturally accompany the genius of invention. This great man was much favoured by Charles I,[4] who gave him the liberty of using all the deer in the royal forests for perfecting his discoveries on the generation of animals. It was remarked, that no physician in Europe, who had reached forty years of age, ever, to the end of his life, adopted Harvey's doctrine of the circulation of the blood, and that his practice in London diminished extremely, from the reproach drawn upon him, by that great and signal discovery. So slow is the progress of truth in every science, even when not opposed by factious or superstitious prejudices! He died in 1657, aged 79. [VI, 153-4]

The Royal Society (established by royal charter 1662)

Amidst the thick cloud of bigotry and ignorance, which overspread the nation, during the Commonwealth and Protectorship, there were a few sedate philosophers, who, in the retirement of Oxford, cultivated their reason, and established conferences for the mutual communication of their discoveries in physics and geometry. Wilkins,[5] a clergyman, who had married Cromwell's sister, and was afterwards Bishop of Chester, promoted these philosophical conversations. Immediately after the Restoration, these men procured a patent, and having enlarged their number, were denominated the *Royal Society*. But this patent was all they obtained from the king. Though Charles[6] was a lover of the sciences, particularly chemistry and mechanics; he animated them by his example alone, not by his bounty. His craving courtiers and mistresses, by whom he was perpetually surrounded, engrossed all his expense, and left him neither money nor attention for literary merit. His contemporary, Louis,[7] who fell short of the king's genius and knowledge in this particular, much exceeded him in

---

[4] Charles I (1600–49), reigned 1625–49; executed by decision of parliament.
[5] John Wilkins (1614–72), mathematician and astronomer. He was Warden of Wadham College, Oxford, and Master of Trinity College, Cambridge, before becoming Bishop of Chester.
[6] Charles II (1630–85), reigned 1660–85.
[7] Louis XIV of France (1638–1715), reigned 1643–1715. He granted royal patronage to the French Academy of Sciences (founded 1666) in 1699.

liberality. Besides pensions conferred on learned men throughout all Europe, his academies were directed by rules and supported by salaries: A generosity which does great honour to his memory; and in the eyes of all the ingenious part of mankind, will be esteemed an atonement for many of the errors of his reign. We may be surprised, that this example should not be more followed by princes; since it is certain that that bounty, so extensive, so beneficial, and so much celebrated, cost not this monarch so great a sum as is often conferred on one useless overgrown favourite or courtier.

But though the French academy of sciences was directed, encouraged and supported by the sovereign, there arose in England some men of superior genius who were more than sufficient to cast the balance, and who drew on themselves and on their native country the regard and attention of Europe. Besides Wilkins, Wren,[8] Wallis,[9] eminent mathematicians, Hooke,[10] an accurate observer by microscopes, and Sydenham,[11] the restorer of true physic; there flourished during this period a Boyle and a Newton; men who trod, with cautious, and therefore the more secure steps, the only road, which leads to true philosophy. [VI, 540-1]

Robert Boyle (1627-91)

Boyle improved the pneumatic engine invented by Otto Guericke,[12] and was thereby enabled to make several new and curious experiments on the air as well as on other bodies: His chemistry is much admired by those who are acquainted with that art: His hydrostatics contain a greater mixture of reasoning and invention with experiment than any other of his works; but his reasoning is still remote from that boldness and temerity, which had led astray so many philosophers. Boyle was a great partisan of the mechanical philosophy; a theory, which, by discovering some of the secrets

---

[8] Sir Christopher Wren (1632–1723), mathematician and architect. Savilian Professor of Astronomy at Oxford; designed the new St Paul's Cathedral after the first was destroyed in the Fire of London (1666).

[9] John Wallis (1616–1703), Savilian Professor of Geometry at Oxford. Disputed with Hobbes over the latter's attempts to square the circle.

[10] Robert Hooke (1635–1703), scientist of great versatility. Best known for the law of elasticity, he proposed the inverse square law of gravitational attraction, and contributed to the development of optics.

[11] Thomas Sydenham (c. 1624–89), physician who studied the causes of epidemics and of neurological disorders; came to be known as 'the English Hippocrates'.

[12] Otto Guericke (1602–86), German engineer and physicist. The first to investigate the properties of a vacuum, and invented the Magdeburg hemispheres to demonstrate atmospheric pressure.

of nature, and allowing us to imagine the rest, is so agreeable to the natural vanity and curiosity of men. He died in 1691, aged 65. [VI, 541]

Sir Isaac Newton (1642–1727)

In Newton this island may boast of having produced the greatest and rarest genius that ever arose for the ornament and instruction of the species. Cautious in admitting no principles but such as were founded on experiment; but resolute to adopt every such principle, however new or unusual: From modesty, ignorant of his superiority above the rest of mankind; and thence, less careful to accommodate his reasonings to common apprehensions: More anxious to merit than acquire fame: He was from these causes long unknown to the world; but his reputation at last broke out with a lustre, which scarcely any writer, during his own life-time, had ever before attained. While Newton seemed to draw off the veil from some of the mysteries of nature, he showed at the same time the imperfections of the mechanical philosophy; and thereby restored her ultimate secrets to that obscurity, in which they ever did and ever will remain. He died in 1727, aged 85. [VI, 542]

Selections from Hume's letters

To Michael Ramsay

Orleans [France]
31 August 1737

My Dear Friend

I have quitted La Fleche two days after receiving yours. I am now at Tours
in my way to Paris, where I do not intend to stay any considerable time,
unless some extraordinary accident intervene: So that I propose to see
you in London about 3 or 4 weeks hence. You may be sure that this
meeting will afford me a very great satisfaction, and it is with the utmost
concern I hear you will leave the city a little after my arrival. Nothing can be
more useful and agreeable than to have an intimate friend with one at any
critical time of life such as that which I am just going to enter upon. And I
must certainly esteem it a great loss to be deprived of your advice, as well in
points that regard my conduct and behaviour, as in those of criticism and
learning. I can assure you I have great confidence in your judgement even
in this last particular, though the state of your health and business have
never permitted you to be a regular student, nor to apply yourself to any
part of learning in a methodical manner, without which it is almost
impossible to make any mighty progress. I shall submit all my
performances to your examination, and to make you enter into them
more easily, I desire of you, if you have leisure, to read once over La

Recherche de la Verite of Pere Malebranche,[1] the Principles of Human Knowledge by Dr Berkeley, some of the more metaphysical articles of Bayle's Dictionary, such as those [of] Zeno and Spinoza. Descartes's Meditations would also be useful, but don't know if you will find it easily among your acquaintances. These books will make you easily comprehend the metaphysical parts of my reasoning,[2] and, as to the rest, they have so little dependence on all former systems of philosophy, that your natural good sense will afford you light enough to judge of their force and solidity ...

Adieu.

To Henry Home

London
2 December 1737

Dear Sir,

I am sorry I am not able to satisfy your curiosity, by giving you some general notion of the plan upon which I proceed. But my opinions are so new, and even some terms I am obliged to make use of, that I could not propose, by any abridgement, to give my system an air of likelihood, or so much as make it intelligible ...

Having a franked letter, I was resolved to make use of it; and accordingly enclose some *Reasonings concerning Miracles*,[3] which I once thought of publishing with the rest, but which I am afraid will give too much offence, even as the world is disposed at present. There is something in the turn of thought, and a good deal in the turn of expression, which will not perhaps appear so proper, for want of knowing the context: But the force of the argument you'll be judge of, as it stands. Tell me your thoughts of it. Is not the style too diffuse? Though, as that was a popular argument, I have spread it out much more than the other parts of the work. I beg of you to

---

[1] *The Search after Truth* by Father Malebranche. (Malebranche was a Catholic priest.)
[2] That is, in Book I of the *Treatise*.
[3] The first version of what would become Section 10 of the first *Enquiry*.

show it to nobody, except to Mr Hamilton,[4] if he pleases; and let me know at your leisure that you have received it, read it, and burnt it. Your thoughts and mine agree with respect to Dr Butler,[5] and I would be glad to be introduced to him. I am at present castrating my work, that is cutting off its noble parts; that is, endeavouring it shall give as little offence as possible, before which, I could not pretend to put it into the Doctor's hands. This is a piece of cowardice, for which I blame myself, though I believe none of my friends will blame me. But I was resolved not to be an enthusiast in philosophy, while I was blaming other enthusiasms. If ever I indulge myself in any, it will be when I tell you that I am, Dear Sir, yours,

DAVID HUME.

To Francis Hutcheson

Ninewells near Berwick
17 September 1739

Sir

I am much obliged to you for your reflections on my papers. I have perused them with care, and find they will be of use to me. You have mistaken my meaning in some passages; which upon examination I have found to proceed from some ambiguity or defect in my expression.

What affected me most in your remarks is your observing, that there wants a certain warmth in the cause of virtue, which, you think, all good men would relish, and could not displease amidst abstract enquiries. I must own, this has not happened by chance, but is the effect of a reasoning either good or bad. There are different ways of examining the mind as well as the body. One may consider it either as an anatomist or as a painter; either to discover its most secret springs and principles or to describe the grace and beauty of its actions. I imagine it impossible to conjoin these two views. Where you pull off the skin, and display all the minute parts, there appears something trivial, even in the noblest

---

[4] Probably William Hamilton of Bangour (1704–54), a Jacobite poet who was a member of the Edinburgh circle of Henry Home (who was himself an ex-Jacobite).
[5] Joseph Butler, the author of *The Analogy of Religion* (1736).

attitudes and most vigorous actions: Nor can you ever render the object graceful or engaging but by clothing the parts again with skin and flesh, and presenting only their bare outside. An anatomist, however, can give very good advice to a painter or statuary: And in like manner, I am persuaded, that a metaphysician may be very helpful to a moralist; though I cannot easily conceive these two characters united in the same work. Any warm sentiment of morals, I am afraid, would have the air of declamation amidst abstract reasonings, and would be esteemed contrary to good taste. And though I am much more ambitious of being esteemed a friend to virtue, than a writer of taste; yet I must always carry the latter in my eye, otherwise I must despair of ever being serviceable to virtue. I hope these reasons will satisfy you; though at the same time I intend to make a new trial, if it be possible to make the moralist and metaphysician agree a little better.

I cannot agree to your sense of *natural*. It is founded on final causes,[6] which is a consideration that appears to me pretty uncertain and unphilosophical. For pray, what is the end of man? Is he created for happiness or for virtue? For this life or for the next? For himself or for his Maker? Your definition of *natural* depends upon solving these questions, which are endless, and quite wide of my purpose ...

I have many other reflections to communicate to you; but it would be troublesome. I shall therefore conclude with telling you, that I intend to follow your advice in altering most of those passages you have remarked as defective in point of prudence; though I must own, I think you a little too delicate. Except a man be in Orders,[7] or be immediately concerned in the instruction of youth, I do not think his character depends upon his philosophical speculations, as the world is now modelled; and a little liberty seems requisite to bring into the public notice a book that is calculated for so few readers. I hope you will allow me the freedom of consulting you when I am in any difficulty; and believe me to be

Dear Sir
Your most obliged humble servant
DAVID HUME

---

[6] One of Aristotle's four 'causes', or kinds of explanation: a final cause is an end or purpose (Aristotle, *Physics*, II.3 (194b16ff)). Hume's rejection of the knowability of final causes is a sceptic's denial of a pillar of Stoic providentialism.
[7] That is, be an ordained priest.

To Gilbert Elliot of Minto

[March or April 1751]

Dear Sir

I am sorry your keeping these papers[8] has proceeded from business and avocations, and not from your endeavours to clear up so difficult an argument. I despair not, however, of getting some assistance from you; the subject is surely of the greatest importance; and the views of it so new as to challenge some attention.

I believe the Philosophical Essays[9] contain every thing of consequence relating to the understanding, which you would meet with in the Treatise; and I give you my advice against reading the latter. By shortening and simplifying the questions, I really render them much more complete. *Addo dum minuo.*[10] The philosophical principles are the same in both: But I was carried away by the heat of youth and invention to publish too precipitately. So vast an undertaking, planned before I was one and twenty, and composed before twenty five, must necessarily be very defective. I have repented my haste a hundred, and a hundred times.

I return Strabo,[11] whom I have found very judicious and useful. I give you a great many thanks for your trouble.

I am Dear Sir Yours
DAVID HUME

---

[8] The manuscript first draft of Hume's posthumously published *Dialogues concerning Natural Religion*.
[9] That is, *An Enquiry concerning Human Understanding*, which was initially published under the title *Philosophical Essays concerning Human Understanding*.
[10] I add while diminishing in size.
[11] Strabo (c. 64 BC–AD 19), author of Greek histories and a geography of the Roman empire.

Exchange with John Stewart, Professor of Natural Philosophy in Edinburgh[12]

Excerpt from John Stewart, Some Remarks on the Laws of Motion, and the Inertia of Matter, in Essays and Observations (Philosophical Society of Edinburgh, 1754)

That something may begin to exist, or start into being without a cause, has indeed been advanced in a very ingenious and profound system of the sceptical philosophy;* but has not yet been adopted by any of the societies for the improvement of natural knowledge. Such sublime conceptions are far above the reach of the greatest physiologist on earth. The man who believes that a perception may exist without a percipient mind or a perceiver, may well comprehend, that an action may be performed without an agent, or a thing produced without any cause of the production. And the author of this new and wonderful doctrine informs the world that, when he looked into his own mind, he could discover nothing but a series of fleeting perceptions; and that from thence he concluded, that he himself was nothing but a bundle of such perceptions.

* *Treatise on Human Nature*. This is the system at large, a work suited only to the comprehension of adepts. An excellent compound or summary whereof, for the benefit of vulgar capacities, we of this nation enjoy in the *Philosophical Essays* and the *Essays Moral and Political*. And to these may be added, as a further help, that useful commentary, the *Essays on Morality and Natural Religion*.[13]

---

[12] In 1754 the Philosophical Society of Edinburgh, of which Hume was a secretary, published a volume entitled *Essays and Observations, Physical and Literary, read before a Society in Edinburgh and published by them*. One of the essays was by John Stewart, and one of Hume's letters (presumably addressed to Stewart) is a reply to its claims.

[13] Henry Home, Lord Kames (1696–1782), *Essays on Morality and Natural Religion* (1751), the first considered reply to the *Treatise*. Stewart's intimation that Kames shared Hume's principles was, apparently, a widespread belief: 'Philosophers must judge of the question, but the clergy have already decided, and say he is as bad as me. Nay some affirm him to be worse, as much as a treacherous friend is worse than an open enemy.' (Hume to Michael Ramsay, 22 June 1751.)

Hume's reply

Tuesday Forenoon
[February, 1754]

Sir –

I am so great a lover of peace, that I am resolved to drop this matter altogether, and not to insert a syllable in the Preface, which can have a reference to your essay. The truth is, I could take no revenge, but such a one as would have been a great deal too cruel, and much exceeding the offence. For though most authors think, that a contemptuous manner of treating their writings, is but slightly revenged by hurting the personal character and the honour of their antagonists, I am very far from that opinion. Besides, I am as certain as I can be of any thing (and I am not such a sceptic, as you may, perhaps, imagine) that your inserting such remarkable alterations in the printed copy proceeded entirely from precipitancy and passion, not from any formed intention of deceiving the Society. I would not take advantage of such an incident to throw a slur on a man of merit, whom I esteem, though I might have reason to complain of him.

When I am abused by such a fellow as Warburton,[14] whom I neither know nor care for, I can laugh at him: But if Dr. Stewart approaches any way towards the same style of writing, I own it vexes me: Because I conclude, that some unguarded circumstance of my conduct, though contrary to my intention, had given occasion to it.

As to your situation with regard to Lord Kames, I am not so good a judge. I only think, that you had so much the better of the argument, that you ought, upon that account, to have been the more reserved in your expressions. All raillery ought to be avoided in philosophical argument; both because it is unphilosophical, and because it cannot but be offensive, let it be ever so gentle. What then must we think with regard to so many insinuations of irreligion, to which Lord Kames's paper gave not the least occasion? This spirit of the Inquisitor is in you the effect of passion, and what a cool moment would easily correct. But where it

---

[14] The Revd William Warburton (1698–1779), Bishop of Gloucester, and the probable author of the hostile review of the *Treatise* that appeared in the *History of the Works of the Learned* (November/ December 1739).

predominates in the character, what ravages has it committed on reason, virtue, truth, liberty, and every thing, that is valuable among mankind?

I shall now speak a word as to the justness of your censure with regard to myself, after these remarks on the manner of it. I have no scruple of confessing my mistakes. You see I have owned, that I think Lord Kames is mistaken in his argument; and I would sooner give up my own cause than my friend's, if I thought that imputation of any consequence to a man's character. But allow me to tell you, that I never asserted so absurd a proposition as *that any thing might arise without a cause*: I only maintained, that our certainty of the falsehood of that proposition proceeded neither from intuition nor demonstration; but from another source. *That Caesar existed, that there is such an island as Sicily*; for these propositions, I affirm, we have no demonstrative nor intuitive proof. Would you infer that I deny their truth, or even their certainty? There are many different kinds of certainty; and some of them as satisfactory to the mind, though perhaps not so regular, as the demonstrative kind.

Where a man of sense mistakes my meaning, I own I am angry: But it is only at myself: For having expressed my meaning so ill as to have given occasion to the mistake.

That you may see I would no way scruple of owning my mistakes in argument, I shall acknowledge (what is infinitely more material) a very great mistake in conduct, viz. my publishing at all the Treatise of Human Nature, a book, which pretended to innovate in all the sublimest parts of philosophy, and which I composed before I was five and twenty. Above all, the positive air, which prevails in that book, and which may be imputed to the ardour of youth, so much displeases me, that I have not patience to review it. But what success the same doctrines, better illustrated and expressed, may meet with, *adhuc sub judice lis est.*[15] The arguments have been laid before the world, and by some philosophical minds have been attended to. I am willing to be instructed by the public; though human life is so short that I despair of ever seeing the decision. I wish I had always confined myself to the more easy parts of erudition; but you will excuse me from submitting to a proverbial decision, let it even be in Greek.

As I am resolved to drop this matter entirely from the Preface; so I hope to persuade Lord Kames to be entirely silent with regard to it in our meeting. But in case I should not prevail, or if any body else start the

---

[15] The case is still before the court.

subject, I think it better, that some of your friends should be there, and be prepared to mollify the matter. If I durst pretend to advise, I should think it better you yourself were absent, unless you bring a greater spirit of composition than you express in your letter. I am persuaded, that whatever a person of Mr. Monro's authority proposes will be agreed to: Though I must beg leave to differ from his judgement, in proposing to alter two pages. That chiefly removes the offence given to me, but what regards Lord Kames is so interwoven with the whole discourse, that there is not now any possibility of altering it. – I am Sir, your most obedient humble servant,

DAVID HUME

To the Reverend George Campbell (1719–96), Principal of Marischal College, Aberdeen

7 June 1762

Dear Sir,

It has so seldom happened that controversies in philosophy, much more in theology, have been carried on without producing a personal quarrel between the parties, that I must regard my present situation as somewhat extraordinary, who have reason to give you thanks for the civil and obliging manner in which you have conducted the dispute against me, on so interesting a subject as that of miracles. Any little symptoms of vehemence, of which I formerly used the freedom to complain, when you favoured me with a sight of the manuscript, are either removed or explained away, or atoned for by civilities, which are far beyond what I have any title to pretend to.[16] It will be natural for you to imagine, that I will fall upon some shift to evade the force of your arguments, and to retain my former opinion in the point controverted between us; but it is impossible for me not to see the ingenuity of your performance, and the great learning which you have displayed against me.

I consider myself as very much honoured in being thought worthy of an answer by a person of so much merit; and as I find that the public does you

---

[16] That is, in the published version of Campbell's *Dissertation on Miracles* (1762).

justice with regard to the ingenuity and good composition of your piece, I hope you will have no reason to repent engaging with an antagonist, whom, perhaps in strictness, you might have ventured to neglect. I own to you, that I never felt so violent an inclination to defend myself as at present, when I am thus fairly challenged by you, and I think I could find something specious[17] at least to urge in my defence; but as I had fixed a resolution, in the beginning of my life, always to leave the public to judge between my adversaries and me, without making any reply. I must adhere inviolably to this resolution, otherwise my silence on any future occasion would be construed an inability to answer, and would be matter of triumph against me.

It may perhaps amuse you to learn the first hint, which suggested to me that argument which you have so strenuously attacked. I was walking in the cloisters of the Jesuits' College of La Fleche, a town in which I passed two years of my youth, and engaged in a conversation with a Jesuit of some parts and learning, who was relating to me, and urging some nonsensical miracle performed in their convent, when I was tempted to dispute against him; and as my head was full of the topics of my Treatise of Human Nature, which I was at that time composing, this argument immediately occurred to me, and I thought it very much gravelled my companion; but at last he observed to me, that it was impossible for that argument to have any solidity, because it operated equally against the Gospel as the Catholic miracles;[18] – which observation I thought proper to admit as a sufficient answer. I believe you will allow, that the freedom at least of this reasoning makes it somewhat extraordinary to have been the produce of a convent of Jesuits, though perhaps you may think the sophistry of it savours plainly of the place of its birth.

Yours sincerely,
DAVID HUME.

---

[17] Plausible; attractive.
[18] The Jesuit's response reflects the fact that eighteenth-century critics of modern miracles were, commonly, Protestant critics of Catholicism, rather than critics of belief in the miraculous *tout court*.

To William Strahan

Edinburgh
26 October 1775

Dear Sir

I have often regretted the interruption of our correspondence: But when you ceased to be a speculative politician and became a practical one,[19] I could no longer expect you would be so communicative or impartial as formerly on that head; and my object with regard to authorship was, for a time, at an end ...

I must, before we part, have a little stroke of politics with you, notwithstanding my resolution to the contrary. We hear that some of the ministers have proposed in Council, that both fleet and army be withdrawn from America, and these colonists be left entirely to themselves. I wish I had been a member of His Majesty's Cabinet Council, that I might have seconded this opinion. I should have said, that this measure only anticipates the necessary course of events a few years; that a forced and every day more precarious monopoly of about six or seven hundred thousand pounds a year of manufactures was not worth contending for; that we should preserve the greater part of this trade even if the ports of America were open to all nations; that it was very likely, in our method of proceeding, that we should be disappointed in our scheme of conquering the colonies; and that we ought to think beforehand how we were to govern them, after they were conquered. Arbitrary power can extend its oppressive arm to the antipodes; but a limited government can never long be upheld at a distance, even where no disgusts[20] have intervened: Much less, where such violent animosities have taken place. We must, therefore, annul all the Charters;[21] abolish every democratical power in every colony; repeal the Habeas Corpus Act with regard to them; invest every governor with full discretionary or arbitrary powers; confiscate the estates of all the chief planters; and hang three fourths of their clergy. To execute such acts of destructive violence twenty thousand men will not be sufficient; nor thirty thousand to maintain them, in so

---

[19] Strahan had become MP for Malmesbury in 1774.   [20] Causes of offence.
[21] The Charters constituting each of the American colonies.

wide and disjointed a territory. And who are to pay so great an army? The colonists cannot at any time, much less after reducing them to a state of desolation: We ought not, and indeed cannot, in the overloaded or rather overwhelmed and totally ruined state of our finances. Let us, therefore, lay aside all anger; shake hands, and part friends. Or if we retain any anger, let it only be against our selves for our past folly; and against that wicked madman, Pitt;[22] who has reduced us to our present condition. *Dixi.*[23]

But we must not part, without my also saying something as an author. I have not yet thrown up so much all memory of that character.[24] There is a short advertisement, which I wish I had prefixed to the second volume of the Essays and Treatises in the last edition.[25] I send you a copy of it. Please to enquire at the warehouse, if any considerable number of that edition remain on hands;[26] and if there do, I beg the favor of you, that you would throw off[27] an equal number of this advertisement, and give out no more copies without prefixing it to the second volume. It is a complete answer to Dr Reid and to that bigoted silly fellow, Beattie.[28]

I believe that I have formerly mentioned to you, that no new editions should be made of any of my writings, without mentioning it to me; I shall still have some corrections to make. By calculation, or rather conjecture from former sales, the last edition of my History should be nearly sold off: Pray inform yourself whether it be not so: And how many remain on hand.

I am with great sincerity Dear Sir
Your affectionate humble servant
DAVID HUME.

[22] William Pitt the Elder (1708–78), 1st Earl of Chatham and Secretary of State (effectively Prime Minister) of Great Britain, 1756–61 and 1766–8. He brought the Seven Years War with France (1756–63) to an end, and masterminded the conquest of French possessions in North America.
[23] I have spoken. (That is, I will say no more on the matter.)
[24] I have not forgotten that I am an author.
[25] The 1772 edition of *Essays and Treatises on Several Subjects*. The second volume contained *An Enquiry concerning Human Understanding*, *A Dissertation on the Passions*, *An Enquiry concerning the Principles of Morals* and *The Natural History of Religion*.
[26] Remain in stock.   [27] Print.
[28] Thomas Reid (1710–96), Professor at Aberdeen (1752–64) before becoming Adam Smith's replacement as Professor of Moral Philosophy at Glasgow (1764–81). He had sought Hume's opinion on the manuscript of his *An Inquiry Into the Human Mind on the Principles of Common Sense* (1764), in which the *Treatise* is criticized for its reliance on the theory of ideas. James Beattie (1735–1803), Scottish poet and essayist, and Professor of Moral Philosophy at Aberdeen. He attacked Hume's philosophy in his *Essay on the Nature and Immutability of Truth* (1770).

My Own Life

It is difficult for a man to speak long of himself without vanity; therefore, I shall be short. It may be thought an instance of vanity that I pretend at all to write my life; but this narrative shall contain little more than the history of my writings; as, indeed, almost all my life has been spent in literary pursuits and occupations. The first success of most of my writings was not such as to be an object of vanity.

I was born the 26th of April 1711, old style,[1] at Edinburgh. I was of a good family, both by father and mother: my father's family is a branch of the Earl of Home's, or Hume's;[2] and my ancestors had been proprietors of the estate, which my brother possesses, for several generations. My mother was daughter of Sir David Falconer, President of the College of Justice: the title of Lord Halkerton came by succession to her brother.

My family, however, was not rich, and being myself a younger brother, my patrimony, according to the mode of my country, was of course very slender. My father, who passed for a man of parts, died when I was an infant, leaving me, with an elder brother and a sister, under the care of our mother, a woman of singular merit, who, though young and handsome, devoted herself entirely to the rearing and educating of her children. I passed through the ordinary course of education with success, and was seized very early with a passion for literature, which has been the ruling

---

[1] Great Britain changed from the Julian calendar (established by Julius Caesar in 46 BC) to the more accurate Gregorian calendar (originally promulgated by Pope Gregory XIII in 1582) in 1752. The changeover meant that Wednesday 2 September 1752 was followed by Thursday 14 September 1752.
[2] Variant spellings of Hume's family name (both pronounced as 'Hume'). Hume was christened 'David Home', but changed the spelling in 1734, when living in Bristol, apparently so the English would know how to pronounce it.

passion[3] of my life, and the great source of my enjoyments. My studious disposition, my sobriety, and my industry, gave my family a notion that the law was a proper profession for me; but I found an insurmountable aversion to every thing but the pursuits of philosophy and general learning; and while they fancied I was poring upon Voet and Vinnius,[4] Cicero and Virgil were the authors which I was secretly devouring.

My very slender fortune, however, being unsuitable to this plan of life, and my health being a little broken by my ardent application, I was tempted, or rather forced, to make a very feeble trial for entering into a more active scene of life. In 1734, I went to Bristol, with some recommendations to eminent merchants, but in a few months found that scene totally unsuitable to me. I went over to France, with a view of prosecuting my studies in a country retreat; and I there laid that plan of life, which I have steadily and successfully pursued. I resolved to make a very rigid frugality supply my deficiency of fortune, to maintain unimpaired my independency, and to regard every object as contemptible, except the improvement of my talents in literature.

During my retreat in France, first at Rheims, but chiefly at La Fleche, in Anjou, I composed my *Treatise of Human Nature*. After passing three years very agreeably in that country, I came over to London in 1737. In the end of 1738, I published my Treatise, and immediately went down to my mother and my brother, who lived at his country-house, and was employing himself very judiciously and successfully in the improvement of his fortune.

Never literary attempt was more unfortunate than my Treatise of Human Nature. It fell *dead-born from the press*,[5] without reaching such distinction, as even to excite a murmur among the zealots. But being naturally of a cheerful and sanguine temper, I very soon recovered the blow, and prosecuted with great ardour my studies in the country. In 1742, I printed at Edinburgh the first part of my Essays: the work was favourably received, and soon made me entirely forget my former disappointment. I continued with my mother and brother in the country, and in that time recovered the knowledge of the Greek language, which I had too much neglected in my early youth.

---

[3] See Alexander Pope, *Epistle to Cobham* ('Of the Knowledge and Characters of Men').
[4] Johannes Voet (1647–1713) and Arnoldus Vinnius (1588–1657), Dutch jurists.
[5] 'All, all but Truth, drops dead-born from the Press'; Pope, *Epilogue to the Satires*, II.226.

In 1745, I received a letter from the Marquis of Annandale, inviting me to come and live with him in England; I found also, that the friends and family of that young nobleman were desirous of putting him under my care and direction, for the state of his mind and health required it. – I lived with him a twelvemonth. My appointments during that time made a considerable accession to my small fortune. I then received an invitation from General St. Clair to attend him as secretary to his expedition, which was at first meant against Canada, but ended in an incursion on the coast of France.[6] Next year, to wit, 1747, I received an invitation from the General to attend him in the same station in his military embassy to the courts of Vienna and Turin. I there wore the uniform of an officer, and was introduced at these courts as aide-de-camp to the general, along with Sir Harry Erskine and Captain Grant, now General Grant. These two years were almost the only interruptions which my studies have received in the course of my life: I passed them agreeably, and in good company; and my appointments, with my frugality, had made me reach a fortune, which I called independent, though most of my friends were inclined to smile when I said so; in short, I was now master of near a thousand pounds.

I had always entertained a notion, that my want of success in publishing the Treatise of Human Nature, had proceeded more from the manner than the matter, and that I had been guilty of a very usual indiscretion, in going to the press too early. I, therefore, cast the first part of that work anew in the Enquiry concerning Human Understanding, which was published while I was at Turin. But this piece was at first but little more successful than the Treatise of Human Nature. On my return from Italy, I had the mortification to find all England in a ferment, on account of Dr. Middleton's Free Enquiry,[7] while my performance was entirely overlooked and neglected. A new edition, which had been published at London of my Essays, moral and political, met not with a much better reception.

Such is the force of natural temper, that these disappointments made little or no impression on me. I went down in 1749, and lived two years with my brother at his country-house, for my mother was now dead. I there composed the second part of my Essays, which I called Political Discourses, and also my Enquiry concerning the Principles of Morals, which is another part of my treatise that I cast anew. Meanwhile, my bookseller,

---

[6] A minor and ill-managed episode in the War of the Austrian Succession (1740–8).

[7] Conyers Middleton (1683–1750), English theologian. His *Free Enquiry into the Miraculous Powers* (1749) denied any special credibility to the early church fathers' reports of miraculous events.

A. Millar, informed me, that my former publications (all but the unfortunate Treatise) were beginning to be the subject of conversation; that the sale of them was gradually increasing, and that new editions were demanded. Answers by Reverends, and Right Reverends, came out two or three in a year; and I found, by Dr. Warburton's railing, that the books were beginning to be esteemed in good company. However, I had fixed a resolution, which I inflexibly maintained, never to reply to any body; and not being very irascible in my temper, I have easily kept myself clear of all literary squabbles. These symptoms of a rising reputation gave me encouragement, as I was ever more disposed to see the favourable than unfavourable side of things; a turn of mind which it is more happy to possess, than to be born to an estate of ten thousand a year.

In 1751, I removed from the country to the town, the true scene for a man of letters. In 1752, were published at Edinburgh, where I then lived, my Political Discourses, the only work of mine that was successful on the first publication. It was well received abroad and at home. In the same year was published at London, my Enquiry concerning the Principles of Morals; which, in my own opinion (who ought not to judge on that subject), is of all my writings, historical, philosophical, or literary, incomparably the best. It came unnoticed and unobserved into the world.

In 1752, the Faculty of Advocates chose me their Librarian, an office from which I received little or no emolument, but which gave me the command of a large library.[8] I then formed the plan of writing the History of England; but being frightened with the notion of continuing a narrative through a period of 1700 years, I commenced with the accession of the House of Stuart, an epoch when, I thought, the misrepresentations of faction began chiefly to take place. I was, I own, sanguine in my expectations of the success of this work. I thought that I was the only historian, that had at once neglected present power, interest, and authority, and the cry of popular prejudices; and as the subject was suited to every capacity, I expected proportional applause. But miserable was my disappointment: I was assailed by one cry of reproach, disapprobation, and even detestation; English, Scotch, and Irish, Whig and Tory,[9] churchman and sectary,

---

[8] The Advocates' Library, now the National Library of Scotland.
[9] Nicknames for the two principal political parties in eighteenth-century Britain. They were originally terms of abuse, meaning, roughly, Scottish rebel (Whig) and Irish thief (Tory). The parties originated in the disputes between royal and parliamentary authority of the seventeenth century, the Tories being royalists, the Whigs parliamentarians. In Hume's day, this had translated into the

freethinker and religionist, patriot and courtier, united in their rage against the man, who had presumed to shed a generous tear for the fate of Charles I and the Earl of Strafford; and after the first ebullitions of this fury were over, what was still more mortifying, the book seemed to sink into oblivion. Mr. Millar told me, that in a twelvemonth he sold only forty-five copies of it. I scarcely, indeed, heard of one man in the three kingdoms, considerable for rank or letters, that could endure the book. I must only except the primate of England, Dr. Herring, and the primate of Ireland, Dr. Stone, which seem two odd exceptions. These dignified prelates separately sent me messages not to be discouraged.

I was, however, I confess, discouraged; and had not the war been at that time breaking out between France and England, I had certainly retired to some provincial town of the former kingdom, have changed my name, and never more have returned to my native country. But as this scheme was not now practicable, and the subsequent volume was considerably advanced, I resolved to pick up courage and to persevere.

In this interval, I published at London my Natural History of Religion, along with some other small pieces: its public entry was rather obscure, except only that Dr. Hurd wrote a pamphlet against it, with all the illiberal petulance, arrogance, and scurrility, which distinguish the Warburtonian school.[10] This pamphlet gave me some consolation for the otherwise indifferent reception of my performance.

In 1756, two years after the fall of the first volume, was published the second volume of my History, containing the period from the death of Charles I till the Revolution. This performance happened to give less displeasure to the Whigs, and was better received. It not only rose itself, but helped to buoy up its unfortunate brother.

But though I had been taught by experience, that the Whig party were in possession of bestowing all places, both in the state and in literature, I was so little inclined to yield to their senseless clamour, that in above a hundred alterations, which farther study, reading, or reflection engaged me to make in the reigns of the two first Stuarts, I have made all of them

question of the legitimacy of the House of Hanover. Hume's 'generous tear' for Charles I provoked hostility from all quarters presumably because it was taken as implicit disloyalty towards the reigning Hanoverian king, George II (reigned 1727–60).

[10] The Revd Richard Hurd (1720–1808), Bishop of Coventry and Worcester. The work in question, the anonymously published *Remarks on Mr. David Hume's Essay on the Natural History of Religion: Addressed to the Rev. Dr. Warburton* (1757), actually consisted of Warburton's marginalia to Hume's book, pieced together and given an introduction by Hurd.

invariably to the Tory side. It is ridiculous to consider the English constitution before that period as a regular plan of liberty.

In 1759, I published my History of the House of Tudor. The clamour
against this performance was almost equal to that against the History of the
two first Stuarts. The reign of Elizabeth was particularly obnoxious. But I
was now callous against the impressions of public folly, and continued very
peaceably and contentedly in my retreat at Edinburgh, to finish, in two
volumes, the more early part of the English History, which I gave to the
public in 1761, with tolerable, and but tolerable success.

But, notwithstanding this variety of winds and seasons, to which my
writings had been exposed, they had still been making such advances, that
the copy-money given me by the booksellers, much exceeded any thing
formerly known in England; I was become not only independent, but
opulent. I retired to my native country of Scotland, determined never
more to set my foot out of it; and retaining the satisfaction of never having
preferred a request to one great man, or even making advances of friendship to any of them. As I was now turned of fifty, I thought of passing all the
rest of my life in this philosophical manner, when I received, in 1763, an
invitation from Lord Hertford,[11] with whom I was not in the least
acquainted, to attend him on his embassy to Paris, with a near prospect of
being appointed secretary to the embassy; and, in the meanwhile, of performing the functions of that office. This offer, however inviting, I at first
declined, both because I was reluctant to begin connexions with the great,
and because I was afraid that the civilities and gay company of Paris, would
prove disagreeable to a person of my age and humour: but on his lordship's
repeating the invitation, I accepted of it. I have every reason, both of
pleasure and interest, to think myself happy in my connexions with that
nobleman, as well as afterwards with his brother, General Conway.

Those who have not seen the strange effect of modes, will never imagine
the reception I met with at Paris, from men and women of all ranks and
stations. The more I recoiled from their excessive civilities, the more I was
loaded with them. There is, however, a real satisfaction in living at Paris,
from the great number of sensible, knowing, and polite company with
which the city abounds above all places in the universe. I thought once of
settling there for life.

---

[11] Francis Seymour Conway (1718–94), Earl of Hertford.

I was appointed secretary to the embassy; and, in summer 1765, Lord Hertford left me, being appointed Lord Lieutenant of Ireland. I was *chargé d'affaires* till the arrival of the Duke of Richmond, towards the end of the year. In the beginning of 1766, I left Paris, and next summer went to Edinburgh, with the same view as formerly, of burying myself in a philosophical retreat. I returned to that place, not richer, but with much more money, and a much larger income, by means of Lord Hertford's friendship, than I left it; and I was desirous of trying what superfluity could produce, as I had formerly made an experiment of a competency. But, in 1767, I received from Mr. Conway an invitation to be Under-secretary; and this invitation, both the character of the person, and my connexions with Lord Hertford, prevented me from declining. I returned to Edinburgh in 1769, very opulent (for I possessed a revenue of 1000 pounds a year), healthy, and though somewhat stricken in years, with the prospect of enjoying long my ease, and of seeing the increase of my reputation.

In spring 1775, I was struck with a disorder in my bowels, which at first gave me no alarm, but has since, as I apprehend it, become mortal and incurable. I now reckon upon a speedy dissolution. I have suffered very little pain from my disorder; and what is more strange, have, notwithstanding the great decline of my person, never suffered a moment's abatement of my spirits; insomuch, that were I to name the period of my life, which I should most choose to pass over again, I might be tempted to point to this later period. I possess the same ardour as ever in study, and the same gaiety in company. I consider, besides, that a man of sixty-five, by dying, cuts off only a few years of infirmities; and though I see many symptoms of my literary reputation's breaking out at last with additional lustre, I know that I have but few years to enjoy it. It is difficult to be more detached from life than I am at present.

To conclude historically with my own character. I am, or rather was (for that is the style I must now use in speaking of myself, which emboldens me the more to speak my sentiments); I was, I say, a man of mild dispositions, of command of temper, of an open, social, and cheerful humour, capable of attachment, but little susceptible of enmity, and of great moderation in all my passions. Even my love of literary fame, my ruling passion, never soured my humour, notwithstanding my frequent disappointments. My company was not unacceptable to the young and careless, as well as to the studious and literary; and as I took a particular pleasure in the company of modest women, I had no reason to be displeased with the reception I met with from them. In a word, though most men any wise eminent, have found reason to complain of calumny, I never was touched, or even attacked by her baleful tooth: and though I wantonly exposed myself to the rage of both civil and religious factions, they seemed to be disarmed in my behalf of their wonted[12] fury. My friends never had occasion to vindicate any one circumstance of my character and conduct: not but that the zealots, we may well suppose, would have been glad to invent and propagate any story to my disadvantage, but they could never find any which they thought would wear the face of probability. I cannot say there is no vanity in making this funeral oration of myself, but I hope it is not a misplaced one; and this is a matter of fact which is easily cleared and ascertained.

April 18, 1776.

[12] Habitual.

Index

definition (*cont.*)
  importance of 73–4, 142–3, 161
  of 'belief' 48, 149
  of 'cause' 29, 70–1, 93
  of 'liberty' 85–6
  of 'miracle' 100, 101
  of 'necessity' 75–85, 86
  of 'proof' 54
Deism 156
Demetrius I of Macedonia 107
demonstration *see* reasoning,
  demonstrative
Demosthenes 103
Descartes, René x, xii, xxiii–xxiv, xxx, xli,
  5, 15, 28, 36, 47, 57, 62, 65, 68, 131, 132,
  133, 134, 135, 157, 159, 204
  see also Cartesian philosophy
design, argument from xx, xxix, 120–30,
  156–8
determinism xi, xxix, 73–91
  see also necessity
deus ex machina 65
Dicker, Georges xxxvi
Diderot, Denis xxxiii
Digby, Sir Kenelm 93
Dio Cassius 118
Diogenes Laertius 43
dogmatic philosophy xii, xxvi, xxxi
  see also under scepticism
Domitian 107, 173
duty
  to God 182–7
  to neighbour 187–8
  to self 188

Edgar, Andrew xl
eggs 37
Elizabeth I 113, 220
Elliot of Minto, Gilbert 119, 207
Elysium 193
enthusiasm xvii, 97, 103, 129, 169, 205
Epictetus 41, 133, 174
Epicurean philosophy xiii–xiv, xvii, xxviii,
  xxix, xxx, xxxi, 41, 117, 118, 123, 140,
  163

Epicurus 117, 118–19, 123, 126, 129, 130,
  159
ether (etherial active fluid) 68, 160
Eucharist 96, 153
Euclid 28, 168
Euripides 65
Eve 24
ex nihilo nihil fit 143
  see also cause, necessity of
experience
  and causal inference xxviii–xxix,
  30–2, 34–40, 43–6, 120–1, 124,
  125, 127–8, 129–30, 139, 143, 150,
  152, 158, 190
  and proof xxviii, xxix, 54, 56, 62, 63,
  70, 71, 76, 79, 84, 97, 98, 100–1,
  112–13, 114, 115, 120, 123, 130, 153,
  200, 210
external world, belief in 133–6

faculties, mental xii, xxvii, 9, 10–11, 14, 16,
  22–30, 42, 44, 60, 61, 67, 68, 73, 82,
  83, 131, 132, 142, 149, 155, 183, 184,
  186, 187, 192, 197
  see also power
faculty psychology xxii–xxiii, 10–11, 14
faith xviii, 115, 144, 156
falsehood upon the very face 108
fame 178, 221
fancy *see* imagination, imagine
fiction 47–9, 55
Flew, Antony xxxv
Fontenelle, Bernard le Bouvier de 175–6
Force, James E. xl
forces of nature 11, 33, 74, 120, 159
Frasca-Spada, Marina xviii, xxxvii
freedom *see* liberty
free will *see* liberty

Gabriel 143
Galilei, Galileo 198–9
Garrett, Don xxv, xxxvi
Gaskin, J. C. A. xxxvii
geometry *see* science, mathematical
George II 219

God 63, 115, 150
    as cause of the world 65−7, 68, 143,
        151−2, 154, 159−60
    as cause of evil xxix, 88−91
    as cause of miracles 101, 114
    duty to 182−7, 206
    existence of 128, 131, 143, 144, 151, 154,
        156, 157, 158, 192
    idea of xxiii, 16, 151−2, 156−8, 170
    and punishment 192−4
    uniqueness of 117−30, 127, 192
    veracity of 135
Golden Age 122
golden mountain 16
gravitation 11, 55, 67, 160, 183, 201
Green, T. H. xxxv
Gregory xiii, 215
Greig, J. Y. T. xl
Grose, T. H. xxxv
Guericke, Otto 201
Gummere, Richard M. xl

habit x, xii, xxviii, 43, 64, 69, 94, 169, 172−3,
    178
    see also custom
Hamilton of Bangour, William 205
happiness xiii−xiv, 163, 169−71, 178,
    179−80, 189, 196, 206
Harris, James xviii, xxxvii
Hartley, David xxxiii
Harvey, William 92, 199−200
Hector 23, 25
Helen of Troy 7, 23
Hera 23
Herodotus 111
Hertford, Francis Seymour Conway, Earl
    of xxxiii, 220−1
Hesiod 122
Hippocrates 76
Hobbes, Thomas xxviii, xxxi, 14, 15, 18, 45,
    85, 92, 93, 133, 153, 199, 201
Holy Spirit 96
Home, Henry xii, xiii, xv, xvi, xxxiii, 147,
    204−5, 208, 209−11
Homer 22, 23, 24, 25, 195

Hooke, Robert 201
Horace 22−23, 47
Houston, J. xxxvii
Huet, Pierre-Daniel 155, 156
human nature xi, xiii, xxix, 3, 5, 9, 12, 37, 42,
    43, 44, 76, 98, 102, 104, 115, 126, 128,
    139, 141, 166, 174, 175, 178, 181, 187
    inferences drawn from 80−2
    uniformity of 75−80, 169
    variety in 77−80
Hurd, Richard 219
Hutcheson, Francis xiii, xiv−xvii,
    xxxii−xxxiii, 11, 20, 21, 43, 47, 160,
    161, 205−6
hypothesis, hypotheses 26, 68, 85, 86, 92,
    121, 123, 152, 159, 160, 193
    religious hypothesis 123, 125, 127, 129

ideas
    abstract xiii−xiv, 136, 138, 158
    association of *see* association of ideas
    clear and distinct 36, 57, 58, 138, 143,
        150
    copies of impressions xxviii, 16−17, 18,
        58, 59, 71
    as if copies of things 134
    faintness of 15, 18
    innate 18
    obscure 58, 72
    relations of 28, 30, 95
    term loosely employed by Locke 18
    theory of 214
    unity of 21, 22, 27
ignorance *see* powers, secret
image, images 22−3, 50, 51, 66, 84, 133−4,
    135, 137
imagination, the x, xxii−xxiv, 3, 14, 15, 17,
    19−21, 26, 47−9, 50, 52, 55, 56, 66, 69,
    71, 90, 94, 103, 111, 125, 137, 138, 141,
    143, 148, 149, 170, 178, 182
imagine, to 60, 18, 30, 31, 32, 37, 47, 84, 104,
    122−3, 124, 128, 185, 187, 195, 202, 205
impressions 15, 29
    as source of ideas xxviii, 16−17, 18, 58,
        59, 71

Peripatetic see Aristotelian

Philip II of Macedon 176

philosophy

abstruse 3–4, 6–12; see also science, metaphysical

easy 3, 4–6

its limited authority 171–3, 178

its practical defects 173–8

and public good 117–18, 119–20, 129

as reflections of common life 142, 177

pious frauds 111

Pitt, William (the Elder) 213

Plato xiii, xxvii, 15, 25, 31, 42, 51, 140

Platonism xxx, 123, 159, 163

Pliny the Elder xl, 189, 196

Plutarch xi, xvii, 100, 106, 107, 111, 174, 175, 176, 178

Polemo 51

Polybius 76

Pompey 26, 111

Pope, Alexander xv, 53, 90, 175, 216

Popkin, Richard xxxvii, xl

Portia 189

Port-Royal 110

power xxii, xxix, 9, 10, 11, 35, 85, 150–1, 183–4, 185, 186, 187, 189, 192

idea of 58–72, 150, 151

mental 15–16, 45, 47, 85

secret xxiv, xxvi, xxix, 11, 25, 31, 32–3, 34–5, 37–8, 43, 52–3, 54, 55, 64, 65, 66, 67, 71, 75, 78–80, 83, 84, 121, 128, 134, 159–60, 201, 202, 205; see also secret connection, secret structures

pre-established harmony 28, 52, 55

prejudice xvi, xxi, 119, 129, 132, 141, 164, 166, 171, 200, 218

Price, John V. xl

primary qualities 135–6

probability 67, 115

and chance 54–5

and causes 55–6

and miracles 99–101

and proofs xxviii, 54, 56, 97–9, 100–1, 112, 114, 210

proof see experience, probability

proof against proof 100, 112

see also mutual destruction of arguments, opposition of arguments

prophecies 115

Protagoras 117

Protestantism xvii–xx, xxxi, 50, 212

see also enthusiasm

Proteus 170

Providence 66, 117, 118, 131, 159, 206

general xiii, xxxi, 117, 183–7, 188, 189, 191–4

particular xxxi, 117, 118, 120–30

Ptolemaic astronomy 140, 167, 168

Ptolemy 140

Pyrrho of Elis 140

Racine, Jean 108, 110

Rackham, H. xl

Radcliffe, Elizabeth xxxvi

Ramsay, Michael xxiii, xl, 203–4, 208

rational animal xii, xiii, xx

Read, Rupert xxxvii

real presence see transubstantiation

reason, faculty of

reducible to experience 44–5

see also understanding, the

reasoning

a priori 30–3, 36, 143, 157, 190

abstract 137–8, 144, 156, 190, 206

analogical 30–1, 32, 46, 48, 49, 52, 67, 92–3, 94, 95, 100, 113, 127, 128, 130, 190, 194–5, 196, 205

animal 92–5

demonstrative 28, 29, 36, 38, 54, 84, 97, 137, 142–3, 150, 154, 156, 210

experimental xxv, 120–1, 124, 125, 127–8, 129–30, 139, 143, 144, 158, 190

hypothetical 46

229

will, the 10, 47, 60–4, 68, 83, 84, 85,
  86, 87
William Rufus 173
Wilkins, John 200, 201
Wishart, William xvi, 147
witchcraft 110
Wollaston, William 160
women
  company of 221

inferiority of 192
wonder, love of 103, 104–5, 111
Wren, Sir Christopher 201
Wright, John P. vii, xxxvi–xxxviii
Xenocrates 51

Zeno of Elea 136
Zeus 121
Zeuxis 121

Titles published in the series thus far

Aquinas *Disputed Questions on the Virtues* (edited by E. M. Atkins and Thomas Williams)

Aquinas *Summa Theologiae, Questions on God* (edited by Brian Davies and Brian Leftow)

Aristotle *Nicomachean Ethics* (edited by Roger Crisp)

Arnauld and Nicole *Logic or the Art of Thinking* (edited by Jill Vance Buroker)

Augustine *On the Trinity* (edited by Gareth Matthews)

Bacon *The New Organon* (edited by Lisa Jardine and Michael Silverthorne)

Boyle *A Free Enquiry into the Vulgarly received Notion of Nature* (edited by Edward B. Davis and Michael Hunter)

Bruno *Cause, Principle and Unity* and *Essays on Magic* (edited by Richard Blackwell and Robert de Lucca with an introduction by Alfonso Ingegno)

Cavendish *Observations upon Experimental Philosophy* (edited by Eileen O'Neill)

Cicero *On Moral Ends* (edited by Julia Annas, translated by Raphael Woolf)

Clarke *A Demonstration of the Being and Attributes of God and Other Writings* (edited by Ezio Vailati)

Classic and Romantic German Aesthetics (edited by J. M. Bernstein)

Condillac *Essay on the Origin of Human Knowledge* (edited by Hans Aarsleff)

Conway *The Principles of the Most Ancient and Modern Philosophy* (edited by Allison P. Coudert and Taylor Corse)

Cudworth *A Treatise Concerning Eternal and Immutable Morality* with *A Treatise of Freewill* (edited by Sarah Hutton)

Descartes *Meditations on First Philosophy*, with selections from the *Objections and Replies* (edited by John Cottingham)

Descartes *The World and Other Writings* (edited by Stephen Gaukroger)

Newton *Philosophical Writings* (edited by Andrew Janiak)

Nietzsche *The Antichrist, Ecce Homo, Twilight of the Idols and Other Writings* (edited by Aaron Ridley and Judith Norman)

Nietzsche *Beyond Good and Evil* (edited by Rolf-Peter Horstmann and Judith Norman)

Nietzsche *The Birth of Tragedy and Other Writings* (edited by Raymond Geuss and Ronald Speirs)

Nietzsche *Daybreak* (edited by Maudemarie Clark and Brian Leiter, translated by R. J. Hollingdale)

Nietzsche *The Gay Science* (edited by Bernard Williams, translated by Josefine Nauckhoff)

Nietzsche *Human, All Too Human* (translated by R. J. Hollingdale with an introduction by Richard Schacht)

Nietzsche *Thus Spoke Zarathustra* (edited by Adrian Del Caro and Robert B. Pippin)

Nietzsche *Untimely Meditations* (edited by Daniel Breazeale, translated by R. J. Hollingdale)

Nietzsche *Writings from the Late Notebooks* (edited by Rüdiger Bittner, translated by Kate Sturge)

Novalis *Fichte Studies* (edited by Jane Kneller)

Reinhold *Letters on the Kantian Philosophy* (edited by Karl Ameriks, translated by James Hebbeler)

Schleiermacher *Hermeneutics and Criticism* (edited by Andrew Bowie)

Schleiermacher *Lectures on Philosophical Ethics* (edited by Robert Louden, translated by Louise Adey Huish)

Schleiermacher *On Religion: Speeches to its Cultured Despisers* (edited by Richard Crouter)

Schopenhauer *Prize Essay on the Freedom of the Will* (edited by Günter Zöller)

Sextus Empiricus *Against the Logicians* (edited by Richard Bett)

Sextus Empiricus *Outlines of Scepticism* (edited by Julia Annas and Jonathan Barnes)

Shaftesbury *Characteristics of Men, Manners, Opinions, Times* (edited by Lawrence Klein)

Adam Smith *The Theory of Moral Sentiments* (edited by Knud Haakonssen)

Voltaire *Treatise on Tolerance and Other Writings* (edited by Simon Harvey)

For EU product safety concerns, contact us at Calle de José Abascal, 56–1°,
28003 Madrid, Spain or eugpsr@cambridge.org.

www.ingramcontent.com/pod-product-compliance
Ingram Content Group UK Ltd.
Pitfield, Milton Keynes, MK11 3LW, UK
UKHW020334140625
459647UK00018B/2140